THE LITTLE BOOK OF RUBY

HUW COLLINGBOURNE

bitwise books

The Little Book Of Ruby
Edition 1
(1st paperback/Kindle edition)

ISBN: 978-1-913132-07-1

This is the first paperback and Kindle edition of The Book Of Ruby. It is based on an earlier PDF-format eBook in these editions: #1: June 2006, #2: March 2008, #3: July 2011, #4: July 201,. #5: August 2019. This paperback/Kindle edition has been full revised, substantially rewritten and completely redesigned, incorporating feedback and suggestions based on the earlier PDF releases.
Minor corrected revision: December 2020

bitwise books is an imprint of **dark neon**

written by
Huw Collingbourne

Download the Source Code

To download **the source code join our mailing list**:

http://www.bitwisebooks.com/subscribe

or scan this QR code:

Contents

Introduction

> Ruby is a cross-platform, object-oriented, interpreted language. Its syntax looks deceptively simple at first sight. In fact, Ruby is a good deal more complex than it may appear.

The Ruby language was created by Yukihiro Matsumoto (commonly known as 'Matz') and it was first released in 1995. There are implementations of Ruby for most widely used operating systems so whether you are running macOS, Windows or Linux, you can easily get started with Ruby programming.

Download the Source Code

All the programs in every chapter in this book are available as a Zip archive. I strongly advise that you download the source code archive and run the sample programs that accompany each chapter.

Join our mailing list and you will be sent a link by email to download the code from the Bitwise Books web site at:

http://www.bitwisebooks.com

What is in this Book?

This book is a step-by-step tutorial to programming in Ruby. It covers everything from the basics of Ruby's object orientation to file-handling, exception-handling, arrays and hashes. I know that there is plenty of information online about Ruby, and I haven't filled the pages of this book with all that readily-available information. Each of the books in *Little Book* series aims to give you *just the stuff you really need* to get straight to the heart of the matter without all the fluff and padding. Exactly how you study this book is entirely up to you. You may prefer to follow it chapter by chapter, reading the text and then running the sample programs. Or you may prefer to skip from topic to topic. There are no monolithic applications in this book – just small, self-contained sample programs – so it's easy to skip from chapter to chapter if you wish.

Who Should Read this Book?

This book is suitable for both beginners and more experienced programmers switching to Ruby from some other language such as C, Java, C# or Python. Whether you are completely new to programming or you are already program other languages and need a fast, simple introduction to Ruby, this book is for you.

Making Sense of the Text

In **The Little Book Of Ruby**, any Ruby source code is written like this:

```
def saysomething
  puts( "Hello world" )
end
```

When there is a sample program to accompany the code, the program name may be shown over the code like this:

hellonamerb

```
def saysomething
  puts( "Hello world" )
end
```

When a program runs and displays something on screen, the program output is shown like this:

```
Hello world
```

Explanatory notes (which generally provide some hints or give a more in-depth explanation of some point mentioned in the text) are shown like this:

Here's Something Interesting!

This is an explanatory note. You can skip it if you like – but if you do so, you may miss something of interest…!

Installing Ruby

If you haven't already done so, you will need to install Ruby on your computer. Some versions of Linux and macOS already have Ruby installed. At any rate, you can download the latest version of Ruby from http://www.ruby-lang.org. Be sure to download the binaries (not merely the source code). For Windows users, the easiest way to set up Ruby on your system is by using the Ruby Installer available from: http://rubyinstaller.org

Ruby Versions

At the time of writing, the latest version of Ruby is Ruby 2.x where 'x' represents the minor version numbers used differentiate specific updates to Ruby 2 (e.g. Ruby 2.6.3, Ruby 2.7.0 and so on). Some versions of Ruby may also be marked as 'preview' or 'rc' (release candidate). I recommend that you install the latest stable release of Ruby (not a preview or release candidate) for your operating system.

Installing a Ruby Editor or IDE

While you could write Ruby programs in any text editor and run them from the command prompt or Terminal, it is a good idea to use (at the very minimum) a Ruby editor with syntax code colouring. You might also consider using a Ruby IDE (Integrated Development Environment) that offers features such as IntelliSense (code completion) and integrated debugging. Some popular Ruby editors and IDEs are listed in the Appendix.

Running Ruby Programs

It is often useful to keep a Command window or Terminal open in the source directory containing your Ruby program files. Assuming that the Ruby interpreter is correctly pathed on your system (that is, that it has been added to the 'search path' which allows programs in other directories to find the Ruby interpreter – see the Appendix for more information), you will then be able to run programs by entering `ruby` followed by a program name like this, which is the command to run a program named *helloworld.rb*:

```
ruby helloworld.rb
```

Running Ruby from a Windows Command Prompt

If you are using Windows, click the *Start* menu. In the *Run* or *Search* text entry field enter:

```
cmd
```

This should open a text-mode window. You can now change to the directory containing the Ruby program you wish to run. To change directory enter `cd` followed by the directory name, like this:

```
cd E:\BOOKS\Programming\Ruby\Code\01
```

Quick-Open Windows Command Prompt

On Windows, you can open a command prompt into whichever directory is currently active in the Windows Explorer. To do that, enter `cmd` in the Explorer address bar.

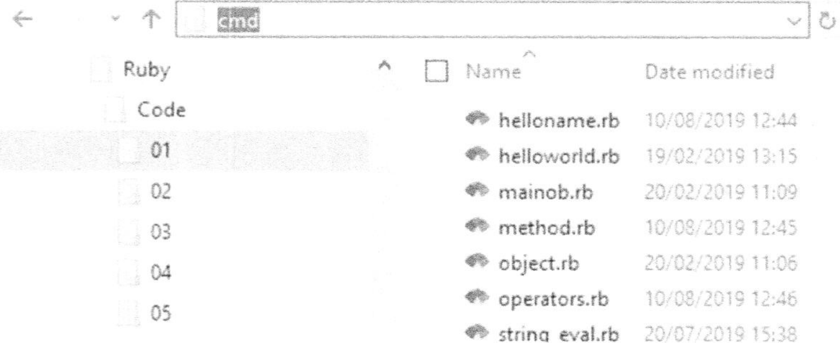

Running Ruby from a macOS Terminal

You need to open a 'Terminal' window. Double-click your hard-drive (e.g. *Macintosh HD*). Open the *Applications* folder. Then open the *Utilities* folder. Double-click the *Terminal* icon. This will open a window into which you can enter commands to run Ruby. To change directory enter `cd` followed by the directory name, like this:

```
cd /myrubyprograms
```

Quick-Open macOS Terminal

Opening a Terminal onto a folder in Finder takes a bit of pre-preparation. You need to set an option as follows: Go to *System Preferences*, then select *Keyboard* then *Shortcuts* and *Services*. In the *Keyboard settings* dialog, scroll down to the entry labelled '*New Terminal at Folder*'. Check it.

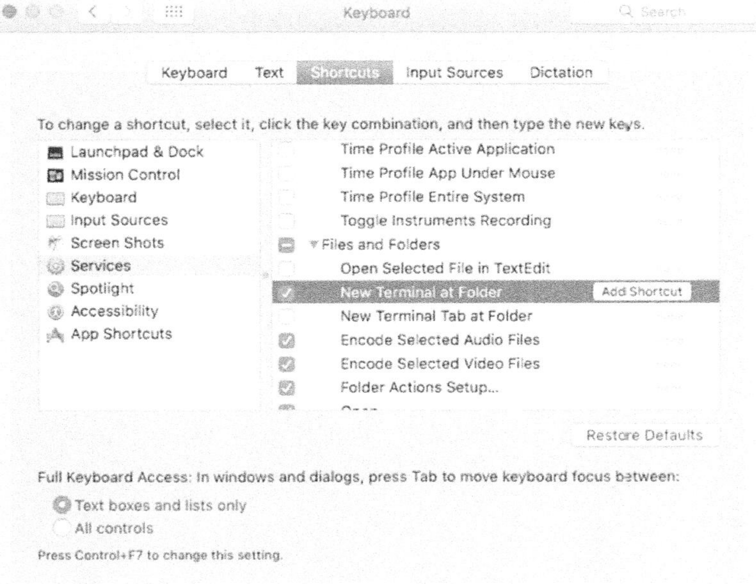

Now in Finder you can navigate to the folder you need (the one containing your Ruby program) – right click the folder. The popup menu will contain an item that pops out from *Services* called '*New Terminal at Folder*', When selected this opens a Terminal on the current folder.

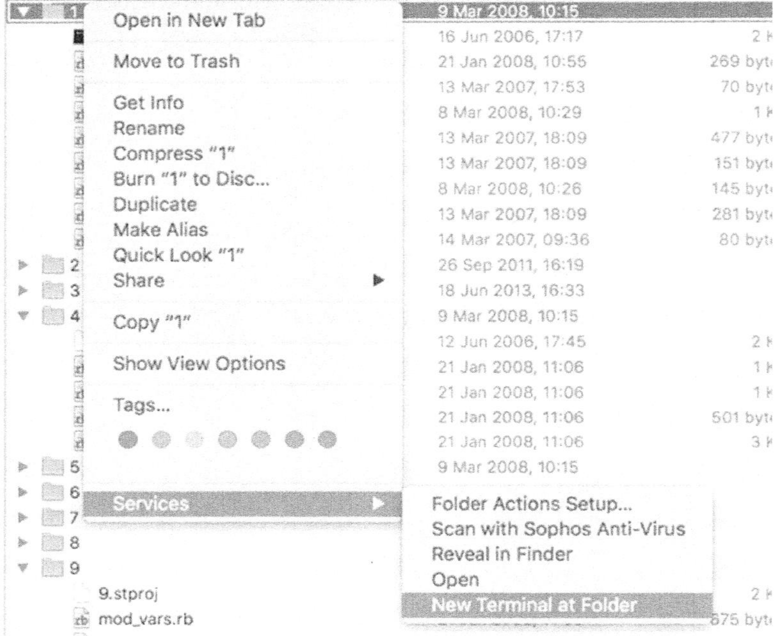

Running a Ruby Program

Open a Command Prompt or Terminal. Make sure the active folder or directory contains the Ruby program, you want to run. For example, you might need to open a Terminal onto the *01* folder (from the source code archive that accompanies this book) which contains the *helloname.rb* program. You then need to enter the command `ruby` to run the Ruby interpreter (which is the tool that runs Ruby programs), followed by the name of the program, like this:

```
ruby helloname.rb
```

Here is a Ruby program being run in a Mac Terminal:

```
Last login: Mon Aug 12 15:41:06 on ttys001
iMac:1 huw$ ruby helloname.rb
Enter your name: Huw
Hello Huw
Enter your name again: Huw
Hello Huw
iMac:1 huw$
```

Here is a Ruby program being run in a Windows Command window:

```
> ruby helloname.rb
Enter your name: Huw
Hello Huw
Enter your name again: Huw
Hello Huw
Enter your name again: Huw
Hello #{name}
```

About the Author

Huw Collingbourne has been a programmer for more than 30 years. He is an online programming instructor with successful courses on Ruby, C, C#, Java, Object Pascal, JavaScript and other topics. For a full list of available courses be sure to visit the Bitwise Courses web site: http://bitwisecourses.com

He is author of *The Little Book Of C*, *The Little Book Of Pointers*, *The Little Book Of C#* and *The Little Book Of Recursion* from Bitwise Books. He is a well-known technology writer in the UK and has written numerous opinion and programming columns for a number of computer magazines, such as Computer Shopper, PC Pro, and PC Plus.

At various times Huw has been a magazine publisher, editor, and TV broadcaster. He has an MA in English from the University of Cambridge and holds a 2nd dan black belt in aikido, a martial art which he teaches in North Devon, UK.

About the Technical Editor

Dr. Dermot Hogan is a software developer who has led major projects written in Assembly Language, C , C# and a number of other programming languages. A specialist in real time trading technologies, he has managed and developed global risk management systems for several international banks and financial institutions. He is the lead developer of the independent software company, SapphireSteel Software. He holds a Ph.D in physics from the University of Cambridge. His current area of research is devoted to robotic control and imaging systems.

1 – Fundamentals of Ruby

In this chapter, we tie up some strings, add up some numbers, mess about with methods and diagnose some conditions…

From the fact that you are reading this, it is safe to deduce that you want to program Ruby – and, if you are anything like me, you will be impatient to get on with it. First, you must be sure that you have Ruby installed, as explained in the Introduction. Now, let's start coding. Start up your editor and enter the following:

helloworld.rb

```
puts 'Hello world'
```

Here `puts` is the name of a function or 'method' that can display or 'put' a string such as `'Hello world'` on screen. A string is a series of characters enclosed by either a pair of single-quotes or a pair of double-quotes. `'Hello'` is a string, and so is `"Goodbye"`.

Save your program with the name *helloworld.rb*. You are now ready to run the program. To do this, open a command window or Terminal and navigate to the directory containing the file that you just saved.

The Command Window

The 'Command Window' or 'Terminal' is a window in which you can enter commands to be run by your operating system. You enter these commands at the 'system prompt'. If you are unfamiliar with this window, go back to the Introduction section of this book which provides more information.

In the command window, enter `ruby` followed by the program name, like this:

```
ruby helloworld.rb
```

All being well, Ruby should display this:

```
Hello world
```

This must be just about the shortest 'Hello world' program in the history of programming. Having 'put' a string on screen, the obvious next step is to 'get' a string from the user. Ruby provides the `gets()` method for this.

Functions and Methods

A function is a 'subroutine' – a block of code with a name. When you want to run the code in a function, you can just 'call' the function by its name. In object oriented languages such as Ruby, the word 'method' is often used to describe a function. 'Method' is the object-oriented term for a function that is bound into an object. A method may sometimes 'return' a value (some piece of data such as an integer or a string) to the code that called it. We'll look more closely at objects and methods later in this chapter.

Here I use three methods: the `print()` method displays a string, the `gets()` method gets a string entered by the user and the `puts()` method displays another string.

helloname.rb

```
print( 'Enter your name: ' )
name = gets()
puts( "Hello #{name}" )
```

While this program is short and simple, there are a few details that need to be explained. First, notice that I've used `print()` rather than `puts()` to display the prompt, `'Enter your name: '`. This is because `puts()` adds a linefeed at the end whereas `print()` does not; in the present case I want the cursor to remain on the same line as the prompt. So when the user enters some text, that text is entered on the same line.

On the next line I use `gets()` to read in a string when the user presses ENTER. This string is assigned to the variable, `name`. I have not pre-declared this variable, nor have I specified its type (which you would have to do in some languages such as C or Pascal).

Variables

A variable is an identifier to which values can be assigned. So if I have a variable called `name` I can assign the value `"Fred"` like this:

```
name = "Fred"
```

The equals sign `=` is the 'assignment operator'. It assigns the value on its right to the variable on its left. The value of a variable can be changed so I can give a new value to a variable such as `name` just by making a new assignment like this:

```
name = "Mary"
```

In Ruby you can create variables as you need them and Ruby 'infers' their types. In the preceding example, I assigned a string to `name` so Ruby knows that the *type* of the `name` variable must be a string.

Ruby is case sensitive.

The 'case' of a variable name (and other code elements) matters in Ruby. Uppercase characters are considered to be different from lowercase characters. So a variable called `myvar` is different from a variable called `myVar`. A variable such as `name` in my sample project must begin with a lowercase character.

Parentheses

You may have noticed that I put a pair of parentheses following `gets()` in the *helloname.rb* program. This shows that `gets()` is the name of a function or method. In Ruby, unlike in many other programming languages, parentheses are optional here.

Similarly the parentheses enclosing the strings after `print()` and `puts()` may also be optionally omitted; the code would run just the same if you removed the parentheses. However, parentheses help to avoid potential ambiguity in code and, in some cases, the Ruby interpreter will warn you if you omit them.

Many Ruby programmers like to omit parentheses whenever possible. I am not one of them; you will, therefore, find parentheses used liberally in my programs. Parentheses do no harm but they can help clarify complex bits of code. They also help to distinguish a variable name from a method name. Without parentheses, I cannot tell if `xxx` is a variable or a method. With parentheses, I know that `xxx()` is a method.

In spite of my prejudice in favour of parentheses, I generally follow the common Ruby practice of omitting parentheses when methods take no arguments; though I may occasionally add them to clarify that the identifier is a method name rather than a variable name. Bear in mind that this is all a matter of personal choice. If you don't like parentheses, in most cases you don't have to use them.

Strings and Embedded Evaluation

The last line in the *helloname.rb* program is rather interesting:

```
puts( "Hello #{name}" )
```

Here the `name` variable is embedded into the string itself. This is done by placing the variable between two curly braces preceded by a hash character `#{ }`. When some code is embedded into a double-quoted string, the code will be automatically evaluated. So the *value* of a variable will be displayed, not the *name* of the variable. Assuming that the user entered `"Mary"` when prompted, then the value of the `name` variable would now be the string `"Mary"`. When the code shown above is run, this is what will be displayed:

```
Hello Mary
```

Double-quoted & Single-quoted Strings

This kind of 'embedded' evaluation only works with strings delimited by double quotes. Let's assume that the `name` variable has been assigned the string `"Mary"`, and I place `#{name}` into a double-quoted string like this:

```
puts "Hello #{name}"
```

When the program runs, Ruby displays this:

```
Hello Mary
```

But what happens if I do the same thing with a single-quoted string?

```
puts 'Hello #{name}'
```

In this case, Ruby does not attempt to evaluate the code and this is displayed:

```
Hello #{name}
```

It isn't only variables which can be embedded in double-quoted strings. You can also embed non-printing characters such as newlines `"\n"` and tabs `"\t"`. You can even embed bits of program code and mathematical expressions. Let's assume that you have a method called `showname()`, which returns the string `"Fred"`.

string_eval.rb

```
def showname
  return "Fred"
end
```

Now I display a double-quoted string, using the `puts()` method. I embed the name of the method name `showname` into this string just as I embedded the name of the variable `name` in a previous example. Since a double-quoted string 'evaluates' any code embedded inside `#{ }`, `showname` is evaluated here. This causes Ruby to run the `showname()` method.

```
puts( "Hello #{showname}" )
```

The `showname()` method runs, it returns the string `"Fred"` and this is what is displayed:

```
Hello Fred
```

See if you can figure out what would be displayed by the following code:

string_eval.rb

```
puts( "\n\t#{(1 + 2) * 3}" )
```

Run the *string_eval.rb* program to see if you were right.

Methods and Objects

Earlier I said that a method is like a function. In non-object-oriented languages, functions or subroutines are free-standing, named blocks of code. So what exactly is a *method*? Put simply, a method is a sort of function that is 'bound into' an object. Which raises the question: what is an object?

In Ruby, everything from an integer to a string is considered to be an object. An object is like a self-contained bundle of data and code. An object may contain some data such as strings or numbers and it may also contain methods to modify the object's data or do other useful things.

To run the code in a method, you generally need to put a dot after the object name, then append the method name. For example, if I assign a string to a variable, that variable can be regarded as a 'string object'. Here I call the `upcase()` method, which returns an uppercase string, from the `mystring` object:

uppercase.rb

```
mystring = "hello world"
puts( mystring.upcase )
```

When this code runs, this is what I see:

```
HELLO WORLD
```

You don't even need a variable to create an object. The string `"hello world"` is itself a string object and it too can call string methods. So this code works too:

```
puts( "hello world".upcase )
```

And it also displays this output:

```
HELLO WORLD
```

Methods without Objects?

Some methods such as `puts()` and `gets()` are available everywhere and don't need to be associated with a specific object. Technically speaking, these methods are provided by Ruby's `Kernel` module and they are *included* in all Ruby objects (Modules and inclusion are explained in Chapter 9). When you run a Ruby application, an object called `main` is automatically created and this object provides access to the `Kernel` methods.

As a consequence of this, if you write any 'free-standing' methods in your own code, these are added to the methods of the `main` object. In the *mainob.rb* program I show a sorted list of the `main` object's methods using this code:

mainob.rb

```
puts( self.private_methods.sort )
```

If you look at the list of methods displayed (the list is too long to show here), you will see that the `main` object has some methods such as `gets()`, `print()` and `puts()` which we've used previously (along with many methods that we haven't). I have also written some 'standalone' methods of my own in this program – namely, `showstring()`, `showname()`, `return_name()` and `return_name2()` – and these methods too 'belong' to the `main` object. So even though some Ruby methods *look* as though they are not bound into an object, this is not in fact the case, because the `main` object 'contains' those methods.

Messages and Methods

A *method* is so called because it provides a method (that is, 'a way') for an object to respond to messages. In strict object-oriented terminology, instead of saying that an object 'calls' a method, you could say that that a message is sent to an object and the object's method receives that message. While it's worth being familiar with these terms, I will generally use the more familiar term 'method-calling' in this book.

Calling Methods from Objects

Let's suppose that you have created an object called `ob` which has a method called `saysomething()`. This is how you would send the `saysomething()` message to the `ob` object (or, in other words, this is how the `ob` object would 'call' the `saysomething()` method):

object.rb

```
ob.saysomething
```

This is the `saysomething()` method in the *object.rb* sample program:

```
def saysomething
  puts( "Hello" )
end
```

The result is, that the code of the `saysomething()` method runs and it displays this:

```
Hello
```

Defining a Method

In Ruby a method is declared with the keyword `def` followed by a method name which should begin with a lowercase letter, like this:

method.rb

```
def showstring
  puts( "Hello" )
end
```

You may optionally put one or more named parameters, separated by commas, after the method name:

```
def showname( aName )
  puts( "Hello #{aName}" )
end

def return_name( aFirstName, aSecondName )
  return "Hello #{aFirstName} #{aSecondName}"
end
```

The parentheses around the parameters are optional. This syntax is also permissible:

```
def return_name2 aFirstName, aSecondName
  return "Hello #{aFirstName} #{aSecondName}"
end
```

As explained previously, for the sake of clarity, I am very much prejudiced in favour of parentheses – especially when arguments (data items) are passed to methods – but you can omit them if you wish.

Arguments and Parameters

Computer scientists sometimes make a distinction between arguments and parameters. Strictly speaking, *parameters* are the variables declared between parentheses in the function itself. Here, the `return_name()` function declares two parameters: `aFirstName` and `aSecondName`:

```
def return_name( aFirstName, aSecondName )
  return "Hello #{aFirstName} #{aSecondName}"
end
```

Arguments are the values that are passed to the function when that function is called. Here I call the `return_name()` function and pass to it the string arguments, `"Mary Mary"` and `"Quite-Contrary"`:

```
return_name( "Mary Mary", "Quite-Contrary"  )
```

When the arguments `"Mary Mary"` and `"Quite-Contrary"` are passed to the `return_name()` function, they will be assigned to the matching parameters: `aFirstName` will have the value `"Mary Mary"`; `aSecondName` will have the value `"Quite-Contrary"`. Programmers commonly use the terms 'argument' interchangeably with 'parameter'.

Returning Values

A method may return some value when it exits. In the *string_eval.rb* program, the `showname()` method returns the string `"Fred"`. I can assign that returned value to a variable, such as `x` and then use that variable in some other code. For example, here, I pass `x` to the `puts()` method in order to display its value:

string_eval.rb

```
def showname
  return "Fred"
end

x = showname
puts( x )
```

Alternatively, I could simply use the returned value 'directly' by calling one method inside another like this:

```
puts( showname )
```

In that case, the call to the method `showname()` returns the string `"Fred"` and that string is then passed to `puts()`. Incidentally, the `return` keyword is optional. Ruby methods always return the last expression evaluated. That means I could have written the `showname()` method like this, without the `return` keyword, and it would still return the string `"Fred"`:

```
def showname
  "Fred"
end
```

For the sake of clarity (and to avoid unexpected results from methods of more complexity than this one!) I shall make a habit of explicitly returning values by placing them after the `return` keyword.

Local and Global Variables

We've seen a few variables in the short code snippets in this chapter. This is how I assigned the string `"hello world"` to the variable named `mystring`:

```
mystring = "hello world"
```

Local Variables

Variables such as `mystring`, which begin with a lowercase character, are local variables. This means that they only exist within a specific part of a program – in other words, they are restricted to a well-defined 'scope'. Here is an example:

variables.rb

```
localvar = "hello"
$globalvar = "goodbye"

def amethod
  localvar = 10
  puts( localvar )
  puts( $globalvar )
end

def anotherMethod
  localvar = 500
  $globalvar = "bonjour"
  puts( localvar )
  puts( $globalvar )
end
```

Here there are three local variables called `localvar`. One is assigned the string value, `"hello"` within the 'main scope' of the program; two others are assigned integers within the scope of two separate methods. Since each local variable has a different scope, the assignments have no effect on the local variables with the same name in different scopes.

Global Variables

A global variable – one that begins with the dollar `$` character - has global scope. That means it is visible, and accessible, from anywhere in the program. When an assignment is made to a global variable inside a method, that affects the value of that variable elsewhere in the program too. Let's see what happens when I call each of my three methods and then print the values of `localvar` and `$globalvar` outside the methods:

```
amethod()
puts
anotherMethod()
puts
amethod()
puts
puts( localvar )
puts( $globalvar )
```

This is what I see:

```
10
goodbye

500
bonjour

10
bonjour

hello
bonjour
```

This shows that `$globalvar` is accessible both inside and outside the methods. That's because it has *global* scope. When I refer to `$globalvar` anywhere in my program, I am always referring to the same variable. If I assign a new value to it, as I do in `anotherMethod()` that value changes the variable everywhere – both inside and outside methods. But `localvar` is *local* to the scope in which it is defined. When it is defined inside a method, it is local to that method alone and it cannot be accessed outside that method. If I change its value in one method it has no effect on the value of a variable with the same name in another method.

In the *variables.rb* program, the `localvar` variable inside `amethod()` is different from `localvar` variable inside `anotherMethod()` and those two variables are both different from the `localvar` variable that is declared at the top of the code file. They all have the same name, `localvar`, but even so, they are different variables.

Numbers

Numbers are just as easy to use as strings. Let's suppose you want to calculate the selling price or 'grand total' of an item based on its ex-tax value or 'subtotal'.

To do this you would need to multiply the subtotal by the tax rate and then add the result to the value of the subtotal. Assuming the subtotal to be $100 and the tax rate to be 17.5%, this Ruby code would do the calculation and display the result:

```
subtotal = 100.00
taxrate = 0.175
tax = subtotal * taxrate

puts( "Tax on $#{subtotal} is $#{tax}, so grand total is $#{subtotal+tax}" )
```

Obviously, it would be more useful if it could perform calculations on a variety of subtotals rather than calculating the same value time after time! Here is a simple version of a Tax Calculator that prompts the user to enter a subtotal:

taxcalc.rb

```
taxrate = 0.175
print( "Enter price (ex tax): " )
s = gets()
subtotal = s.to_f()
tax = subtotal * taxrate

puts( "Tax on $#{subtotal} is $#{tax}, so grand total is $#{subtotal+tax}" )
```

If you run this and enter `100` when prompted, this is what you will see:

```
Enter price (ex tax): 100
Tax on $100.0 is $17.5, so grand total is $117.5
```

Here `to_f()` is a method of the `String` class. The variable `s` is assigned a string entered by the user. The `to_f()` method attempts to convert the string to a floating point number. For example, the string `"145.45"` would be converted to the floating point number, `145.45`. If the string cannot be converted, `0.0` is returned. So, for instance, `"Hello world".to_f()` would return `0.0` and this is what you would see:

```
Enter price (ex tax): Hello world
Tax on $0.0 is $0.0, so grand total is $0.0
```

The problem with the simple tax calculator code shown above is that it accepts *minus* subtotals and calculates *minus* tax on them. Try it out by entering `-100` and this is what you will see:

```
Enter price (ex tax): -100
Tax on $-100.0 is $-17.5, so grand total is $-117.5
```

Testing a Condition: if...then

Buying things with negative amounts of money is an activity of which the Government is very likely to disapprove! I therefore need to check for minus figures and, when found, do something to avoid ending up with negative tax calculations. This is my new version of the code:

taxcalc2.rb

```
taxrate = 0.175
print "Enter price (ex tax): "
s = gets
subtotal = s.to_f

if (subtotal < 0.0) then
  subtotal = 0.0
end

tax = subtotal * taxrate
puts "Tax on $#{subtotal} is $#{tax}, so grand total is $#{subtotal+tax}"
```

In this program, if the value of the `subtotal` variable is less than `0.0`, the code sets the value of `subtotal` to `0.0`. That ensures that the calculation will never result in negative totals.

Once again, the parentheses around the test condition are optional, as is the keyword `then`. However, if you were to write the following, with no line break after the test condition, the `then` would be obligatory:

```
if (subtotal < 0.0) then subtotal = 0.0 end
```

The `end` keyword that terminates the `if` block is *not* optional. Forget to add it and your code will not run.

Operators

Operators are special symbols that are used to do specific operations such as the addition and subtraction of numbers. There are also operators for assigning values to variables and testing conditions. Let's look at the most commonly used Ruby operators.

Assignment Operator

One of the most important operators is the assignment operator, `=`, which assigns the value on its right to a variable on its left. Note that the type of data assigned must be compatible with the type of the variable. This is an assignment of a floating point number, `0.175`, to a variable, `taxrate`:

taxcalc.rb

```
taxrate = 0.175
```

Arithmetic Operators

We've already used some arithmetic operators in previous programs – for example, in *taxcalc.rb*, I used the multiplication operator `*` to multiply `subtotal` by `taxrate`. I then used the assignment operator `=` to assign the result of that calculation to the `tax` variable:

taxcalc.rb

```
tax = subtotal * taxrate
```

The principal arithmetic operators are the division `/` and multiplication `*` operators which divide and multiply one value by the other and the remainder (or 'modulus') operator `%` which calculates the remainder after a division. These are examples of these operators:

operators.rb

```
x = 100
y = 100
z = 200

puts( z + y )
puts( z - y )
puts( z * y )
puts( z / y )
puts( 10 % 3 )
```

When you run this code, this is the output:

```
300
100
20000
2
1
```

Comparison Operators

In the *taxcalc2.rb* program, I tested if the value of the `subtotal` variable was less than `0.0`. If that test succeeded my code set the value of `subtotal` to `0.0`:

```
if (subtotal < 0.0) then
  subtotal = 0.0
end
```

The < is the 'less than' comparison operator. There are other operators that can be used in tests of this sort. These are the most common comparison operators:

`==`	equals
`!=`	not equals
`>`	greater than
`<`	less than
`<=`	less than or equal to
`>=`	greater than or equal to

Here are a few examples of these operators in use:

operators.rb

```
x = 100
y = 100
z = 200

if (x < z)
  puts( "x is less than z" )
end

if (z > x)
  puts( "z is greater than z" )
end

if (x == y)
  puts( "x equals y ")
end

if (x <= y)
  puts( "x is less than or equal to y " )
end

if (z >= y)
  puts( "z is greater than or equal to y " )
end

if (x >= z)
  puts( "x is greater than or equal to z " )
else
  puts( "x is not greater than or equal to z " )
end

if (x != z)
  puts( "x is not equal to z " )
end
```

This program produces this output:

```
x is less than z
z is greater than z
x equals y
x is less than or equal to y
z is greater than or equal to y
x is not greater than or equal to z
x is not equal to z
```

Operators are Methods

In many programming languages, operators are special, pre-defined symbols. Most of Ruby's operators are, in fact, methods. For example, the addition and subtraction operators, `+` and `-`, are methods of numeric objects such as `Fixnum` (integer) and `Float` objects. The implementation details need not concern you. In most cases, Ruby's operator methods work much the same ways as operators in other programming languages.

Keywords

Ruby defines a number of keywords that mean specific things to the language. Keywords include words such as `if`, `else`, `for` and `while`. The keyword `def` is used when defining methods. The keyword `class` is used when defining classes. The keywords `begin` and `end` are used in various places to mark the start and end of blocks of code.

Comments

If you've been studying the code samples that accompany this chapter, you will have noticed that some of them contain some lines of explanatory text like these from the *method.rb* program:

```
# Here I define some free-standing methods. I use a mix of acceptable Ruby syntax
# (both with and without parentheses), and define methods with 0, 1 and 2
# arguments.
```

Lines beginning with a # character are treated as comments (they are ignored by the Ruby interpreter). You can also add a comments after some Ruby code on the same line as the comment, like this:

```
puts( "Hello" )    # This is a comment
```

2 – Constructing Objects

So far we've used a number of 'standard' Ruby objects such as numbers and strings. Let's now find out how to create new types of objects.

As in most other OOP (Object Oriented Programming) languages, a Ruby object is defined by a class. A class is like a blueprint from which individual objects can be constructed. This is a very simple class:

```
class MyClass
end
```

This is how I would create a usable object from it:

```
ob = MyClass.new
```

In its present form, I can't do much of interest with my `ob` object – for the simple reason that I haven't written any Ruby code in the `MyClass` class. In fact, even though `MyClass` appears to be an 'empty' class, the objects created from it will not be totally useless. That's because all Ruby classes automatically inherit the features of the `Object` class. So my `ob` object can make use of `Object` methods such as `class` (which tells an object display its class).

Try this:

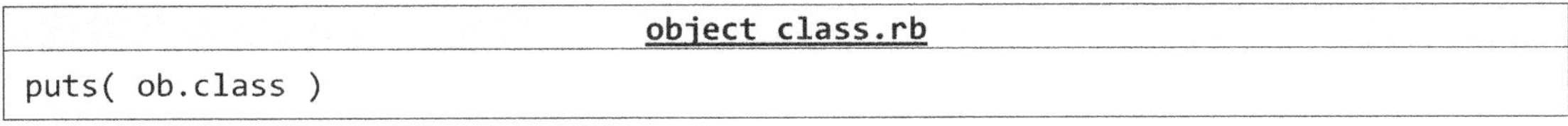

object_class.rb

```
puts( ob.class )
```

When it is run, this code displays the following:

```
MyClass
```

To make `MyClass` a bit more useful, I need to give it a method or two. In this example (which was mentioned briefly in the last chapter), I've added a method called `saysomething`:

```
class MyClass
  def saysomething
   puts( "Hello" )
  end
end
```

Now, when I create a `MyClass` object, I can call this method in order to get that object to say `"Hello"`:

```
ob = MyClass.new
ob.saysomething()
```

This is the output:

```
Hello
```

Instances and Instance Variables

Let's create some more useful objects. No home (or computer program) should be without a dog. So let's make ourselves a `Dog` class:

dogs_and_cats.rb

```
class Dog
  def set_name( aName )
    @myname = aName
  end
end
```

Note that the class definition begins with the keyword **`class`** (all lowercase) and is followed by the name of the class itself, which must begin with an uppercase letter.

My `Dog` class contains a single method, `set_name()`. This takes an incoming argument, `aName`. The body of the method assigns the value of `aName` to a variable called `@myname`.

@variables

Variables beginning with the `@` character are 'instance variables' – that means that they belong to individuals objects – or 'instances' of the class. It is not necessary to pre-declare variables (as would be required in many other languages such as C or Pascal).

I can create instances of the `Dog` class (that is, 'Dog objects') by calling the `new()` method. Here I am creating two `Dog` objects (remember that class names begin with uppercase letters; object names begin with lowercase letters):

```
mydog = Dog.new
yourdog = Dog.new
```

At the moment, these two dog objects have no names. So the next thing I do is call the `set_name()` method to give them names:

```
mydog.set_name( 'Fido' )
yourdog.set_name( 'Bonzo' )
```

Having given names to the dogs, I need to have some way to find out their names later on. Each dog needs to know its own name, so I've written a `get_name()` method:

```
def get_name
  return @myname
end
```

Finally, let's give the dog some behaviour with a `talk()` method. Here is the `Dog` class:

dogs_and_cats.rb

```
class Dog
  def set_name( aName )
    @myname = aName
  end

  def get_name
    return @myname
  end

  def talk
    return 'woof!'
  end
end
```

For the sake of variety – and to show that I am not biased against our feline friends – I have added a `Cat` class in my program, *dogs_and_cats.rb*. The `Cat` class is similar to the `Dog` class apart from the fact that its `talk()` method, naturally enough, returns a *miaow* instead of a *woof*.

dogs_and_cats.rb

```
class Cat
  def set_name( aName )
    @myname = aName
  end

  def get_name
    return @myname
  end

  def talk
    return 'miaow!'
  end
end
```

Now, I can create dog and cat objects, give them names, display their names and ask them to talk, like this:

dogs_and_cats.rb

```
# --- Create instances (objects) of the Dog and Cat classes

mydog = Dog.new
yourdog = Dog.new
mycat = Cat.new
yourcat = Cat.new
someotherdog = Dog.new

# --- Name them

mydog.set_name( 'Fido' )
yourdog.set_name( 'Bonzo' )
mycat.set_name( 'Tiddles' )
yourcat.set_name( 'Flossy' )


# --- Get their names and display them

# Dogs
p( mydog.get_name )
p( yourdog.get_name )
# hmmm, but what happens here if the dog has no name?
p( someotherdog.get_name )
```

dogs and cats.rb (contirued)

```
# Cats
p( mycat.get_name )
p( yourcat.get_name )

# --- Ask them to talk
p( mydog.talk )
p( yourdog.talk )
p( mycat.talk )
p( yourcat.talk )
```

This is what I see:

```
"Fido"
"Bonzo"
nil
"Tiddles"
"Flossy"
"woof!"
"woof!"
"miaow!"
"miaow!"
```

A Dog With No Name?

This program contains an error. The object named `someotherdog` never has a value assigned to its `@name` variable. Fortunately, Ruby doesn't crash out when we try to display this dog's name. Instead it just prints `nil`. In a short while, I'll explain a simple way of making sure that errors like this don't happen again.

Constructors

Let's take a look at another example of a user-defined class. If you are following along using the samples in the code archive, load up *treasure.rb*. This the basis of a very simple text adventure game. It contains two classes, `Thing` and `Treasure`. The `Thing` class is broadly similar to the `Dog` class from the last program – well, apart from the fact that it doesn't woof, that is:

treasure.rb

```
class Thing
  def set_name( aName )
    @name = aName
  end

  def get_name
    return @name
  end
end

class Treasure
    def initialize( aName, aDescription )
      @name        = aName
      @description  = aDescription
    end

    def to_s # override default to_s method
       "The #{@name} Treasure is #{@description}\n"
    end
end

thing1 = Thing.new
thing1.set_name( "A lovely Thing" )
puts( thing1.get_name )

t1 = Treasure.new( "Sword", "an Elvish weapon forged of gold" )
t2 = Treasure.new( "Ring", "a magic ring of great power" )
puts( t1.to_s )
puts( t2.to_s )
```

When you run this, the program displays:

```
A lovely Thing
The Sword Treasure is an Elvish weapon forged of gold
The Ring Treasure is a magic ring of great power
```

The `Treasure` class has a few interesting extras. First of all, it hasn't got a `get_name()` or a `set_name()` method. Instead, it contains a method named `initialize()` which takes two arguments whose values are assigned to the `@name` and `@description` variables.

When a class contains a method named `initialize()` this is automatically called when an object is created using the `new()` method. If you write an `initialize()` method you will be able to set the values of an object's instance variables each time a new object is created. This has two clear benefits over setting the values of instance variables one by one using methods such `set_name()`. First, a complex class may contain numerous instance variables and you can set the values of all of them with the single `initialize()`

method rather than with many separate 'set' methods; secondly, if the variables are all automatically initialized at the time of object creation, you will never end up with an 'empty' variable (like the `nil` value returned when we tried to display the name of `someotherdog` in the previous program).

new() and initialize()

The `new()` method creates an object so it can be thought of as the object's 'constructor'. The constructor is responsible for bringing an object into being: setting aside some memory for it and making it ready for use in your program. If you define a method named `initialize()`, this method will be called immediately after the new object has been created. The `initialize()` method is a good place to set the starting values of an object's instance variables.

My `Treasure` class also contains a method called `to_s()` which is intended to return a string representation of a `Treasure` object. The method name, `to_s()`, is not arbitrary. The same method name is used throughout the standard Ruby class hierarchy. In fact, the `to_s()` method is defined for the `Object` class itself which is the ultimate ancestor of all other classes in Ruby.

Overridden Methods

By redefining the `to_s()` method, I have added new behaviour which is more appropriate to the `Treasure` class than the default method. In other words, I have 'overridden' the `Object` class `to_s()` method. We'll see why this method is important when we look at how to 'inspect' an object shortly.

Object and BasicObject

I said earlier that the `Object` class is the ultimate ancestor of all other classes in Ruby. In versions of Ruby prior to Ruby 1.9 that was literally true However, in Ruby 1.9 and later, the `Object` class is the descendent of another class called `BasicObject`. The Ruby class library documentation describes `BasicObject` as a "blank class" which can be used to create "object hierarchies independent of Ruby's object hierarchy". As this is something we definitely do not want to do, it is safe to consider `Object` as the base class or "root" of all the other classes we shall ever use in this book.

Inspecting Objects

Right at the end of the code in the *treasure.rb* program you will see that I have 'looked inside' the `Treasure` object, `t1`, using the `inspect()` method: `t1.inspect`. In fact, I have embedded this into a double-quoted string which, as explained in Chapter 1, causes the code to be evaluated:

```
puts( "Inspecting 1st treasure: #{t1.inspect}" )
```

The `inspect()` method is defined for all Ruby objects. It returns a string containing a human-readable representation of the object. Running the code shown above displays something like this:

```
Inspecting 1st treasure: #<Treasure:0x00000000031066b8 @name="Sword",
@description="an Elvish weapon forged of gold">
```

This begins with the class name, `Treasure`. Then there is `0x00000000031066b8` – the actual number may vary each time the program runs. It is Ruby's internal identification code for this particular object; then there are the names and values of the object's variables.

p() – inspect and puts

Ruby provides the `p()` method as a shortcut to inspect and display the internal details of an object:

```
p( anobject )
```

This is equivalent to writing:

```
puts( anobject.inspect )
```

The actual output will depend on the type of object being inspected. For example, if the object is an integer, the integer itself is displayed. If it is a string, the string (including a pair of string delimiters – the quotation marks) will be displayed:

```
a = "hello"
b = 123
p( a )
p( b )
```

The preceding code produces the following output:

```
"hello"
123
```

to_s()

Earlier in this chapter (in the *treasure.rb* program) I wrote a `Treasure` class that contained a method called `to_s()` which returned a description of a `Treasure` object. I mentioned that `to_s()` is a method that is provided for other objects too and that my version of `to_s()` 'overrode' (or replaced) the default `to_s()` method. This fact becomes significant when we want to inspect an object, because `inspect()`, and some other methods, rely on `to_s()` to provide a string representation of an object.

To see how `to_s()` can be used with a variety of objects and to test how a `Treasure` object would be converted to a string in the absence of an overridden `to_s()` method, try out the *to_s.rb* program:

to_s.rb

```
class Treasure
  def initialize( aName, aDescription )
    @name      = aName
    @description   = aDescription
  end
end

t = Treasure.new( "Sword", "A lovely Elvish weapon" )
print( "Class.to_s: " )
puts( Class.to_s )
print( "Object.to_s: " )
puts( Object.to_s )
print( "String.to_s: " )
puts( String.to_s )
print( "100.to_s: " )
puts( 100.to_s )
print( "Treasure.to_s: " )
puts( Treasure.to_s )
print( "t.to_s: " )
puts( t.to_s )
print( "t.inspect: " )
puts( t.inspect )
```

As you will see when you run this program, *classes* such as `Class`, `Object`, `String` and `Treasure` simply return their names when the `to_s()` method is called:

```
Class.to_s: Class
Object.to_s: Object
String.to_s: String
Treasure.to_s: Treasure
```

But an *object*, such as the `Treasure` object, `t`, returns its identifier, the unique number that ruby associates with the object:

```
t.to_s: #<Treasure:0x0000000003228050>
```

The identifier displayed by `to_s()` is the *same identifier* shown by the `inspect` method.

```
t.inspect: #<Treasure:0x0000000003228050 @name="Sword", @description="A lovely
Elvish weapon">
```

Object Identifiers

When you run this code the *actual* number, such as `0x0000000003228050` will almost certainly be different from the one shown above. That is because the number is Ruby's internal identifier for the object, it is based on the object's location in memory, and this will probably be different each time the code is run.

Looking over my *treasure.rb* program I can't help thinking that its code is a bit repetitive. After all, why have a `Thing` class which contains a name and a `Treasure` class which also contains a name (that is, the `@name` instance variable)?

It would make more sense to regard a `Treasure` as a 'type of' `Thing`. Each `Thing` would have a name and any object that is a 'type of' thing would, automatically, also have a name. If I were to develop this program into a complete adventure game, other objects such as Rooms and Weapons might be yet other 'types of' `Thing`. It is clearly time to start working on a proper class hierarchy. That's what we shall do in the next chapter.

3 – Classes and Subclasses

We ended the last chapter by creating two new classes: *Thing* and *Treasure*. In spite of the fact that these two classes shared some features, there was no direct connection between them. To make a connection we need to create a class hierarchy.

The `Thing` and `Treasure` classes which I wrote in the *treasure.rb* program from the last chapter both included an assignment to the `@name` variable in their `initialize()` methods. Generally I try to avoid programming the same bit of code twice. But in this case, the repetition is so trivial that it doesn't really matter.

However, when you start writing real programs of greater complexity, your classes will frequently contain numerous variables and methods. For example, I might decide to write a `get_name()` and a `set_name()` methods for the `Treasure` class. I've already written those methods in my `Thing` class and now I'll have to write the same code all over again. What's more, if I create another ten classes with `@name` variables, I would have to rewrite the `get_name()` and a `set_name()` methods ten more times – once in each of the ten classes. However, with an object oriented language like Ruby, I can avoid this repetition by creating classes that 'inherit' the features of other classes.

Creating a Class Hierarchy

In my simple adventure game, a `Treasure` is a special type of `Thing`. The `Thing` class, we might say, is the 'base class' of the game – it defines the features such as a name and, eventually, a description – which will be needed by every other class too.

The behaviour of Things in general will be coded in the `Thing` class. I want the `Treasure` class to 'inherit' all the features of the `Thing` class, so I won't need to recode them. The `Treasure` class will then add some additional features, specific to Treasures.

When creating a class hierarchy or 'family tree' of classes, the classes with the most generalised behaviour will be closer to the 'root' of the tree than the classes with more specialist behaviour. So a `Thing` class with just a name and a description, would be the ancestor of a `Treasure` class which has a name, a description and, additionally, a value.

The `Thing` class might also be the ancestor of some other specialist class such as a `Room` which has a name, a description and also exits – and so on.

Class Hierarchies – Ancestors and Descendants

In this book, I often talk about 'descendant' classes 'inheriting' features from their 'ancestor' classes. These terms deliberately suggest a kind a family tree of 'related' classes. In Ruby, each class only has one parent. A class may, however, descend from a long and distinguished family tree with generations of grandparents, great-grandparents and so on.

One Parent, Many Children...

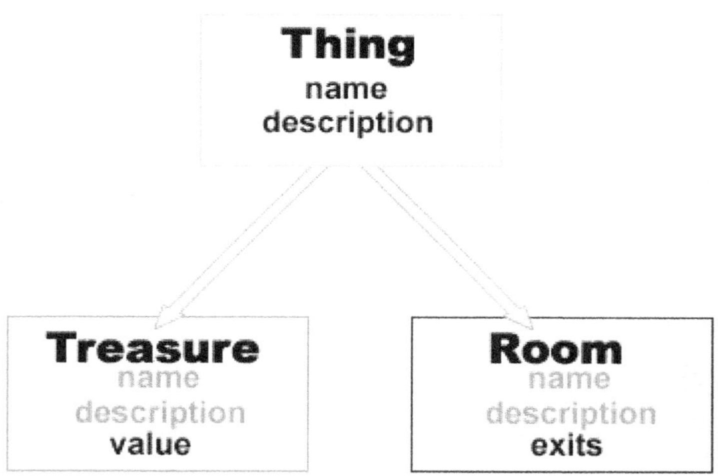

The diagram above shows a `Thing` class which has a *name* and a *description* (in a Ruby program, these might be internal variables such as `@name` and `@description` plus some methods to access them).

The `Treasure` and `Room` classes both descend from the `Thing` class so they automatically 'inherit' a *name* and a *description*. The `Treasure` class adds one new item: *value* – so it now has *name*, *description* and *value*; The `Room` class adds *exits* – so it has *name*, *description* and *exits*. Let's see how to create a descendant class in Ruby. Look at the *adventure1.rb* program:

adventure1.rb

```
class Thing
  def initialize( aName, aDescription )
    @name    = aName
    @description  = aDescription
  end

  def get_name
    return @name
  end

  def set_name( aName )
    @name = aName
  end

  def get_description
    return @description
  end

  def set_description( aDescription )
    @description = aDescription
  end
end

class Treasure < Thing  # Treasure descends from Thing
  def initialize( aName, aDescription, aValue )
    super( aName, aDescription )
    @value = aValue
  end

  def get_value
    return @value
  end

  def set_value( aValue )
    @value = aValue
  end
end
```

This program starts simply enough with the definition of a `Thing` class which has two instance variables, `@name` and `@description`. These variables are assigned values in the `initialize()` method when a new `Thing` object is created.

Instance variables generally cannot (and *should* not) be directly accessed from the world outside the class itself due the principle of encapsulation (see next page). In order to obtain the value of each variable in a `Thing` object we need a *get* accessor method such as `get_name()` and to assign a new value we need a *set* accessor method such as `set_name()`:

```
def get_name
  return @name
end

def set_name( aName )
  @name = aName
end
```

Encapsulation and Information Hiding

Encapsulation is a core idea of Object Oriented programming but not all programmers agree on exactly what it means. As the simplest level, encapsulation refers to the grouping together of an object's 'state' (its data) and the operations which may alter or interrogate its state (its methods). A related idea is called '*Information hiding*'. This describes a situation when an object's data (its fields or variables) cannot be directly accessed by code outside the object. To access the data, you would need to make use of well-defined routes into and out and out of the object. In other words, you would need to use methods to obtain or change the values of an object's data. The benefit of information hiding is that the programmer is able to change the implementation of methods without having to worry that some external code elsewhere in the program relies upon some specific detail of the previous implementation. Ruby usually hides data but there are exceptions to that rule.

Superclasses and Subclasses

Look at the `Treasure` class. Notice how it is declared:

```
class Treasure < Thing
```

Here the angle bracket `<` indicates that `Treasure` is a 'subclass' or descendant of `Thing` and therefore it inherits the data (variables) and behaviour (methods) from the `Thing` class. Since the `get_name`, `set_name`, `get_description` and `set_description` methods already exist in the ancestor class (`Thing`) these don't need to be re-coded in the descendant class (`Treasure`).

Descendent < Ancestor

Don't be confused between the use of the angle-bracket < here and in expressions such as `if(x < y)`. The < character is used as a conditional 'less than' operator when used in tests but as an indicator of the 'ancestor' class or 'superclass' (to the right of the <) when it occurs in a class definition.

The `Treasure` class has one additional piece of data, its value. This is stored by the `@value` variable and I have written *get* and *set* accessor methods for this. When a new `Treasure` object is created (with `new`), its `initialize()` method is automatically called. A `Treasure` object has three variables to initialize (`@name`, `@description` and `@value`), so its `initialize()` method takes three arguments:

```
def initialize( aName, aDescription, aValue )
```

The first two arguments are passed, using the `super` keyword, to the `initialize()` method of the superclass (`Thing`) so that the `Thing` class's `initialize()` method can deal with them:

```
super( aName, aDescription )
```

When used inside a method, the `super` keyword calls a method *with the same name* in the ancestor or 'super' class. The current method in the `Treasure` class is called `initialize()` so when code inside this method passes the two arguments `aName` and `aDescription` to `super()` it is actually passing them to the `initialize()` method of its superclass, `Thing`.

If the `super` keyword is used on its own, without any arguments being specified, all the arguments sent to the current method are passed to the ancestor method.

4 – Methods, Attributes and Class Variables

In this chapter we delve more deeply into Object Orientation and take a look at attributes, class variables and superclasses.

In the little adventure game from the last chapter, whenever I wanted to provide some way of getting or setting the values of an object's variables I wrote a special *get* or *set* accessor method: `get_name()`, `set_name()`, `get_description()`, `set_description()` and so on. This is fine for objects that have just a few variables. But if my objects happen to have lots of variables, it is soon going to be quite messy and time-consuming to write *get* and *set* accessors for every one of them. In fact, there is a much simpler way to do this.

Accessor Methods

I could get and set the value of the `@description` instance variable with two different methods, `get_description()` and `set_description()`, like this:

```
puts( t1.get_description )
t1.set_description( "Some description" )
```

However, Ruby also gives me the ability to retrieve and assign values like this:

```
puts( t1.description )
t1.description = "Some description"
```

In the example above, it may look, at first sight, as though `description` is a variable. Certainly the assignment of a string to `t1.description` using the `=` operator looks very much like an assignment to a variable. In fact `description` isn't a variable. The variable `@description` is 'hidden' inside the `t1` object so I can't access it directly. It turns out that `description` is a special sort of accessor method – in fact, a *pair* of accessor methods. I've had to modify the `Treasure` class definition to create these. Here are the two accessor methods for `@description`:

accessors.rb

```
def description
  return @description
end

def description=( aDescription )
  @description = aDescription
end
```

There are two differences from the *get* and *set* accessors which I wrote previously. First, both of the accessors are called `description` rather than `get_description()` and `set_description()`; secondly the *set* accessor appends an equals sign (=) to the method name. With a *set* accessor of this sort, it is now possible to assign a new string to the `@description` variable like this:

```
t.description = "a bit faded and worn around the edges"
```

And with this sort of *set* accessor, I can retrieve the value of `@description` like this:

```
puts( t.description )
```

Take Care With the =

When you write a *set* accessor in this way, you must append the = character directly to the method name, not merely place it somewhere between the method name and the arguments. So this is correct:

```
def name=( aName )
```

But this is an error:

```
def name =( aName )
```

Attribute Readers and Writers

There is an even simpler way of creating accessors. All you have to do is use two special methods, `attr_reader()` and `attr_writer()`, followed by a *symbol* like this:

```
attr_reader :description
attr_writer :description
```

This code should be placed inside the class definition but outside any methods, like this:

accessors2.rb

```
class Thing
  attr_reader :description
  attr_writer :description
    # some methods here…
end
```

Symbols

In Ruby, a symbol is a name preceded by a colon. `Symbol` is defined in the Ruby class library to represent names inside the Ruby interpreter. Symbols have a number of special uses. For example, when you pass one or more symbols as arguments to `attr_reader` (while it may not be obvious, `attr_reader` is, in fact, a method of the `Module` class), Ruby creates an instance variable and a *get* accessor method to return the value of that variable; both the instance variable and the accessor method will have the same name as the specified symbol.

Calling `attr_reader()` with a symbol has the effect of creating an instance variable with a name matching the symbol and a *get* accessor for that variable. Calling `attr_writer()` similarly creates an instance variable with a *set* accessor. Here, the variable would be called `@description`. Instance variables are considered to the 'attributes' of an object, which is why the `attr_reader()` and `attr_writer()` methods are so named.

The *accessors2.rb* program contains some working examples of attribute readers and writers. The listing of this program is shown on the next page. Notice that the `Thing` class defines a short-form *set* accessor (using `attr_writer()` plus a symbol) for the `@name` variable:

```
attr_writer :name
```

But it has a long-form *get* accessor – a hand-coded method – for the same variable:

```
def name
  return @name.capitalize
end
```

accessors2.rb

```
class Thing

  attr_reader :description
  attr_writer :description
  attr_writer :name

  def initialize( aName, aDescription )
    @name = aName
    @description = aDescription
  end

  # 'long-form' get accessor for @name
  def name
    return @name.capitalize
  end
end

class Treasure < Thing  # Treasure descends from Thing
  attr_accessor :value

  def initialize( aName, aDescription )
    super( aName, aDescription )
  end

end

# This is where our program starts...
t1 = Treasure.new( "sword", "an Elvish weapon forged of gold" )
t1.value = 100
t2 = Treasure.new( "dragon horde", "a huge pile of jewels" )
t2.value = 500

puts( "t1 name=#{t1.name}, description=#{t1.description}, value=#{t1.value}" )
puts( "t2 name=#{t2.name}, description=#{t2.description}, value=#{t2.value}" )
puts( "This is treasure1: #{t1.inspect}" )
puts( "This is treasure2: #{t2.inspect}" )
```

The advantage of writing a long-form accessor method like the *get* accessor for `name` is that it gives you the opportunity to do some extra processing rather than simply reading and writing an attribute value. Here the *get* accessor uses the `String` class's `capitalize()` method to return the string value of `@name` with its initial letter in uppercase.

I've decided that the `@description` attribute needs no special processing so I have used both `attr_reader()` and `attr_writer()` to get and set the value of the `@description` variable.

Attributes or Properties?

Don't be confused by the terminology. In Ruby, an 'attribute' is the equivalent of what many other programming languages call a 'property'. That is, it is a function or method-based interface to retrieve or assign a value to an object's variable.

When you want to read *and* write a variable, the `attr_accessor()` method provides a shorter alternative to using both `attr_reader()` and `attr_writer()`. I have made use of this to access the `value` attribute in the `Treasure` class:

```
attr_accessor :value
```

This is equivalent to:

```
attr_reader :value
attr_writer :value
```

Attributes Create Variables

Earlier I said that calling `attr_reader()` with a symbol creates a variable with the same name as the symbol. The `attr_accessor()` method also does this. In the code for the `Thing` class, this behaviour is not obvious since the class has an `initialize()` method which explicitly creates the variables. The `Treasure` class, however, makes no reference to the `@value` variable in its `initialize()` method:

accessors2.rb

```
class Treasure < Thing
    attr_accessor :value

    def initialize( aName, aDescription )
       super( aName, aDescription )
    end
end
```

The only indication that an `@value` variable exists at all is this accessor definition which declares a `value` attribute:

```
attr_accessor :value
```

The code down at the bottom of the source file sets the value of each `Treasure` object:

```
t1.value = 100
t2.value = 500
```

Even though it has never been formally declared, the `@value` variable really does exist, and we are able to retrieve its numerical value using the *get* accessor `value`.

To be absolutely certain that the attribute accessor really has created an `@value` instance variable, you can look inside the object using the `inspect()` method. I have done this in the final two code lines in this program:

```
puts( "This is treasure1: #{t1.inspect}" )
puts( "This is treasure2: #{t2.inspect}" )
```

This is the output, showing the `@value` variable inside the two `Treasure` objects:

```
This is treasure1: #<Treasure:0x00000000031bf8e8 @name="sword", @description="an
Elvish weapon forged of gold (now somewhat tarnished)", @value=100>
This is treasure2: #<Treasure:0x00000000031bf870 @name="dragon horde",
@description="a huge pile of jewels", @value=500>
```

Attribute accessors can initialize more than one attribute at a time if you send them a list of symbols in the form of arguments separated by commas. As always in Ruby parentheses around the arguments are optional.

accessors3.rb

```
attr_reader :name, :description
attr_writer(:name, :description)
attr_accessor(:value, :id, :owner)
```

Now let's see how to put attribute readers and writers to use in my little adventure game. If you look at the code of the *adventure2.rb* program, you will see that I have created two readable attributes in the `Thing` class: `name` and `description`. I have also made `description` writeable; however, as I don't plan to change the names of any `Thing` objects, the `name` attribute is not writeable:

adventure2.rb

```
attr_reader( :name, :description )
attr_writer( :description )
```

I have also created a `to_s()` method which returns a string that describes a `Thing` object:

```
def to_s
  return "(Thing.to_s):: The #{@name} Thing is #{@description}"
end
```

Recall that all Ruby classes have a `to_s()` method as standard. The `to_s()` method in the `Thing` class overrides the default method.

Overriding methods

As we saw in Chapter 2 with `to_s()`, when you define a method in a subclass with the same name as a method in its superclass, you are said to 'override' the superclass's method. In effect, an overridden method replaces the method in the superclass. You can override existing methods when you want to implement new behaviour appropriate to the specific class type.

Calling Methods of a Superclass

In the *adventure2.rb* program (see the listing on the next page), I have decided that my game will have two classes (`Treasure` and `Room`) descending from `Thing`. The `Treasure` class adds a `value` attribute which can be both read and written. Note that its `initialize()` method calls its superclass in order to initialize the `@name` and `@description` variables before initializing the new `@value` variable:

```
class Treasure < Thing
  attr_reader :value
  attr_writer :value

  def initialize( aName, aDescription, aValue )
    super( aName, aDescription )
    @value = aValue
  end
end
```

Here, if I had omitted to call the superclass's method, `@name` and `@description` would never be initialized. This is because the `Treasure` class's `initialize()` method overrides `Thing` class's `initialize()` method; so when a `Treasure` object is created, the code of the `initialize()` method of `Thing` will not automatically be executed.

adventure2.rb

```
class Thing
  @@num_things = 0 # class variable

  attr_reader( :name, :description )
  attr_writer( :description )

  def initialize( aName, aDescription )
    @name    = aName
    @description  = aDescription
    @@num_things +=1  # increment @@num_things
  end

  def to_s # override default to_s method
    return "(Thing.to_s):: The #{@name} Thing is #{@description}"
  end

  def show_classvars
    return "There are #{@@num_things} Thing objects in this game"
  end

end

class Room < Thing
    # TODO: Add Room-specific behaviour
end

class Treasure < Thing
  attr_reader :value
  attr_writer :value

  def initialize( aName, aDescription, aValue )
    super( aName, aDescription )
    @value = aValue
  end
end

class Map
  def initialize( someRooms )
    @rooms = someRooms
  end

  def to_s
    @rooms.each {
      |a_room|
      puts( a_room )
  }
  end
end
```

Just like the `Treasure` class, the `Room` class, descends from `Thing`. However, unlike `Treasure`, the `Room` class has no `initialize()` method (in fact, I have yet to add any code to the `Room` class).

When a new `Room` object is created Ruby tries to find an `initialize()` method because, if one exists, it will be run immediately after the object is constructed, as I explained in Chapter 2. Since `Room` has no `initialize()` method, Ruby goes scrambling back up the class hierarchy looking for one. The first `initialize()` method it finds is in the `Room` class's superclass, `Thing`; so a `Room` object's `name` and `description` attributes are initialised there:

```
class Room < Thing
  # TODO: Add Room-specific behaviour
end
```

Class Variables

There are a few other interesting things going on in this program. Right at the top of the `Thing` class you will see this:

adventure2.rb

```
@@num_things = 0
```

The two `@` characters at the start of this variable name, `@@num_things`, define this to be a 'class variable'. The variables we've used inside classes up to now have been *instance* variables, preceded by a single `@`, like `@name`. Each new object (or 'instance') of a class assigns its own values to its own *instance* variables. But all objects derived from a specific class share the same *class* variables. I have assigned `0` to the `@@num_things` variable to ensure that it has a meaningful value at the outset.

Here, the `@@num_things` class variable is used to keep a running total of the number of `Thing` objects in the game. It does this simply by incrementing the value of the class variable (it uses `+=` to add 1 to it) in the `initialize()` method every time a new object is created:

```
@@num_things +=1
```

If you look lower down in my code, you will see that I have created a `Map` class to contain an array (a sequential list) of rooms. This includes a version of the `to_s()` method which prints information on each room in the array:

```
class Map
  def initialize( someRooms )
    @rooms = someRooms
  end

  def to_s
    @rooms.each {
      |a_room|
      puts( a_room )
  }
  end
end
```

Don't worry about the implementation of the `Map` class; we'll be looking at arrays and their methods in the next chapter.

Compound Assignment Operators

Before moving on, let me just say a few words about the `+=` operator from the last example (`@@num_things +=1`). This is one of Ruby's 'compound assignment operators'. These are similar to operators found in languages such as C, C# and Java. Compound assignment operators first do a calculation and then assign the result to a variable. The list below shows some examples of common 'compound assignment operators along with the non-compound equivalent.

operator	example	equivalent to
`+=`	`a += b`	`a = a + b`
`-=`	`a -= b`	`a = a - b`
`*=`	`a *= b`	`a = a * b`
`/=`	`a /= b`	`a = a / b`

Here are some examples:

compound_ops.rb

```
a = 100
b = 50

a += b
  puts( a )
a -= b
  puts( a )
```

compound ops.rb (continued)

```
a *= b
  puts( a )
a /= b
  puts( a )
```

This produces this output:

```
150
100
5000
100
```

Objects Share Class Variables

Let's be clear about the difference between the class variable `@@num_things` and the instance variable `@name`, both of which are defined in the `Thing` class. Here is a diagram representing a `Thing` class definition (the rectangle) and three 'Thing objects' – that is, 'instances' of the `Thing` class (the three oval shapes).

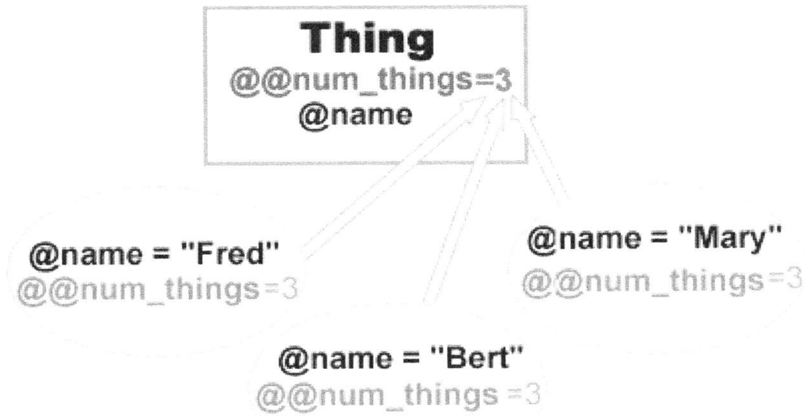

This is a simplified version of the `Thing` class containing only the code related to the `@name` and `@@num_things` variables:

things.rb

```
class Thing
  @@num_things = 0 # class variable

  def initialize( aName, aDescription )
    @name = aName    # instance variables
    @description = aDescription
    @@num_things +=1    # increment @@num_things
  end

  def count
     return @@num_things
  end
end
```

I now create and initialize the three `Thing` objects shown in the diagram: `"Fred"`, `"Mary"` and `"Bert"`:

```
t1 = Thing.new( "Fred", "A cheerful chap" )
t2 = Thing.new( "Mary", "A jolly woman" )
t3 = Thing.new( "Bert", "A grumpy fellow" )
```

When one of these objects assigns a value to its instance variable, `@name`, that value only affects the `@name` variable in the object itself – so here, each of the three objects has a different value for `@name` (and also for `@description`). I can verify that by using `p()` to inspect and display the objects:

```
p( t1 )
p( t2 )
p( t3 )
```

This displays:

```
#<Thing:0x000000000305d400 @name="Fred", @description="A cheerful chap">
#<Thing:0x000000000305d270 @name="Mary", @description="A jolly woman">
#<Thing:0x000000000305d068 @name="Bert", @description="A grumpy fellow">
```

But when an object assigns a value to the class variable, `@@num_things` (this variable's value is incremented in the `initialize()` method every time a new object is created) that value 'lives inside' the `Thing` class and it is 'shared' by all instances of that class.

Here `@@num_things` equals 3 and that is true for all three `Thing` objects. I can verify that by calling the `count()` method from each object:

```
p( t1.count )
p( t2.count )
p( t3.count )
```

In each case, the same value is returned:

```
3
3
3
```

In the *adventure2.rb* program, I don't directly create any `Thing` objects. I do, however, create two `Treasure` objects and three `Room` objects:

adventure2.rb

```
t1 = Treasure.new( "Sword", "an Elvish weapon forged of gold", 800 )
t2 = Treasure.new( "Dragon Horde", "a huge pile of jewels", 550 )

room1 = Room.new( "Crystal Grotto", "A glittery cavern" )
room2 = Room.new( "Dark Cave", "A gloomy hole in the rocks" )
room3 = Room.new( "Forest Glade", "A clearing filled with shimmering light" )
```

The `Treasure` class and the `Room` class are both descendants of the `Thing` class. The `Room` class doesn't define an `initialize()` method, which means that the first `initialize()` defined by an ancestor class will be run when a new `Room` object is created – that's the `initialize()` method of `Thing`:

```
class Room < Thing

end
```

The `Treasure` class *does* define an `initialize()` method. This would normally 'replace' the `initialize()` method of its ancestor class. But the `initialize()` method of `Treasure` calls `super()`, which, remember, has the effect of calling a method with the same name in its superclass – so this again runs the `initialize()` method of `Thing`, and that increments the class variable `@@num_things`:

```
class Treasure < Thing
  attr_reader :value
  attr_writer :value

  def initialize( aName, aDescription, aValue )
    super( aName, aDescription )
    @value = aValue
  end
end
```

When I run the program I can check the value the `@@num_things` class variable by calling the `show_classvars()` method from any object that descends from the `Thing` class. This method simply returns a nicely formatted string showing the value of `@@num_things`:

```
def show_classvars
  return "There are #{@@num_things} Thing objects in this game"
end
```

In this example, the `Treasure` object `t1` calls the `show_classvars()` method (but any `Thing`, `Treasure` or `Room` object could also call the method:

```
puts( t1.show_classvars )
```

And this shows me the total of all the `Thing` objects (including the descendent objects, `Treasure` and `Room`):

```
There are 5 Thing objects in this game
```

5 – Arrays

In this chapter we'll find out how to create a list of objects, starting with the most common type of list – an array.

An array is a sequential collection of items in which each item can be indexed. In Ruby, (unlike many other languages) a single array can hold items of mixed data types such as strings, integers and floating-point numbers. An array can even include method-calls which return some value. This program contains two arrays, `a0` and `a1`. The first array `a0` contains five integers. The second array `a1` contains an integer, a string, a floating-point number and a method-call which returns an integer:

array0.rb

```
def array_length( anArray )
  return anArray.length
end

a0 = [1, 2, 3, 4, 5]
a1 = [1, 'two', 3.0, array_length( a0 )]

p( a0 )
p( a1 )
puts( "Item index #0 of a1 is #{a1[0]}, item #3 is #{a1[3]}" )
```

This is what you will see if you run this code:

```
[1, 2, 3, 4, 5]
[1, "two", 3.0, 5]
Item index #0 of a1 is 1, item #3 is 5
```

The first item in an array has the index `0`, which means that the last item has an index equal to the total number of items in the array minus 1. This explains why `a1[3]` returns the fourth item in the `a1` array (that's the integer 5, which is the length, returned by the `array_length()` method, of `a0`). Given the array, `a1`, shown above, this is how to obtain the values of the first and last items:

```
a1[0]   # returns 1st item (at index 0)
a1[3]   # returns 4th item (at index 3)
```

We've already used arrays a few times – for example, in *adventure2.rb* in Chapter Four I used an array to store a map of `Room` objects:

```
mymap = Map.new( [room1,room2,room3] )
```

Creating Arrays

In common with many other programming languages, Ruby uses square brackets to delimit an array. You can easily create an array, fill it with some comma-delimited values and assign it to a variable. As with most other things in Ruby, arrays are objects. They are defined, as you might guess, by the `Array` class and, just like strings, they are indexed from 0, which means that the first element in the array is at position 0 in the array.

You can reference an item in an array by placing its index between square brackets. If the index is invalid, `nil` is returned:

array1.rb

```
arr = ['a', 'b', 'c']

puts( arr[0] )
puts( arr[1] )
puts( arr[2] )
puts( arr[3] )
```

This produces the following output:

```
"a"
"b"
"c"
nil
```

nil

You can think of `nil` as being a 'non-thing'. It is a special value that is used to indicate that an object of some kind doesn't exist or isn't valid. When some operations fail, a `nil` value is returned and you can test this in your code to try to trap errors. In fact, in Ruby, `nil` itself is an object. It is defined by the class `NilClass`.

In addition to placing multiple data types into a single array, you can also include expressions – that is, bits of Ruby code which return some value. In *array0.rb* I showed an example of an array that included a call to a method that returned an integer. I could equally include other bits of executable code in an array:

array2.rb

```
def hello
  return "hello world"
end

x = [1+2, hello, Dir.entries(".")]
puts( x.inspect )
```

In *array2.rb* I create an array `x` in which the first element is the integer 3 which is the result of the arithmetic expression `1+2`. The second element is the string `"hello world"` which is returned by the method `hello()`. The third element is itself an array containing a the names of all the files in the active directory. Here `"."` indicates the current directory and this is passed as an argument to the `entries()` method of Ruby's `Dir` class. That returns an array of file names. When I look into the `x` array, using the `inspect()` method, which was explained in Chapter Two, this is what I see:

```
[3, "hello world", [".", "..", "array0.rb", "array1.rb", "array2.rb",
"array_assign.rb", "array_index.rb", "array_new.rb", "dir_array.rb",
"multi_array.rb"]]
```

Other Ways to Create an Array

If you want to create an array of strings but can't be bothered typing all the quotation marks, a shortcut is to put unquoted text separated by spaces between parentheses preceded by `%w` like this:

array2.rb

```
y = %w( this is an array of strings )
```

You can also create arrays using the usual object construction method, `new`. Optionally, you can pass an integer to `new` to create an empty array of a specific size (with each element set to `nil`), or you can pass two arguments – the first to set the size of the array and the second to specify the element to place at each index of the array. Here is how I create an empty array, an array with two nil elements and an array with two string elements, both of which are `"hello world"`:

```
a = Array.new                        # an empty array []
a = Array.new( 2 )                   # [nil, nil]
a = Array.new( 2, "hello world" )    # ["hello world", "hello world"]
```

Concatenating Strings and Arrays

In the *array2.rb* program you will see that I join one string to another using the `<<` operator like this:

```
puts( "Array.new : " << a.inspect )
```

It is also possible to concatenate one string to another using the `+` operator, like this:

```
puts( "Array.new : " + a.inspect )
```

So what's the difference? The `+` 'concatenate operator' adds a string or an array to the end of another string or array but it does not modify the string or array to which second string or array is added. The `<<` 'append operator' adds one string or array to another and it also modifies the string or array to which the second string or array is added. Look at this example:

concat.rb

```
s1 = "hello"
s2 = " world"
s3 = " moon"

s1 + s2
p( s1 )

s1 << s2
p( s1 )
```

Here, after the expression `s1 + s2`, the string `s1` remains unmodified (it is still `"hello"`). But after the expression `s1 << s2`, the string `s1` *is* modified (it is now `"hello world"`):

```
"hello"
"hello world"
```

In order to modify a string after using the `+` operator, I need to make an assignment:

```
s4 = s2 + s3
p( s4 )
```

This is now the value of `s4`:

```
" world moon"
```

You can think of strings as being *like* arrays of characters. In fact, the `String` class in Ruby does not descend from the `Array` class. Even so, arrays and strings can often be used in similar ways. The `+` and `<<` operators have the same effects on arrays as on strings. Look at this example:

concat.rb

```
a = [1, 2, 3]
b = [4, 5, 6]
c = [7, 8, 9]

a + b
p( a )

a << b
p( a )

d = b + c
p( d )
```

This shows:

```
[1, 2, 3]
[1, 2, 3, [4, 5, 6]]
[4, 5, 6, 7, 8, 9]
```

There is, however, one other important difference when using these operators with arrays. From the output above, you can see that the `<<` operator inserts the array on the right – here that's `[4, 5, 6]` – as the final element of the array on the left – here that's `[1, 2, 3]` – so the end result is that the concatenated array takes this form:

```
[1, 2, 3, [4, 5, 6]]
```

The `+` operator, on the other hand, inserts the *individual elements* of the array on the right – here that's the integers, `7, 8, 9` – directly into the array on the left, so this is the result:

```
[4, 5, 6, 7, 8, 9]
```

At first sight, this may seem a trivial difference but it is worth bearing in mind since one array contains just 4 elements (the last of which is itself an array) whereas the other contains 6 (all of which are integers). In a real-world program, that would be a significant difference.

Multi-Dimensional Arrays

To create a multi-dimensional array, you can create one array and then add other arrays to each of its 'slots'. For example, this creates an array containing two elements, each of which is itself an array of two elements:

array2.rb

```
a = Array.new( 2 )
a[0]= Array.new( 2, 'hello' )
a[1]= Array.new( 2, 'world' )
```

I can 'look inside' a by inspecting it with `p()` as explained in Chapter 2. This is what I see:

```
[["hello", "hello"], ["world", "world"]]
```

You could nest arrays inside one another using square brackets. This creates an array of four arrays. Each of the four arrays contains four integers:

```
a = [ [1, 2, 3, 4],
      [5, 6, 7, 8],
      [9, 10, 11, 12],
      [13, 14, 15, 16] ]
```

Now when I inspect `a`, I see this:

```
[[1, 2, 3, 4], [5, 6, 7, 8], [9, 10, 11, 12], [13, 14, 15, 16]]
```

In the code shown above, I have placed the four 'sub-arrays' on separate lines. This is not obligatory but it does help to clarify the structure of the multi-dimensional array by displaying each sub-array as though it were a row, similar to the rows in a spreadsheet. When talking about arrays within arrays, it is convenient to refer to each nested array as a 'row' of the 'outer' array.

You can also create an Array object by passing an array as an argument to the new() method of the Array class. Be careful, though. It is a quirk of Ruby that, while it is legitimate to pass an array argument either with or without enclosing parentheses, Ruby considers it a syntax error if you fail to leave a space between the new() method and the opening square bracket. These are all correct:

array_new.rb

```
arrayob = Array.new( [1, 2, 3] )
arrayob = Array.new( [1, 2, 3] )
arrayob = Array.new [1, 2, 3]
```

But this is an error:

```
arrayob = Array.new[1, 2, 3]
```

This is yet another good reason for making a habit of using parentheses when passing arguments to methods.

To see some examples of using multi-dimensional arrays, load up the *multi_array.rb* program. This starts by creating an array, multiarr, containing two other arrays. The first of these arrays, ['one', 'two', 'three', 'four'], is at index 0 of multiarr and the second array, [1, 2, 3, 4], is at index 1:

multi_array.rb

```
multiarr = [['one', 'two', 'three',' four'], [1, 2, 3, 4]]
```

Iterating over Arrays

You can access the elements of an array by iterating over them using a for loop. In my code, the for loop iterates over two elements: namely, the sub-arrays at index 0 and 1:

multi_array.rb

```
for i  in multiarr
  p( i )
end
```

This displays:

```
["one", "two", "three", "four"]
[1, 2, 3, 4]
```

Iterators and for loops

The code inside a `for` loop is executed for each element in an expression. The syntax is summarized like this:

```
for <one or more variables> in <expression> do
    <code to run>
end
```

When more than one variable is supplied, these variables are passed to the code inside the `for...end` block just as you would pass arguments to a method. Here, for example, you can think of `(a,b,c,d)` as four arguments which are initialised, at each turn through the `for` loop, by the four values from a row of `multiarr`:

multi_array.rb

```
for (a, b, c, d) in multiarr
   print( "a=#{a}, b=#{b}, c=#{c}, d=#{d}\n" )
end
```

This processes the two elements of the `multiarr` array – that is, the two sub-arrays which `multiarr` contains: `['one','two','three','four']` and `[1,2,3,4]`. The arguments passed into the loop, `a, b, c, d`, are assigned the matching elements of each of these arrays, so this is the output:

```
a=one, b=two, c=three, d=four
a=1, b=2, c=3, d=4
```

Indexing into Arrays

You can index from the end of an array using minus figures, where `-1` is the index of the last element, `-2` is the index of the last-but-one element and so on. You can also use ranges (values between a start index and an end index separated by two dots) like this: `arr[0..4]` or, using minus values to index from the end of the array back to the start (in this case, assuming an array length of 5 characters), like this: `arr[-5..-1]`. The *array_index.rb* program shows some examples of indexing into an array of characters, `arr`:

array_index.rb

```
arr = ['h', 'e', 'l', 'l', 'o', ' ', 'w', 'o', 'r', 'l', 'd']

print( arr[0,5] )
print( arr[-5,5] )
print( arr[0..4] )
print( arr[-5..-1] )
```

This code produces the following output:

```
["h", "e", "l", "l", "o"]
["w", "o", "r", "l", "d"]
["h", "e", "l", "l", "o"]
["w", "o", "r", "l", "d"]
```

Notice that, as with strings, when provided with two integers separated by a comma, in order to return a number of contiguous items from an array, the first integer is the start *index* while the second integer is a *count* of the number of items (*not* an index):

```
p( arr[0, 5] )    # print 5 items starting from the item at index 0
```

The code above produces the following output:

```
["h", "e", "l", "l", "o"]
```

You can also make assignments by indexing into an array. Here I create an empty array then put items into indexes `0`, `1` and `3`:

array_assign.rb

```
arr = []
arr[0] = [0]
arr[1] = ["one"]
arr[3] = ["a", "b", "c"]
```

I now inspect and print `arr`:

```
p( arr )
```

This is what I see:

```
[[0], ["one"], nil, ["a", "b", "c"]]
```

Notice that 'empty' slot at number 2 contains a nil value. You can also use start and end indexes, ranges and negative index values as shown before:

```
arr2 = ['h', 'e', 'l', 'l', 'o', ' ', 'w', 'o', 'r', 'l', 'd']

arr2[0] = 'H'
arr2[2,2] = 'L', 'L'
arr2[4..6] = 'O', '-', 'W'
arr2[-4,4] = 'a', 'l', 'd', 'o'
```

Let me now inspect and print arr2:

```
p( arr2 )
```

This is what I see:

```
["H", "e", "L", "L", "O", "-", "W", "a", "l", "d", "o"]
```

6 – Hashes

Sometimes it is useful to create collections that are indexed by a string or some other type of object instead of an integer as with an array. Ruby's Hash class can do that – as we'll discover in this chapter.

While arrays provide a simple way to store a collection of items that can be indexed by their numerical position, there may be times when it would be more convenient to index them in some other way. If, for example, you were creating a collection of recipes, it would be more meaningful to have each recipe indexed by name such as "Rich Chocolate Cake" and "Coq au Vin" rather than by numbers: 23, 87 and so on.

Ruby has a class that lets you do just that. It's called a `Hash`. This is the equivalent of what some other languages call an 'associative array' or 'Dictionary'. Just like a real-world dictionary, the entries are indexed by a unique key (in a dictionary, this would be a word) and a value (in a dictionary, this would be the definition of the word).

Creating Hashes

You can create a hash by creating a new instance of the `Hash` class:

```
h1 = Hash.new
h2 = Hash.new( "Some kind of ring" )
```

Both the examples above create an empty `Hash`. A `Hash` object always has a default value – that is, a value that is returned when no *specific* value is found at a given index. In this case, `h2` is initialized with the default value, `"Some kind of ring"`; `h1` is not initialized with a value so its default value will be `nil`.

Having created a `Hash` object, you can add items to it using an array-like syntax – that is, by placing the index (or, in the case of a hash, we should say 'the key') inside a pair of square brackets and using the assignment operator `=` to assign a value. With an array we can only assign a value using an integer array index. With a `Hash`, we can use any sort of data item as a 'key'. The key, however, must be unique because later on we want to be able to use that key to find a specific value stored in the hash.

Here I create a hash containing four values: `'Silver ring'`, `'Gold ring'`, `'Ruby ring'` and `'Sapphire ring'`. Each value is associated with a unique key each of which is a string: `'treasure1'`, `'treasure2'`, `'treasure3'` and `'treasure4'`:

hash1.rb

```
h2['treasure1'] = 'Silver ring'
h2['treasure2'] = 'Gold ring'
h2['treasure3'] = 'Ruby ring'
h2['treasure4'] = 'Sapphire ring'
```

Here the keys are all strings. In principle, however, a key can be any type of object. Given some class, `X`, the following assignment is perfectly legal:

```
x1 = X.new( 'my Xobject' )
h2[x1] = 'Diamond ring'
```

There is a shorthand way of creating hashes and initializing them with key-value pairs. Just add a key followed by `=>` and the value that you want to associate with the key; each key-value pair should be separated by a comma and the whole lot placed inside a pair of curly brackets like this:

```
h1 = {
  'room1'  => 'The Treasure Room',
  'room2'  => 'The Throne Room',
  'loc1'   => 'A Forest Glade',
  'loc2'   => 'A Mountain Stream'
}
```

Unique Keys?

Take care when assigning keys to hashes. If you use the same key twice in a hash, you will end up over-writing the original value. This is just like assigning a value twice to the same index in an array. Consider this example:

```
h2['treasure1'] = 'Silver ring'
h2['treasure2'] = 'Gold ring'
h2['treasure3'] = 'Ruby ring'
h2['treasure1'] = 'Sapphire ring'
```

Here the key `'treasure1'` has been used twice. As a consequence, the original value, `'Silver ring'` has been replaced by `'Sapphire ring'`, resulting in this:

```
{"treasure1"=>"Sapphire ring", "treasure2"=>"Gold ring", "treasure3"=>"Ruby
ring"}
```

Getting and Setting Default Values

You can use the `default` method to get the default value and the `default=` method to set it (see Chapter 4 for more information on *get* and *set* methods). Here, for example, I display the default value for `h1` (which is `nil`), then I give it a new default value, the string `'A mysterious place'` and then display the default value once again.

```
p( h1.default )
h1.default = 'A mysterious place'
p( h1.default )
```

This produces the following output:

```
nil
"A mysterious place"
```

Indexing Into a Hash

To access a *value* stored in a hash, place its *key* between square brackets:

```
puts( h1['room2'] )
```

As the `h1` hash contains the key-value pair: `'room2'=>'The Throne Room'` , the code above displays this:

```
"The Throne Room"
```

If you specify a key that does not exist, the default value is returned. So what happens when I try to obtain a value using an invalid key, like this?

```
p( h1['unknown_room'] )
p( h2['unknown_treasure'] )
```

This is what I see:

```
nil
"Some kind of ring"
```

That is because I did not specify a default value for `h1` but I did for `h2`. Its default value was the string I placed between parentheses when I created the `h2` object:

```
h2 = Hash.new( "Some kind of ring" ).
```

Since `h1` was not explicitly given a default value, its default value is `nil`.

Hash Operations

The `keys()` and `values()` methods of `Hash` each return an array containing all the keys defined for the hash or all the values that have been added to the hash. Once you have obtained arrays of keys or values, so you can use various `Array` methods to manipulate them. Here are a few simple examples. These are my two hashes, `h1` and `h2`:

hash2.rb

```
h1 = {'key1'=>'val1', 'key2'=>'val2', 'key3'=>'val3', 'key4'=>'val4'}
h2 = {'key1'=>'val1', 'KEY_TWO'=>'val2', 'key3'=>'VALUE_3', 'key4'=>'val4',
'key5'=>'val5'}
```

When I use the `keys()` and `values()` methods, I am able to obtain these arrays:

```
h1.keys= ["key1", "key2", "key3", "key4"]
h2.keys= ["key1", "KEY_TWO", "key3", "key4", "key5"]

h1.values= ["val1", "val2", "val3", "val4"]
h2.values= ["val1", "val2", "VALUE_3", "val4", "val5"]
```

Set Intersection

Create a new array containing elements common to two arrays, A and B, excluding any duplicates. The order is preserved from the original array. Set intersection may be done using an array of the keys of two hashes:

```
p( h1.keys & h2.keys )     # set intersection (keys)
```

This displays:

```
["key1", "key3", "key4"]
```

Set intersection may also be done using an array of the values of two hashes:

```
p( h1.values & h2.values )    # set intersection (values)
```

This displays:

```
["val1", "val2", "val4"]
```

Sets

A set is a collection of distinct objects. The intersection of two sets, A and B, is a set that contains only those elements that are found in both A and B.

Concatenation

Create an array containing the elements of one array added to another array:

```
p( h1.keys + h2.keys )      # concatenation
```

This displays:

```
[ "key1", "key2", "key3", "key4", "key1", "key3", "key4", "KEY_TWO"]
```

Appending

Add a second array as the final element of the first array:

```
p( h1.keys << h2.keys )    # append
```

This displays:

```
["key1", "key2", "key3", "key4", ["key1", "key3", "key4", "KEY_TWO"] ]
```

Concatenate or Append?

The append operator << adds an object to the end of an array. The concatenation operator + returns a *new* array that includes all the elements of the array to the right of the + operator, added to the array on its left. If you need to revise array appending and concatenation, refer to the section on *Concatenating Strings and Arrays* in Chapter 5.

Difference

Return an array containing only elements which are found in the first array but not in the second array:

```
p( h1.values - h2.values )
p( h2.values - h1.values )
```

This displays:

```
["val3"]
["VALUE_3", "val5"]
```

7 – Loops

Much of programming is concerned with repetition. In this chapter we'll look at a few common ways of running blocks of code time after time.

There are lots of reasons for repeating some action in a program. You may want to calculate the total of 100 sales; or read lines of text from a file on disk just so long as there are more lines left to read; or repeatedly display some instructions on screen until the user presses a specific key to exit the program. Ruby provides a number of ways of performing this kind of repetition. First we'll look at its `for` loop – which, if you have come to Ruby from more other language – may not be quite what you were expecting.

for Loops

In many programming languages, when you want to run a bit of code a certain number of times you can just put it inside a `for` loop. In most languages, a `for` loop is controlled using a variable that is initialized with a starting value which is incremented by 1 on each turn through the loop. The loop stops running when that variable meets some specific ending value. Here's a version of this traditional type of `for` loop written in Pascal which increments and then displays the variable `i` from the values 1 to 3 :

```
(* This is Pascal code, not Ruby! *)
for i := 1 to 3 do
  writeln( i );
```

Here's a `for` loop written in C. This initializes the variable `i` with the value 1, tests if it is less than 100 and adds 1 to the value of `i` (`i++`). The `dosomething()` function is called inside the loop. When the value of `i` is no longer less than 100 (`i < 100`) the loop exits.

```
// This is C, not Ruby!
for (i = 1; i < 100; i++) {
  dosomething();
}
```

You may recall from Chapter 5 (arrays) that Ruby's `for` loop doesn't work like this at all! Instead of giving it a starting and ending value, we give the `for` loop a list of items and it iterates over them, one by one, assigning each value in turn to a loop variable until it gets to the end of the list. For example, here is a `for` loop that iterates over the items in an array, displaying each in turn:

for_loop.rb

```
# This is Ruby code…
for i in [1, 2, 3] do
  puts( i )
end
```

This is the output:

```
1
2
3
```

Ruby's `for` loop is more like the 'for each' iterator which you may have come across in some other programming languages. Indeed, the author of Ruby describes `for` as "syntax sugar" for the `each()` method which is implemented by Ruby's collection types such as Arrays, Sets, Hashes and Strings (a String being, in effect, a collection of characters). For the sake of comparison, I've rewritten the `for` loop shown above using the `each` method:

each_loop.rb

```
[1, 2, 3].each  do |i|
  puts( i )
end
```

As you can see, there isn't really all that much difference in the code – and the output is exactly the same:

```
1
2
3
```

Let's consider what I had to do in order to convert the `for` loop to an `each()` iterator. First, I had to delete `for` and `in` and append `.each` directly to the array. Then I put the iterator variable, `i`, between a pair of upright bars after `do`. Compare the following examples to see just how similar `for` loops are to `each` iterators:

for_each.rb

```
# i) for
for s in ['one', 'two', 'three'] do
  puts( s )
end

puts

# ii) each
['one', 'two', 'three'].each do |s|
  puts( s )
end
```

Again, the `for` and `each()` examples produce exactly the same results:

```
one
two
three

one
two
three
```

Note, incidentally, that the `do` keyword is optional in a `for` loop that spans multiple lines but it is obligatory when it is written on a single line:

```
# Here the 'do' keyword can be omitted
for s in ['one', 'two', 'three']
  puts( s )
end

# But here it is required
for s in ['one', 'two', 'three'] do puts( s ) end
```

How to Write a Traditional for Loop

If you miss the traditional type of `for` loop, you can always 'fake' it in Ruby by using a `for` loop to iterate over the values in a range. For example, this is how to use a `for` loop variable to count up from 1 to 10, displaying its value at each turn through the loop:

for_to.rb

```
for i in (1..10) do
  puts( i )
end
```

Once again, this can be rewritten using `each()` to iterate over a range of integers:

```
(1..10).each do |i|
  puts( i )
end
```

A range expression such as `1..3` must be enclosed between parentheses when used with the `each()` method, otherwise Ruby assumes that you are attempting to use `each()` as a method of the final integer rather than of the entire expression. The parentheses are optional when a range is used in a `for` loop.

When iterating over items using `each()` the block of code between `do` and `end` is called (predictably, perhaps?) an 'iterator block'.

Block Parameters

In Ruby any variables declared between upright bars at the top of a block are called 'block parameters'. Here `i` is a block parameter:

```
(1..10).each do |i|
```

In a way, a block works like a function and the block parameters work like a function's argument list. The `each()` method runs the code inside the block and passes to it the arguments supplied by a collection (for example, an array or a range). While the collections I've used in the preceding examples happen to be integers, that isn't obligatory. If you look back at the *for_each.rb* program, you'll see that I initialized the block variable, `s`, with strings:

```
['one', 'two', 'three'].each do |s|
```

As we'll see soon, blocks can be used to iterate over other types of object too.

Blocks

Ruby has an alternative syntax for delimiting blocks. You may use `do` and `end`, like this:

block_syntax.rb

```
[1, 2, 3].each do |x| puts( x ) end
```

Or you can use curly braces { } like this:

```
[1, 2, 3].each{ |x| puts( x ) }
```

In each case, the end result is the same: each element of the array (first 1, then 2, then 3) is passed into the block, so here the code inside the block runs three times – once for each array element. The block parameter, x, is assigned the value of the element each time the code inside the block runs and, here it just displays the value of x:

```
1
2
3
```

The elements passed into a block could be other types too. Here is an example, in which each element in the source array is itself an array.

```
[[1, 2, 3], [3, 4, 5], [6, 7, 8]].each{
  |a|
    puts( "#{a}" )
}
```

The array that calls the `each()` method still contains three elements (the three arrays of integers) so the code in the block runs three times. Each time, the block parameter, a, is initialized with one of the arrays of integers and this is the output:

```
[1, 2, 3]
[3, 4, 5]
[6, 7, 8]
```

But wouldn't it be more useful if we could process the individual elements – here, the integers – contained in each of these arrays? Well, it turns out that is really easy to do. We just have to define the same number of block parameters as there are elements in the arrays. Here's how I do that (again this works with either block syntax):

block_syntax.rb

```
#do...end
[[1, 2, 3], [3, 4, 5], [6, 7, 8]].each do
  |a, b, c|
    puts( "#{a}, #{b}, #{c}" )
end
```

This time, the three block parameters, `a`, `b` and `c` are assigned the matching elements of the integer array passed into the block. There are three integer arrays so the block still runs three times and this is the output:

```
1, 2, 3
3, 4, 5
6, 7, 8
```

No matter which block delimiters you use, you must ensure that the opening delimiter (which is either `{` or `do`), is placed on the same line as the `each()` method. Inserting a line break between `each` and the opening block delimiter is a syntax error.

while Loops

Ruby has a few other loop constructs too. This is how to do a `while` loop:

```
while tired
  sleep
end
```

Or, to put it another way:

```
sleep while tired
```

Even though the syntax of these two examples is different they perform the same function. In the first example, the code between `while` and `end`, which is here a call to a method named `sleep()`, executes just as long as the Boolean condition – which, in this case, is the value returned by a method called `tired()` – evaluates to `true`.

As in `for` loops the keyword `do` may optionally be placed between the test condition and the code to be executed when these appear on separate lines; the `do` keyword is obligatory when the test condition and the code to be executed appear on the same line.

Boolean conditions

A Boolean condition is a test that evaluates to either `true` or `false`. Whenever you test something using `if` or `while` you are testing a Boolean condition. Usually you would want to run one piece of code when a condition is `true` and a different piece of code when it is `false`.

while Modifiers

In the second version of the `while` loop shown earlier (`sleep while tired`), the code to be executed (`sleep`) precedes the test condition (`while tired`). This syntax is called a 'while modifier'. When you want to execute several expressions using this syntax, you can put them between the `begin` and `end` keywords:

```
begin
  sleep
  snore
end while tired
```

This is an example showing the various alternative syntaxes:

while.rb

```
$hours_asleep = 0

def tired
  if $hours_asleep >= 8 then
    $hours_asleep = 0
    return false
  else
    $hours_asleep += 1
    return true
  end
end

def snore
  puts( 'snore....' )
end

def sleep
  puts( "z" * $hours_asleep )
end

while tired do sleep end   # a single-line while loop

while tired                # a multi-line while loop
  sleep
end

sleep while tired          # single-line while modifier
```

while.rb (continued)

```
begin                          # multi-line while modifier
  sleep
  snore
end while tired
```

The last example above (the multi-line `while` modifier) needs close consideration as it introduces some important new behaviour. When a block of code which is delimited by `begin` and `end` precedes the `while` test, that code always executes at least once. In the other types of `while` loop, the code may never execute at all if the Boolean condition initially evaluates to `true`. The *while2.rb* sample program clearly shows the differences in behaviour of these alternatives types of `while` loop:

while2.rb

```
puts( "starting 1st while loop" )
# This executes 0 or more times
i = 10
while(i < 10)
  puts(i)
  i += 1
end
puts( "1st while loop ended" )

i = 10
# This executes 1 or more times
puts( "\nstarting 2nd while loop" )
begin
  puts(i)
  i += 1
end while(i < 10)
puts( "2nd while loop ended" )
```

Here the two loops test if the value of `i` is less than 10. Since the value of `i` is 10, this test always evaluates to `false`. The first loop places its test *before* the code between `while` and `end` so that code is never run. The second loop encloses some code between `begin` and `end`. That code is run and then the condition `while(i < 10)` is tested. It is found to be `false` so the code is not run again. The consequence of this is that the code in the first loop *never* runs. The code in the second loop runs *once*:

```
starting 1st while loop
1st while loop ended

starting 2nd while loop
10
2nd while loop ended
```

Here are some more examples. In each of the three lines of code shown below, a test is made to determine if the value of `x` is less than 100. Since the value of `x` is 100, this test always evaluates to `false`:

while2.rb

```
puts( "\nStarting 3 'while' tests")
x = 100
  # code in loop 3 never runs
while(x < 100) do puts('loop 3: x < 100') end

  # code in loop 4 never runs
puts('loop 4: x < 100') while (x < 100)

  # code in loop 5 runs once
begin puts('loop 5: x < 100') end while (x < 100)
```

In the first case (loop 3), the test is done *before* the code enclosed by `do` and `end`. It evaluates to `false`, so the code is never run. In the second case (loop 4), even though the test appears *after* the code to be run, it is still evaluated *before* the code is run. It too evaluates to `false`, so the code never is run. In the third case (loop 5), the code is enclosed by `begin` and `end` and the test is placed *after* the code. Only in this case is the code is run *before* the test is evaluated. So this code runs once. You can verify that from the program output:

```
Starting 3 'while' tests
loop 5: x < 100
```

Loop confusion?

The Ruby language provides many alternative ways of performing the same operations. This has the advantage of giving programmers a broad choice of programming syntax. It has the disadvantage that the sheer variety of ways available for doing similar operations can seem bewildering and confusing to new Ruby programmers (and sometimes to experienced Ruby programmers too). Don't panic! The fact of the matter is that you may only need to use two or three types of loop when writing your own programs. However, you need to *understand* all the various types of loop when reading other programmers' code.

until Loops

Ruby also has an `until` loop which can be thought of as a 'while not' loop. Its syntax and options are the same as those applying to `while` – that is, the test condition and the code to be executed can be placed on a single line (in which case the `do` keyword is obligatory) or they can be placed on separate lines (in which case `do` is optional). There is also an `until` modifier which lets you put the code before the test condition; and there is the option of enclosing the code between `begin` and `end` in order to ensure that the code block is run at least once. Here are some simple examples of `until` loops:

until.rb

```
i = 10
# one line until
puts( "until 1" )
until(i == 10) do puts( i ) end # never executes

# multiple-line until where the do keyword is optional
puts( "\nuntil 2" )
until(i == 10) # do # never executes
  puts( i )
  i += 1
end

# one line until modifier
puts( "\nuntil 3" )
puts(i) until( i == 10) # never executes

# multi-line until modifier, executes 1 or more times
puts( "\nuntil 4" )
begin         # executes once
  puts( i )
end until(i == 10)
```

The code above produces this result:

```
until 1

until 2

until 3

until 4
10
```

Earlier I described `until` loops as being like 'while not' loops. To understand that, try changing the `until` loops above into `while` loops. To do to obtain the same results, you also need to change the test condition from a testing if `i` is *equal* to 10 `(i == 10)` to a test that `i` is *not equal* to 10 `(i != 10)`. The sample program, *until.rb* provides some examples of this.

Both `while` and `until` loops can, just like a `for` loop, be used to iterate over arrays and other collections. This is how to iterate over all the elements in an array:

array_iteration.rb

```
arr = [1,2,3,4,5]

i = 0
while( i < arr.length )
  puts(arr[i])
  i += 1
end

i = 0
until( i == arr.length )
  puts(arr[i])
  i +=1
end
```

8 – Tests and Conditions

When you want your programs to take different actions depending on the value of a variable or expression, you need to perform conditional tests. Let's see how to do that in Ruby.

Computer programs are full of decisions waiting to be made. Things like: if I stay in bed I will get more sleep, else I will have to go to work; if I go to work I will earn some money, else I will lose my job. Let's see how Ruby can help out.

We've already performed a number of `if` tests in previous programs. To take a simple example, this is from the Tax calculator program in Chapter 1:

```
if (subtotal < 0.0) then
  subtotal = 0.0
end
```

In that program, the user was prompted to enter a value, `subtotal`, which was then used in order to calculate the tax due on it. The test above ensures that `subtotal` is never a minus figure.

If the user, in a fit of madness, enters a value less than `0`, the `if` test spots this since the condition `(subtotal < 0.0)` evaluates to `true`, which causes the body of the code between the `if` test and the `end` keyword to be executed; here, this sets the value of `subtotal` to `0`.

Equals once = or equals twice == ?

In common with many other programming languages, Ruby uses one equals sign to *assign* a value two equals signs to *test* a value:

```
x = 10              # assign the value 10 to x
if(x == 10)         # test if the value of x is 10
```

if...else

A simple `if` test has only one of two possible results. Either a bit of code is run or it isn't, depending on whether the test evaluates to true or not. But often, you will need to have more than two possible outcomes. Let's suppose, for example, that your program needs to follow one course of action if the day is a weekday and a different course of action if it is a weekend. You can test these conditions by adding an `else` section after the `if` section, as I have done in the `dayIs()` method this:

if_else.rb

```
def dayIs( aDay )
  if aDay == 'Saturday' or aDay == 'Sunday'
    daytype = 'weekend'
  else
    daytype = 'weekday'
  end
  return daytype
end
```

The `if` condition here is straightforward. It tests two conditions:

1) if the value of the variable, `aDay` is equal to the string `'Saturday'` or..
2) if the value of `aDay` is equal to the string `'Sunday'`.

If either of those conditions is true then the next line of code executes and assigns the string `'weekend'` to the `daytype` variable. In all other cases, the code after `else` executes and that assigns the string `'weekday'` to the `daytype` variable. You can test this by passing it various strings like this:

```
day1 = "Monday"
day2 = "Saturday"
print( day1 + " is a " + dayIs( day1 ) + "\n" )
print( day2 + " is a " + dayIs( day2 ) + "\n" )
```

The output is predictable:

```
Monday is a weekday
Saturday is a weekend
```

if...then

When an `if` test and the code to be executed are placed on separate lines, the `then` keyword is optional. Both these bits of code run without problem:

if_then.rb

```
x = 1
if x == 1 then        # with 'then'
  puts( 'ok' )
end

if x == 1         # without 'then'
  puts( 'ok' )
end
```

When the `if` test and the code are placed on a single line, the `then` keyword is obligatory:

```
if x == 1 then puts( 'ok' ) end    # this works
if x == 1 puts( 'ok' ) end         # this is an error
```

Testing Multiple Conditions

An `if` test isn't restricted to evaluating just two conditions. Let's suppose you want to test this set of conditions to determine if a certain day is a working day or a holiday:

1. All weekdays are working days.
2. All Saturdays are holidays.
3. Sundays are only holidays when you are not working overtime.

This is my first attempt to write a test to evaluate all these conditions:

and_or_buggy.rb

```
def dayIs( aDay )
  working_overtime = true
  if aDay == 'Saturday' or aDay == 'Sunday' and not working_overtime
    daytype = 'holiday'
    puts( "Hurrah! I'm on holiday!" )
  else
    daytype = 'working day'
  end
  return daytype
end
```

I test this by sending some strings to the `dayIs()` method:

```
day1 = "Monday"
day2 = "Saturday"
day3 = "Sunday"
print( day1 + " is a " + dayIs( day1 ) + "\n" )
print( day2 + " is a " + dayIs( day2 ) + "\n" )
print( day3 + " is a " + dayIs( day3 ) + "\n" )
```

Unfortunately, I can see at once that this doesn't work as intended:

```
Monday is a working day
Saturday is a working day
Sunday is a working day
```

Remember that, according to my rules, Saturday is always a holiday. But this program insists that Saturday is a working day. This is because of the way that Ruby evaluates this test:

```
  if aDay == 'Saturday' or aDay == 'Sunday' and not working_overtime
```

I had intended it to mean:

"If the day is Saturday; or if the day is Sunday and I am not working overtime".

But Ruby interprets it as:

"If the day is Saturday and I am not working overtime, or if the day is Sunday and I am not working overtime".

Since the `working_overtime` variable has been set to `true`, according to this test, Saturday can never be a holiday! The easiest way to resolve this ambiguity is to put parentheses around any code to be evaluated as a single unit, like this:

and_or.rb

```
if aDay == 'Saturday' or (aDay == 'Sunday' and not working_overtime)
```

That simple change completely alters the behaviour of my program. Now it displays the following:

```
Monday is a working day
Hurrah! I'm on holiday!
Saturday is a holiday
Sunday is a working day
```

and...or...not

Incidentally, Ruby has two different syntaxes for testing Boolean (`true`/`false`) conditions. In the previous example, I used the English-language style operators: `and`, `or` and `not`. If you prefer you could use alternative operators similar to those used in many other programming languages, namely: `&&` (and), `||` (or) and `!` (not). So, for example, you could rewrite the test condition in the last program like this:

```
if aDay == 'Saturday' || (aDay == 'Sunday' && !working_overtime)
```

Note that the two sets of operators aren't interchangeable. They have different 'precedence' which means that when multiple operators are used in a test, the parts of the test may be evaluated in different orders depending on which operators you use. As a general rule, it is a bad idea to mix these two variations of operators in a program.

if...elsif

There may be occasions when you need to take different actions based on several alternative conditions. One way of doing this is by evaluating an `if` condition followed by a series of other test conditions placed after the keyword `elsif`. The whole lot must then be terminated using the `end` keyword. For example, here I repeatedly take input from a user inside a `while` loop; an `if` condition tests if the user enters `'q'` (I've used the `chomp()` method to remove the carriage return from the input); if `'q'` is not entered the first `elsif` condition tests if the integer value of the input (`input.to_i`) is greater than 800; if this test fails the next `elsif` condition tests if it is less than or equal to 800:

if_elsif.rb

```
while input != 'q' do
  puts( "Enter a number between 1 and 1000 (or 'q' to quit)" )
  print( "?- " )
  input = gets().chomp()
  if input == 'q'
    puts( "Bye" )
  elsif input.to_i > 800
    puts( "That's a high rate of pay!" )
  elsif input.to_i <= 800
    puts( "We can afford that" )
  end
end
```

At first sight, this code seems to work correctly. It prompts me to enter a number. If I enter 800 or less it displays `"We can afford that"`. If I enter a number greater than 800, it displays: `"That's a high rate of pay!"`. Even so, it contains a bug. It asks for a number between 1 and 1000 but it accepts other numbers. It's perfectly acceptable for me even to enter nonsensical negative numbers such as -100. If I try that, this is what I see:

```
Enter a number between 1 and 1000 (or 'q' to quit)
?- -100
We can afford that
```

If you've been studying this chapter carefully, you will now have the knowledge needed to rewrite this code to fix this bug and display different messages if the number entered is greater than 1000 or less than 1. You may want to see if you can rewrite the tests so that the code correctly deals with any number entered.

? :

Ruby also has a short-form notation for `if...then...else` in which a question mark `?` replaces the `if...then` part and a colon `:` acts as `else`, like this:

```
<Test Condition> ? <if true do this> : <else do this>
```

This is a working example:

```
x == 10 ? puts( "it's 10" ) : puts( "it's some other number" )
```

When the test condition is complex (if it uses multiple `and` / `or` tests) you should enclose it in parentheses for clarity. If the tests and code span several lines the `?` must be placed on the same line as the preceding condition and the `:` must be placed on the same line as the code immediately following the `?`. In other words, if you put a newline before the `?` or the `:` you will generate a syntax error. This is an example of a valid multi-line code block:

```
(aDay == 'Saturday' or aDay == 'Sunday') ?
  daytype = 'weekend' :
  daytype = 'weekday'
```

Here is a more complete example of some code using this syntax:

if_else_alt.rb

```
def dayIs( aDay )
  (aDay == 'Saturday' or aDay == 'Sunday') ?
    daytype = 'weekend' :
    daytype = 'weekday'
  return daytype
end

x = 10
x == 10 ? puts( "it's 10" ) : puts( "it's some other number" )
x = 11
x == 10 ? puts( "it's 10" ) : puts( "it's some other number" )

day1 = "Monday"
day2 = "Sunday"
print( day1 + " is a " + dayIs( day1 ) + "\n" )
print( day2 + " is a " + dayIs( day2 ) + "\n" )
```

This displays the following:

```
it's 10
it's some other number
Monday is a weekday
Sunday is a weekend
```

unless

Ruby also can also perform `unless` tests, which are the opposite of `if` tests:

unless.rb

```
unless aDay == 'Saturday' or aDay == 'Sunday'
  daytype = 'weekday'
else
  daytype = 'weekend'
end
```

Think of `unless` as being an alternative way of expressing 'if not'. So when you test a condition with `unless` you could equally test that condition with `if` followed by the `!` negation operator. In the following example, I've rewritten the code shown above using `if` and `!`:

```
if !(aDay == 'Saturday' or aDay == 'Sunday')
  daytype = 'weekday'
else
  daytype = 'weekend'
end
```

if and unless Modifiers

You may recall the alternative syntax for `while` loops in Chapter 7. Instead of writing this…

```
while tired do sleep end
```

…we can write this:

```
sleep while tired
```

This alternative syntax, in which the `while` keyword is placed between the code to execute and the test condition, is called a 'while modifier'. It turns out that Ruby has `if` and `unless` modifiers too. Here are a few examples:

if_unless_mod.rb

```
sleep if tired

begin
  sleep
  snore
end if tired

sleep unless not tired

begin
  sleep
  snore
end unless not tired
```

The terseness of this syntax is useful when, for example, you repeatedly need to take some well-defined action if some condition is `true`. This is how you might pepper your code with debugging output if a constant called `DEBUG` is `true`:

```
puts( "somevar = #{somevar}" ) if DEBUG
```

case Statements

When you need to take a variety of different actions based on the value of a single variable, multiple `if...elsif` tests are verbose and repetitive. A neater alternative is provided by a `case` statement.

This begins with the word `case` followed by the variable name (or some other expression) to test. Then comes a series of `when` sections, each of which specifies a 'trigger' value followed by some code. The code executes only when the test variable (here, that's `i`) equals the trigger value. For instance, in the *case.rb* program, when `i` has the value 2, `"It's Tuesday"` is displayed; when `i` has the value 6 or 7, `"Yippee! It's the weekend! "` is displayed; when `i` has a value that does not occur in any of the `when` sections (that is, any value that is not between 1 and 7), the code in the `else` section runs and `"That's not a real day!"` is displayed:

case.rb

```
case( i )
  when 1 then puts( "It's Monday" )
  when 2 then puts( "It's Tuesday" )
  when 3 then puts( "It's Wednesday" )
  when 4 then puts( "It's Thursday" )
  when 5 then puts( "It's Friday" )
  when (6..7) then puts( "Yippee! It's the weekend! " )
  else puts( "That's not a real day!" )
end
```

This is how I test values from 1 to 8:

```
for i in 1..8 do
  showDay( i )
end
```

And this is what is displayed:

```
It's Monday
It's Tuesday
It's Wednesday
It's Thursday
It's Friday
Yippee! It's the weekend!
Yippee! It's the weekend!
That's not a real day!
```

The `then` keyword can be omitted *only* if the test and the code to be executed are on separate lines, like this:

```
when 1
puts( "It's Monday" )
```

In Ruby, once a match is made the `case` statement exits:

```
case( i )
  when 5 then puts( "It's Friday" )
    puts( "...nearly the weekend!" )
  when 6 then puts( "It's Saturday!" )
    # the following never executes
  when 5 then puts( "It's Friday all over again!" )
end
```

break?

Unlike `case` statements in C-like languages, there is no need to enter a `break` keyword when a match is made in a `case` block in order to prevent execution trickling down through the remainder of the sections.

You can include several lines of code between each `when` condition and you can include multiple values separated by commas to trigger a single `when` block, like this:

```
when 6, 7 then puts( "Yippee! It's the weekend! " )
```

The condition in a `case` statement is not obliged to be a simple variable; it can be an expression like this:

```
case( i + 1 )
```

You can also use non-integer types such as string. If multiple trigger values are specified in a `when` section, they may be of varying types – for example, both string and integers:

```
when 1, 'Monday', 'Mon' then puts( "Yup, '#{i}' is Monday" )
```

Here is a longer example, illustrating some of the syntactical elements mentioned earlier:

case2.rb

```
def showDay( i )
  case( i )
    when 1 then puts( "It's Monday" )
    when 2 then puts( "It's Tuesday" )
    when 3 then puts( "It's Wednesday" )
    when 4 then puts( "It's Thursday" )
    when 5 then puts( "It's Friday" )
      puts( "...nearly the weekend!")
    when 6, 7
      puts( "It's Saturday!" ) if i == 6
      puts( "It's Sunday!" ) if i == 7
      puts( "Yippee! It's the weekend! " )
      # the following never executes
    when 5 then puts( "It's Friday all over again!" )
    else puts( "That's not a real day!" )
  end
end

for i in 1..8 do
  showDay( i )
end
```

This shows:

```
It's Monday
It's Tuesday
It's Wednesday
It's Thursday
It's Friday
...nearly the weekend!
It's Saturday!
Yippee! It's the weekend!
It's Sunday!
Yippee! It's the weekend!
That's not a real day!
```

Here's an example that uses a mix of strings and integers when trying to match the variable t:

case2.rb

```
def showTreasures( t )
  case( t )
    when "ring" then puts( "It's a magical ring")
    when "axe", "sword" then puts( "The #{t} a dwarvish weapon")
    when 1, 2, "XII" then puts( "#{t} is a number of power")
    else puts( "I have no idea what a #{t} is")
  end
end

showTreasures("ring")
showTreasures("axe")
showTreasures("sword")
showTreasures(1)
showTreasures(2)
showTreasures("XII")
showTreasures("wombat")
```

This shows:

```
It's a magical ring
The axe a dwarvish weapon
The sword a dwarvish weapon
1 is a number of power
2 is a number of power
XII is a number of power
I have no idea what a wombat is
```

9 – Modules

A Ruby module is like a class which contains code but can't be used to create objects. To use the code in a module you need to 'mix it in' to a class. In this chapter, we look at modules and mixins.

As mentioned in Chapter 3, each Ruby class can only have one immediate 'parent', though each parent class may have many 'children'. That means that a single class cannot inherit the features from two unrelated classes.

But there are occasions when it might be useful for a class to be able to implement features taken from more than one other pre-existing class. For example, a Sword might be a type of Weapon but also a type of Treasure; a House might be a type of Building but also a type of Investment and so on.

A Module is like a Class

Ruby's solution to this problem is provided by Modules. At first sight, a module looks very similar to a class. Just like a class, a module can contain constants, methods and classes. Here's a simple module:

```
module MyModule
  GOODMOOD = "happy"
  BADMOOD = "grumpy"

  def greet
   return "I'm #{GOODMOOD}. How are you?"
  end
end
```

As you can see, this contains a constant, `GOODMOOD` and an 'instance method', `greet()`. To turn this into a class you would only need to replace the word `module` in its definition with the word `class`.

Module Methods

In addition to instance methods, a module may also have 'module methods' which are preceded by the name of the module:

```
def MyModule.greet
  return "I'm #{BADMOOD}. How are you?"
end
```

In spite of their similarities, there are two major features which classes possess but which modules do not: **instances** and **inheritance**. Classes can have instances (objects created from the class); and classes can both inherit *from* superclasses ('ancestor' classes) and they may have subclasses ('descendent' classes) which inherit *from them*; modules can have none of these.

If you can't create an object from a module, then what are modules for? This question can be answered in two words: **namespaces** and **mixins**. Ruby's 'mixins' provide a simple alternative to multiple inheritance which I mentioned earlier. We'll come to mixins shortly. First though, let's look at namespaces.

Modules as Namespaces

You can think of a module as a sort of named 'wrapper' around a set of methods, constants and classes. The various bits of code inside the module share a 'namespace' - which means that they are all visible to each other but they are not visible to code outside the module.

The Ruby class library defines a number of modules such as `Math` and `Kernel`. The `Math` module contains mathematical methods such as `sqrt()` to return a square root, and constants such as `PI`. The `Kernel` module contains many of the methods we've been using from the outset such as `print()`, `puts()` and `gets()`.

Constants

In Ruby it is a convention that identifiers that start with a capital letter should be treated as constants. Constants are like variables except their values do not (or *should* not!) change. In fact, Ruby does not have true constants because the value of a constant *can* be changed. However, Ruby will warn you if you change the value of a constant.

Let's assume we have this module:

modules1.rb

```
module MyModule
  GOODMOOD = "happy"
  BADMOOD = "grumpy"

  def greet            # instance method
   return "I'm #{GOODMOOD}. How are you?"
  end

  def MyModule.greet    # module method
   return "I'm #{BADMOOD}. How are you?"
  end
end
```

From outside the module, we can access the constants using :: like this:

```
puts( MyModule::GOODMOOD )
```

This code prints this:

```
happy
```

We can similarly access module methods using dot notation – that is, by specifying the module name followed by a full stop and the method name.

```
puts( MyModule.greet )
```

The code above prints this:

```
I'm grumpy. How are you?
```

From this, we can see that the call to `MyModule.greet` has run the module method named `MyModule.greet()` rather than the instance method named `greet()`. This just leaves us with the problem of how to access the instance method.

Module 'Instance Methods'

As the module defines a closed namespace, code outside the module won't be able to 'see' the `greet()` method so, writing this outside the module *won't* work:

```
puts( greet )
```

If `MyModule` were a class rather than a module we would, of course, create objects from the class using the `new()` method – and each separate object would have access to the instance methods. But you cannot create instances of modules. So how the heck can we use their instance methods? This is where those mysterious mixins enter the picture.

Included Modules or 'Mixins'

An object can access the instance methods of a module by including that module using the `include()` method. If you were to include `MyModule` into your program, everything inside that module would suddenly pop into existence within the current scope. So the `greet` method of `MyModule` will now be accessible:

modules2.rb

```
module MyModule
   GOODMOOD = "happy"
   BADMOOD = "grumpy"

  def greet
    return "I'm #{GOODMOOD}. How are you?"
  end

  def MyModule.greet
    return "I'm #{BADMOOD}. How are you?"
  end
end

include MyModule            # include MyModule here
puts( greet )
puts( MyModule.greet )
```

Now when the two puts() statements at the end execute, this is what is shown:

```
I'm happy. How are you?
I'm grumpy. How are you?
```

The process of including a module in a class is also called 'mixing in' the module – which explains why included modules are often called 'mixins'. When you mix a module into the main scope of a program, as I've done here, you are actually mixing it into the Ruby `Object` class so that module is now available to *all objects* in Ruby.

You probably don't really want to do this so, while this is fine in a very simple sample program like this, I wouldn't advise you to make a habit of including modules in the main scope of any real-world Ruby programs.

When you include a module in a class, objects created from that class can use the instance methods of the included module as though they were defined in the class itself:

modules3.rb

```
module MyModule
  GOODMOOD = "happy"
  BADMOOD = "grumpy"

  def greet
    return "I'm #{GOODMOOD}. How are you?"
  end

  def MyModule.greet
    return "I'm #{BADMOOD}. How are you?"
  end
end         # end of module

class MyClass
  include MyModule   # mix in the MyModule module

  def sayHi
    puts( greet )
  end

  def sayHiAgain
    puts( MyModule.greet )
  end
end
```

Not only can the methods of this class access the `greet()` method from `MyModule`, but so too can any objects created from the class, like this:

```
ob = MyClass.new
ob.sayHi
ob.sayHiAgain
puts(ob.greet)
```

This gives the following output:

```
I'm happy. How are you?
I'm grumpy. How are you?
I'm happy. How are you?
```

In short, modules can be used as a way of grouping together related methods, constants and classes within a named scope. On the other hand, you might be more interested in using modules as an alternative to multiple inheritance. Returning to an example which I mentioned at the start of this chapter, let's assume that you have a `Sword` class which is not only a type of `Weapon` but also of `Treasure`. Maybe `Sword` is a descendant of the `Weapon` class (so inherits methods such as `deadliness` and `power`), but it also needs to have the methods of a `Treasure` (such as `value` and `insurance_cost`). If you define these methods inside a `Treasure` *module* rather than a `Treasure` *class*, the `Sword` class would be able to include the `Treasure` module in order to add ('mix in') the `Treasure` methods to the `Sword` class's own methods.

In fact, it could mix in more than one module if it needed to access methods from those too. Here, for example, my `Sword` class descends from the `Weapon` class and mixes in the `Treasure` and `MagicThing` modules (it then adds a `name` attribute):

modules4.rb

```
module MagicThing
  def m_power
    return @m_power
  end

  def m_power=(aPower)
    @m_power=aPower
  end
end

module Treasure
  attr_accessor :value
  attr_accessor :insurance_cost
end

class Weapon
  attr_accessor :deadliness
  attr_accessor :power
end

class Sword < Weapon     # Descends from Weapon
  include Treasure       # Mixes in Treasure
  include MagicThing     # Mixes in MagicThing
  attr_accessor :name
end
```

Now, when I create a `Sword` object, I can access its `name` (defined in the `Sword` class), its `deadliness` and `power` (inherited from its superclass, `Weapon`), its `value` and `insurance_cost` (mixed in from the `Treasure` module) and its `m_power` (mixed in from the `MagicThing` module):

```
s = Sword.new
s.name = "Excalibur"
s.deadliness = 10
s.power = 20
s.value = 100000
s.insurance_cost = 500
s.m_power = "Glows when Orcs Appear"

puts( s.name )
puts( s.deadliness )
puts( s.power )
puts( s.value )
puts( s.insurance_cost )
puts( s.m_power )
```

This is the output:

```
Excalibur
10
20
100000
500
Glows when Orcs Appear
```

Note, incidentally, that any variables which are *local* to a module cannot be accessed from outside the module. This is the case even if a method inside the module tries to access a local variable and that method is invoked by code from outside the module – for example, when the module is mixed in through inclusion. The *mod_vars.rb* program illustrates this.

mod_vars.rb

```
x = 1   # x is local to this program

module Foo
  x = 50   # x is local to module Foo

  def no_bar
   return x
  end
```

mod_vars.rb (continued)

```
  def bar
   @x = 1000
   return  @x
  end

  puts( "In Foo: x = #{x}" )  # this is the module-local x (50)
end

include Foo

puts( x )      # this is the 'program-local' x (1)
puts( bar )
puts( no_bar )  # ERROR: Cannot access module-local variable x needed by no_bar
```

This code produces the following valid output:

```
In Foo: x = 50
1
1000
```

When an attempt is made to execute the `no_bar()` method an error message is displayed:

```
`no_bar': undefined local variable or method `x' for main:Object (NameError)
```

Including Modules from Files

So far, when I've included modules, those modules have been defined in the same source file as the code that includes them. Often it is more useful to define modules in separate files and include them in other files as needed. The first thing you have to do in order to use code from another file is to load that file using the `require()` method, like this:

requiremodule.rb

```
require( "./testmod.rb" )
```

The required file must be in the specified directory (in the example above `"./"` indicates the current directory or on the search path or in a folder listed in the predefined array variable `$:`. You can add a directory to this array variable using the usual array-append method, `<<` in this way:

```
$: << "C:/mydir"
```

$: The Dollar-Colon Constant

The `$:` global variable stores the paths to the directories from which programs and code can be loaded or required by Ruby programs. `$:` returns an array of path names. On my PC I can enter this:

```
p( $: )
```

And this is shown:

```
["C:/Ruby25-x64/lib/ruby/gems/2.5.0/gems/did_you_mean-
1.2.0/lib", "C:/Ruby25-x64/lib/ruby/site_ruby/2.5.0",
"C:/Ruby25-x64/lib/ruby/site_ruby/2.5.0/x64-msvcrt",
"C:/Ruby25-x64/lib/ruby/site_ruby", "C:/Ruby25-
x64/lib/ruby/vendor_ruby/2.5.0", "C:/Ruby25-
x64/lib/ruby/vendor_ruby/2.5.0/x64-msvcrt", "C:/Ruby25-
x64/lib/ruby/vendor_ruby", "C:/Ruby25-x64/lib/ruby/2.5.0",
"C:/Ruby25-x64/lib/ruby/2.5.0/x64-mingw32"]
```

If I wanted to add the current directory to the paths searched by Ruby and then require files from that directory using the file names only, I could rewrite my code like this:

```
$: << "./"
require( "testmod.rb" )
```

File load error?

If you run the program from within an editor or IDE you may see an error message due to the required file not being found in the current directory. That is because some editors and IDEs default to some other directory when running programs. Try running this program from the command prompt, as explained in the Introduction to this book. Open a command prompt containing the source code file, *requiremodule.rb* and enter this command:

```
ruby requiremodule.rb
```

require_relative

In older versions of Ruby (prior to 1.9), you could require files from the current directory without having to include the "./" path. In Ruby 1.9 and Ruby 2 you can do this using the method `require_relative()` like this:

```
require_relative( "testmod.rb" )
```

Pre-Defined Modules

The following modules are built into the Ruby interpreter:

```
Comparable, Enumerable, FileTest, GC, Kernel, Math, ObjectSpace, Precision,
Process, Signal
```

The most important of the pre-defined modules is `Kernel` which, as mentioned earlier, provides many of the 'standard' Ruby methods such as `gets()`, `puts()`, `print()` and `require()`. In common with much of the Ruby class library, `Kernel` is written in the C language. While `Kernel` is, in fact, 'built into' the Ruby interpreter, conceptually it can be regarded as a mixed-in module which, just like a normal Ruby mixin, makes its methods directly available to any class that requires it; since it is mixed in to the `Object` class, from which all other Ruby classes descend, the methods of `Kernel` are universally accessible.

10 – Files and Exceptions

We are nearly at the end of *The Little Book Of Ruby*. Let's finish by looking at a simple database project. We'll also take a look at exception-handling – for when things go wrong!

At some point, most desktop applications will need to save and load data to and from disk. Sometimes you might want to save data stored by user-defined objects or even lists of objects. There are various ways of doing this in Ruby. Here we will look YAML which is a fairly easy-to-use format for saving data.

YAML

YAML is an acronym which is (debatably) either short for "Yet Another Markup Language" or for "YAML Ain't Markup Language".

What this Program Does

The *data_save.rb* program implements a simple CD database. The techniques shown here could equally well be used to create a database of other types too: DVDs, MP3s, Games or Books, for example. My program defines three types of CD object – a basic `CD`, a `PopCD` and a `ClassicalCD`. This is the `CD` class:

data_save.rb

```
class CD

  def initialize( arr )
    @name         = arr[0]
    @artist       = arr[1]
    @numtracks    = arr[2]
  end

  def getdetails
    return [@name, @artist, @numtracks]
  end
end
```

Following the principles of object oriented design, the generic `CD` is my 'base' class while the more specialised classes, `PopCD` and `ClassicalCD` are descendant classes. In other words, `CD` is the superclass of `PopCD` and `ClassicalCD`. The `CD` class contains three fields to store the name, the artist and number of tracks. Here are the two descendant classes:

```
class PopCD < CD

  def initialize( arr )
    super( arr  )
    @genre = arr[3]
  end

  def getdetails
    return ( super << @genre )
  end
end

class ClassicalCD < CD

  def initialize( arr )
    super( arr )
    @conductor  = arr[3]
    @composer   = arr[4]
  end

  def getdetails
   return ( super << @conductor << @composer )
  end
end
```

These two classes descend from the `CD` class – as is shown by the `<` in their declarations:

```
class PopCD < CD
class ClassicalCD < CD
```

Descendent classes inherit the features of their superclass so both `PopCD` and `ClassicalCD` inherit the `@name`, `@artist` and `@numtracks` fields as well as the `getdetails()` method which returns those fields in an array.

`PopCD` adds data on `@genre` (this might, for example, be a string such as 'rock' or 'country') while `ClassicalCD` adds `@conductor` and `@composer`. They define their own `getdetails()` methods because they need to return an array containing the extra fields in addition to the fields defined by their ancestor class. Here, I call the superclass's `getdetails()` method to obtain an array of the fields defined by the `CD` class, then I add on the additional fields using the append operator `<<` before returning the array:

```
def getdetails
  return ( super << @conductor << @composer )
end
```

Overriding and Calling Superclass Methods

If you need to revise overridden methods, refer to Chapter 4. Calling overridden methods using the `super` keyword is explained in Chapter 3 ('Superclasses and Subclasses').

When the program is run, the user can enter data to create new `CD` objects of any of these three types. I won't explain the entire code of this program here. Having read this book, you have all the information you need to be able to understand the code. So use the project for revision. If there is anything in the code that you don't fully understand, go back to the relevant section in this book to revise that topic.

Here's a brief summary of the *data_save.rb* project. Each new `CD` object is created by calling the `otherCD()` method to initialize the name, the artist name and the number of tracks (all this information is required for every `CD` object), then it calls, if necessary, either the `classicCD()` or `popCD()` methods to initialize the additional fields needed for those object types.

When the program is run, the loop shown below runs. It prompts the user to enter data to create new `CD` objects of any of the three defined types. The user can enter either `'p'`, `'c'` or `'o'` to create a new pop, classical or generic ('other') `CD`:

```
ans = ''
until ans == 'q' do
  puts( "Create (P)op CD (C)lassical CD, (O)ther CD - (S)ave or (Q)uit?" )
  print( "> " )
  ans = gets[0].chr().downcase()
  case ans
  when 'p' then addCD( PopCD.new( popCD() ) )
  when 'c' then addCD( ClassicalCD.new( classicCD() ) )
  when 'o' then addCD( CD.new( otherCD() ) )
    when 's' then saveDB
  end
  showData
end
```

There is also an option to save data (`'s'`) to disk. This is the code that saves the data. Given the fact that it may need to save an array of mixed object types – `CD`, `PopCD` and `ClassicalCD` – you might be surprised to see how short and simple this code is:

```
def saveDB
  File.open( $fn, 'w' ) {
    |f|
      f.write($cd_arr.to_yaml)
  }
end
```

Here `open()` is a method of the `File` class, the global variable `$fn` is the file name, *'cd_db.yml'*, which is assigned earlier in my code and `'w'` is a 'file-mode' argument which causes the file to be opened for writing – so that I can save data into it.

The file object is passed into the block delimited by curly brackets and it is assigned to the block parameter `f`. Now I simply call the `write()` method of the file (this method is, in fact, inherited from the `IO` class from which `File` descends) to write my array of data in YAML format (thanks to the `to_yaml()` method) into the named file.

When the application is run subsequently, the existing data is reloaded. Again, this is quite simple, thanks to the `File.read()` method which opens the file and reads in its data. The `YAML.load()` method 'unpacks' the data so that I can assign it into the array `$cd_arr`:

```
def loadDB
  input_data = File.read( $fn )
  $cd_arr = YAML.load( input_data )
end
```

Files

I've made use of the `File` class several times in this program. I use `File.open()` to open a file before reading data from it; I use `File.read()` to do the data-reading and I now I use `File.exist?()` to test if the file name given by `$fn` can actually be found on disk:

```
if File.exist?( $fn ) then
  loadDB
  showData
else
  puts( "The file #{$fn} cannot be found." )
end
```

Here, `exist?()` is a 'class method' – that is, it 'belongs to' the `File` class rather than to an instance of the `File` class. That explains how we can invoke the method from `File` itself rather than having to create a new `File` object and then call the method from that object. This may remind you of the module methods discussed in Chapter 9 – another example of the similarities between modules and classes. Class methods provide a useful way of creating utility methods that act on other objects or data rather than upon a specific object.

The Program Listing

The *data_save.rb* program is longer than the other sample programs that accompany this book. As always, the full source code is available in the code archive from the Bitwise Books web site. The full listing of this program can also be found in the appendix of this book.

Class Methods

To create your own class methods, precede the method name with the keyword `self` or the actual class name and a dot. Here I define one instance method, `instanceMethod()`, and two class methods, `MyClass.classMethod()` and `self.anotherClassMethod()`:

class_methods.rb

```
class MyClass

  def MyClass.classMethod
    puts( "This is a class method" )
  end

  def self.anotherClassMethod
    puts( "This is a another class method" )
  end

  def instanceMethod
    puts( "This is an instance method" )
  end

end
```

There are other ways of defining class methods too. Currently the most commonly-used syntax is the one that uses `self` as in `self.methodname()`. You should use the class name when calling a class method and the object name when calling an instance method:

```
ob = MyClass.new
MyClass.classMethod
MyClass.anotherClassMethod
ob.instanceMethod
```

This code produces this output:

```
This is a class method
This is a another class method
This is an instance method
```

A specific object (such as `ob` in the code above) cannot call a class method. Nor can a class call an instance method. An instance method is a 'normal' method – one which belongs to an 'instance' of a class. If I try to call `instanceMethod()` from the `MyClass` class I get an error:

```
MyClass.instanceMethod
```

If I do that, Ruby displays an error message something like this:

```
undefined method `instanceMethod' for MyClass:Class (NoMethodError)
```

Similarly, if I try to call `classMethod()` from an instance of `MyClass`, here that's the object called `ob`, I also get an error:

```
ob.classMethod
```

This time, I see a message similar to this:

```
undefined method `classMethod' for #<MyClass:0x0000000003112328> (NoMethodError)
```

It is possible that you may rarely need to define class methods in your own programs. However, you need to be familiar with them, as they are provided by a number of standard Ruby classes such as `File` and `IO`.

Exception Handling

Even the most carefully written program will sometimes encounter unforeseen errors. For example, a program such as my CD database (which needs to read some data from disk), works on the assumption that the specified disk is actually available and the data is valid. If your program does calculations based on user input, it works on the assumption that the input is suitable to be used in a calculation. But what happens if the specified disk or file can't be found or the user enters an alphabetic character when your program expects an integer?

You may try to anticipate some potential problems before they arise – for example, by writing code to check that a file exists before reading data from it. Or checking that user input is numerical before doing a calculation.

Even so, you will never be able to predict every possible problem in advance. To avoid problems that may occur due to unforeseen circumstances at runtime, you can use 'exception handling'.

An 'exception' is an error which is packaged up into an object. The object is an instance of the `Exception` class (or one of its descendants). You can handle exceptions by trapping the `Exception` object, optionally using information which it contains (to print an appropriate error message, say) and taking any actions needed to recover from the error – perhaps by closing any files that are still open or by assigning a sensible value to a variable which may have been assigned some nonsensical value as the result of an error.

Here is a summary of the basic syntax of some exception handling code, where `<ExceptionClass>` would be replaced by the actual class name of an exception:

```
begin
   # Some code which may cause an exception
rescue <ExceptionClass>
   # Code to recover from the exception
end
```

Let's look at an example. Suppose we have a program that prompts the user to enter a number that will be used to divide some other number. Unfortunately, a user enters `0`. Dividing by zero is impossible and it will inevitably cause an error if the program tries to do so. The *div_by_zer.rb* sample program simulates this problem by trying to divide `1` by `0` and then attempting to display the result:

div_by_zero.rb

```
x = 1/0
puts( x )
```

Immediately the program crashes and shows me an error message:

```
divided by 0 (ZeroDivisionError)
```

I clearly need to make sure that something as simple as entering the wrong number is not going to crash my program. So I rewrite the code, but this time I add an exception handler which deals with an attempt to divide by zero:

exception1.rb

```
begin
   x = 1/0
rescue Exception
   x = 0
   puts( $!.class )
   puts( $! )
end
```

By placing the troublesome code inside an exception handling block (between `begin` and `end`), I have been able to trap the `Exception` in the section beginning with `rescue`. First I set the variable, `x`, to a meaningful value. Next come these two inscrutable statements:

```
puts( $!.class )
puts( $! )
```

In Ruby, `$!` is a global variable to which the most recent exception is assigned. Printing `$!.class` displays the class name of the exception object. Here this is `ZeroDivisionError`. Printing the variable `$!` alone has the effect of displaying the error message contained within the `Exception` object which here is `"divided by 0"`. So this time, my program shows those messages, sets `x` to `0`, and – most important of all – doesn't crash!

```
ZeroDivisionError
divided by 0
```

I am not generally too keen on relying upon global variables, particularly when they have 'names' as undescriptive as `$!`. Fortunately, there is an alternative. You can associate a variable name with the exception by placing the 'assoc operator', `=>`, after the class name of the exception and before the variable name:

```
rescue Exception => exc
```

You can then use the variable name (here `exc`) to refer to the `Exception` object:

exception2.rb

```
begin
  x = 1/0
rescue Exception => exc
  x = 0
  puts( exc.class )
  puts( exc )
end
```

Exceptions have a Family Tree

In Ruby, exceptions are objects and, like all other objects, they are defined by a class. There is, moreover, a clear 'line of descent' which starts, like all Ruby objects, with the `BasicObject` class.

The *exception_tree.rb* program displays the ancestry of the `ZeroDivisionError` object by climbing back through its class hierarchy using the recursive `showFamily()` function:

exception_tree.rb

```
def showFamily( aClass )
  if (aClass != nil) then
    puts( "#{aClass}" )
    showFamily( aClass.superclass )
  end
end

begin
  x = 1/0
rescue Exception => exc
  x = 0
  puts( exc )
  puts( "Family Tree of this exception..." )
  showFamily( exc.class )
end
```

A recursive function is one that calls itself. In this case, the `showFamily()` method displays the class of an exception, then it calls *itself* with the superclass of that class. It prints the superclass's class then it calls itself again to print the class of the next superclass and so on until there are no more superclasses (at which point `aClass` will be `nil`). The output shows the ancestors of the current exception like this:

```
divided by 0
Family Tree of this exception...
ZeroDivisionError
StandardError
Exception
Object
BasicObject
```

Sometimes it may be useful to take different actions for different exceptions. You can do that by adding multiple `rescue` sections. Each `rescue` section can handle multiple exception types by specifying exception class names separated by commas.

In the *multi_exception.rb* sample program, the `calc()` method has one `rescue` section that handles both `TypeError` and `NoMethodError` exceptions. That's followed by another `rescue` section with a catch-all `Exception` handler to deal with other exception types:

multi_exception.rb

```
def calc( val1, val2 )
  begin
    result = val1 / val2
  rescue TypeError, NoMethodError => e
    puts( e.class )
    puts( e )
    puts( "One of the values is not a number!" )
    result = nil
  rescue Exception => e
    puts( e.class )
    puts( e )
    result = nil
  end
  return result
end
```

I can test this by passing to it a variety of problematic arguments which will generate different types of exceptions:

```
calc( 20, 0 )
puts
calc( 20, "100" )
puts
calc( "100", 100 )
```

The program handles these exceptions, sets the result to a valid value (here that's `nil`), displays an error message and – most important of all – doesn't crash!

```
ZeroDivisionError
divided by 0

TypeError
String can't be coerced into Integer
One of the values is not a number!

NoMethodError
undefined method `/' for "100":String
One of the values is not a number!
```

Exception-handling exercises

To become familiar with exception-handling, you could try rewriting some of the programs supplied in the code archive so that they can recover from unexpected errors. Try adding exception-handling to the tax calculator from Chapter 1 so that it can recover from incorrect input (if the use enters the alphabetic characters `IO` instead of the integer characters `10`, for example). Add exception-handling to the *data_save.rb* program from this chapter so that it if it tries to read in data from a file that contains invalid data, it prints an error message but doesn't crash.

Moving On...

So now we've arrived at the end of this book. What next?

If you want to take your study of Ruby further, take a look at some of the resources – books and web sites – listed in the Appendix. Also, be sure to visit the Bitwise Books web site (http://www.bitwisebooks.com) where you will not only find details of our full range of books but you will also be able to sign up to our newsletter and download a number of free resources.

In conclusion, I hope you've enjoyed this little introduction to Ruby programming and that it may be just the start of many years of enjoyable and productive development using the Ruby language.

Download the Source Code

To download **the source code join our mailing list**:

http://www.bitwisebooks.com/subscribe

or scan this QR code:

A Message from the Author

Thank you for reading my book. I hope you've found it useful – and, with luck, even enjoyable! I've been programming, and writing about programming, since the early 1980s. In the series of 'Little Books' I hope to be able to pass on some of the knowledge that I've gained over the years and provide readers with the sort of books I wish had been available (but weren't!) when I was learning to program.

Writing these books takes a great deal of time and effort and, while I enjoy writing them – because, after all, programming is something I love – it is really hard for me for my books to compete against books produced by big publishing companies.

You can help me!

Reviews are incredibly important to me. They let potential readers know if my books have been useful to other people so that they can decide whether they might also be useful to them. I would therefore be really grateful if you could take a few moments to leave a short review on Amazon. You can do that by clicking one of the two links below or (on other Amazon sites) by clicking the 'Write a Customer Review' button on the book page.

Thanks again for reading my book!

Huw Collingbourne

Leave a Review

Amazon (USA):

https://tinyurl.com/y5jdkbem
or
https://www.amazon.com/review/create-review?asin=1913132072

Amazon (UK);

https://tinyurl.com/yy9mjotx
or
https://www.amazon.co.uk/review/create-review?asin=1913132072

Appendix

Ruby Editors and IDEs

For an easy (and free) way to get started with Ruby, I would suggest that you choose one of the relatively simple text editors such as Komodo Edit, NotePad++, SciTE or Visual Studio Code. Commercial editors and IDEs may have the best combination of Ruby development features and ease of use but these are not required when following this book.

Need Help?

For the latest information and help with installing and using any of these products, refer to the product web site. Most of these sites provide online help and documentation and they may also have a forum where you can post questions. The author and publisher of *The Little Book Of Ruby* cannot provide any help in using IDEs or editors.

Komodo Edit

Free editor for multiple programming languages including Ruby. A more powerful commercial edition, Komodo IDE, is also available. Runs on Windows, Linux, macOS:

http://komodoide.com/komodo-edit

Komodo IDE

The commercial alternative to Komodo Edit which has a much larger feature set including an integrated debugger:

https://www.activestate.com/products/komodo-ide

NotePad++

Free multi-language programmer's editor for Windows:

https://notepad-plus-plus.org

RubyMine

Commercial cross-platform IDE that is tailored for Ruby On Rails users. Runs on Windows, Linux, macOS:

http://www.jetbrains.com/ruby

SciTE

Free programmers' editor with some basic support for Ruby editing:

http://www.scintilla.org/SciTE.html

Sublime Text

Commercial multi-language editor for Windows, macOS, Linux:

http://www.sublimetext.com

TextMate

Commercial programmers' editor, with Ruby coding features, for Mac users:

http://macromates.com

Visual Studio Code

Free, cross-platform, multi-language IDE.

https://code.visualstudio.com

Visual Studio Code requires add-in Ruby support:

https://marketplace.visualstudio.com/items?itemName=rebornix.Ruby

Installing Ruby

Ruby Downloads

Some versions of Linux and macOS already have Ruby installed. You can download the latest version of Ruby from www.ruby-lang.org. Be sure to download the binaries (not merely the source code). For Windows users, the easiest way to set up Ruby on your system is by using the Ruby Installer available from: http://rubyinstaller.org

Ensure Ruby is on the Search Path

If you want to be able to run the Ruby interpreter from any directory, you will need to ensure that it is on the 'search path'. Ruby installers may offer an option to add the Ruby interpreter to the path. You should accept that option when installing Ruby.

Ruby Documentation

Ruby-Doc

The definitive documentation on the Ruby class library (the API) can be found on the Ruby-Doc web site. Bookmark this in your browser. You should always refer to the latest API documentation to understand the features and behaviour of the standard Ruby classes and methods. Ruby-Doc also has links to other useful sources of Ruby information: https://ruby-doc.com

More Resources

If you want to continue your exploration Ruby programming, you may want to get a copy of my more advanced Ruby guide, **The Book Of Ruby**, which is published as a paperback and eBook by No Starch Press: http://www.nostarch.com/boruby.htm

While that book is not necessary to your understanding of Ruby programming (this *Little Book* should be sufficient for that), it does explain the language in more depth, including some of the more obscure features and various potential pitfalls.

Bitwise Books and Courses

For our full range of paperback books and eBooks plus free downloads, be sure to visit the **Bitwise Books** web site:

http://www.bitwisebooks.com

For video-based programming tutorials, go to the **Bitwise Courses** web site:

http://www.bitwisecourses.com

Visit the *Facebook* page of Bitwise Books & Courses:

https://www.facebook.com/BitwiseCourses

Subscribe to our *Twitter* feed:

https://twitter.com/bitwisecourses

The Data Save (CD Database) Listing

This is the full listing of the *data_save.rb* project described in Chapter 10. I recommend that you run this from the command prompt. If you run the program from an IDE or editor it is possible that it will run in some other directory and then it may fail to load any saved data files. Running from the command prompt is explained in the Introduction to this book. Log into the directory containing the source code file *datasave.rb* (e.g. *C:\RubyCodeArchive\10*) and enter this command:

```
ruby datasave.rb
```

data_save.rb

```
require 'yaml'

#array for cd objects
$cd_arr = Array.new

# file name for saving/loading
$fn = 'cd_db.yml'

# ancestor generic CD class
class CD

  # initialize variables parsed from array argument ( arr )
  def initialize( arr )
    @name           = arr[0]
    @artist         = arr[1]
    @numtracks      = arr[2]
  end

  # return an array containing all instance variables of a CD object
  def getdetails
    return [@name, @artist, @numtracks]
  end
end

# PopCD is a 'child' class of CD
class PopCD < CD

  # call super to pass array, arr, to parent (CD) class which initializes three
  # instance variables. Thismethod the initializes one more: @genre
  def initialize( arr )
    super( arr )
    @genre = arr[3]
  end
```

data_save.rb (continued)

```
  # calls sup to get array from CD class getdetails
  # method. Then adds @genre to the end of the array
  # and returns the entier 4-item array
  def getdetails
    return ( super << @genre )
  end
end

class ClassicalCD < CD
  def initialize( arr )
    super( arr )
    @conductor  = arr[3]
    @composer   = arr[4]
  end

  def getdetails
   return ( super << @conductor << @composer )
  end
end

# some methods to get data from the user
def otherCD
    print( "Enter CD name: " )
    cd_name = gets().chomp()
    print( "Enter artist's name: " )
    a_name = gets().chomp()
    print( "Enter number of tracks: " )
    num_tracks = gets().chomp().to_i
    return [cd_name, a_name, num_tracks]
end

def classicCD
    cdInfo= otherCD
    print( "Enter conductor's name: " )
    con_name= gets().chomp()
    print( "Enter composer's name: " )
    comp_name = gets().chomp()
    cdInfo << con_name << comp_name
    return cdInfo
end

def popCD
    cdInfo= otherCD
    print( "Enter genre of music: " )
    genre = gets().chomp()
    cdInfo << genre
    return cdInfo
end
```

data_save.rb (continued)

```
# adds a CD object to the array variable, $cd_arr
def addCD( aCD )
    $cd_arr << aCD
end

# saves data to disk in YAML format - the to_yaml method converts to YAML format
def saveDB
    File.open( $fn, 'w' ) {
        |f|
        f.write($cd_arr.to_yaml)
    }
end

# loads data from disk and recreates the array of
# cd objects, $cd_arr, from the data
def loadDB
    input_data = File.read( $fn )
    $cd_arr = YAML.load( input_data )
end

# prints the data from the array to screen in human-
# readable (YAML) format
def showData
    puts( $cd_arr.to_yaml )
end

# Start of Program

if File.exist?( $fn ) then
  loadDB
  showData
else
  puts( "The file #{$fn} cannot be found." )
end

# 'main' loop
ans = ''
until ans == 'q' do
  puts( "Create (P)op CD (C)lassical CD, (O)ther CD - (S)ave or (Q)uit?" )
  print( "> " )
  ans = gets[0].chr().downcase()
  case ans
    when 'p' then addCD( PopCD.new( popCD() ) )
    when 'c' then addCD( ClassicalCD.new( classicCD() ) )
    when 'o' then addCD( CD.new( otherCD() ) )
    when 's' then saveDB
  end
  showData
end
```

Little Books Of ...

The Little Book Of Ruby is one of a series of '*Little Books Of ...*' for programmers. In each *Little Book* we aim to give you *just the stuff you really need* to get straight to the heart of the matter without all the fluff and padding.

We know that there is plenty of information online about standard code libraries, so we don't fill the pages of these books by duplicating that information. Instead, we aim to explain the really important details that you need to gain a solid understanding of each subject and start hands-on programming as quickly as possible.

Some other '*Little Books Of ...*' are:

The Little Book of Pointers

An in-depth guide to pointers in C:

- Indirection
- Pointer arithmetic
- Data Alignment
- Linked Lists (single/double)
- Stacks & Queues
- Function Pointers
- Common Pointer Problems

The Little Book of C

A beginners guide to the C language:

- Fundamentals of C
- Variable & Types
- Operators & Tests
- Functions & Arguments
- Arrays & Strings
- User-Defined Types

The Little Book of Recursion
Understanding recursion techniques in C:

- Recursive Functions
- The Call Stack
- Stack Frames
- Stack Corruption
- Recursion & Scope
- Tree Structures
- Disk Directory Recursion

The Little Book of C#
A beginners guide to the C# language:

- Object Orientation
- Classes and Methods
- Methods & Arguments
- Arrays & Strings
- Exception-handling
- Lists & Generics

You can also download a number of useful free resources from the Bitwise Books web site: http://www.bitwisebooks.com

Made in the USA
Coppell, TX
27 May 2021

BAPTISTWAY®

Adult Bible Study Guide

The Gospel of Luke

Parables Jesus Told

Jim Denison
Ebbie Smith
Ray Pollard

BAPTISTWAY PRESS®
Dallas, Texas

Luke: Parables Jesus Told—Adult Bible Study Guide—Large Print

BAPTISTWAY PRESS® Management Team
Executive Director, Baptist General Convention of Texas: Charles Wade
Coordinator, Church Health and Growth Section: H. Lynn Eckeberger
Director, Bible Study/Discipleship Center: Dennis Parrott

Publishing consultant: Ross West, Positive Difference Communications
Cover and Interior Design and Production: Desktop Miracles, Inc.
Front Cover Photo: The Mount of Beatitudes in Galilee, BiblePlaces.com

First edition: March 2004
ISBN: 1–931060–46–0

How to Make the Best Use of This Issue

Whether you're the teacher or a student—

1. Start early in the week before your class meets.
2. Overview the study. Review the table of contents and read the study introduction. Try to see how each lesson relates to the overall study.
3. Use your Bible to read and consider prayerfully the Scripture passages for the lesson. (You'll see that each writer has chosen a favorite translation for the lessons in this issue. You're free to use the Bible translation you prefer and compare it with the translation chosen for that unit, of course.)
4. After reading all the Scripture passages in your Bible, then read the writer's comments. The comments are intended to be an aid to your study of the Bible.
5. Read the small articles—"sidebars"—in each lesson. They are intended to provide additional, enrichment information and inspiration and to encourage thought and application.
6. Try to answer for yourself the questions included in each lesson. They're intended to encourage further thought and application, and they can also be used in the class session itself.

If you're the teacher—

A. Do all of the things just mentioned, of course.
B. In the first session of the study, briefly overview the study by identifying with your class the date on which each lesson will be studied. Lead your class to write the date in the table of contents on page 7 and on the first page of each lesson. You might also find it helpful to make and post a chart that indicates the date on which each lesson will be studied. If all of your class has e-mail, send them an e-mail with the dates the lessons will be studied. *Note*: An Easter lesson is included. If your class uses the Easter lesson, you may need to decide whether to combine two lessons or study the missed lesson at a special class meeting.
C. Get a copy of the *Teaching Guide*, a companion piece to this *Study Guide*. The *Teaching Guide* contains additional Bible comments plus two teaching plans. The teaching plans in the *Teaching Guide* are intended to provide practical, easy-to-use teaching suggestions that will work in your class.
D. After you've studied the Bible passage, the lesson comments, and other material, use the teaching suggestions in the *Teaching Guide* to help you develop your plan for leading your class in studying each lesson.
E. You may want to get the additional adult Bible study comments—*Adult Online Bible*

Commentary—by Dr. Jim Denison, pastor of Park Cities Baptist Church, Dallas, Texas, that are available at www.baptistwaypress.org and can be downloaded free. An additional teaching plan plus teaching resource items are also available at www.baptistwaypress.org.

F. You also may want to get the enrichment teaching help that is provided in the *Baptist Standard*, in either the printed or the internet editions. Call 214–630–4571 to begin your subscription to the *Baptist Standard*. Access the internet information by checking the *Baptist Standard* website at http://www.baptiststandard.com. (Other class participants may find this information helpful, too.)

G. Enjoy leading your class in discovering the meaning of the Scripture passages and in applying these passages to their lives.

The Gospel of Luke: Parables Jesus Told

Introducing

The Gospel of Luke: Parables Jesus Told

Often in the Gospel of Luke we read that Jesus "told them a parable" (see 5:1; 6:39; 8:4; 12:16; 13:6; 14:7; 15:3; 18:1, 9, 11; 20:9, 19; 21:29).[1] The parables occupy a large place in the Gospels of Matthew and Mark as well as Luke, in fact.[2] The count of the number of parables in these gospels varies according to how the one counting defines a parable, but New Testament scholar A. M. Hunter counted sixty different parables in the gospels.[3] Other Bible students find fewer parables than this, and some find more. Whatever the exact number, another groundbreaking student of the parables, C. H. Dodd, said that "the parables are perhaps the most characteristic element in the teaching of Jesus Christ as recorded in the gospels."[4] A significant percentage of the teachings of Jesus in the gospels consists of parables.

The intent of this study is to focus on the parables in the Gospel of Luke, giving special emphasis to those parables that appear *only* in the Gospel of Luke. Focusing the study in this manner will permit us to study the parables in more detail, without skipping from gospel to gospel and perhaps wresting the parable out of its context in that particular gospel.

Studying Luke's parables in this manner also keeps us from slighting the parables that are in Luke's Gospel only.

An additional reason for focusing mainly on the parables in Luke is to give these parables a biblical context. That context is the Gospel of Luke, with Luke's own unique approach to telling the story of Jesus. An important and helpful way of studying the Bible is to focus on the message of a given book of the Bible. As is almost always the case in this series of Bible study lessons, we will use that method as we study these parables in Luke's Gospel, following the biblical order of the parables in doing so.

What is a parable, anyway? As might be expected, there are different answers to that question. A helpful one, though, is from one of the great interpreters of parables, C. H. Dodd, who wrote, "At its simplest the parable is a metaphor or simile drawn from nature or common life, arresting the hearer by its vividness or strangeness, and leaving the mind in sufficient doubt about its precise application to tease it into active thought."[5] A parable is more than an attractive story with a "moral," as, for example, with one of Aesop's fables. Indeed, a parable is quite different from that. A parable is intended to provoke serious thought and call for decision.

What you likely will find as you study these parables is that the meaning of each of them is not as cut-and-dried as you might have thought it was. That is the nature of parables. Parables were intended to call hearers and readers to turn the parable around and upside-down—and to turn themselves and their views around and upside-down—so as to view life in a fresh way.

Jesus' identity and the kingdom of God he proclaimed were revolutionary. Jesus used parables to stimulate fresh ways of thought, decision, and action.

Earlier in the Christian era, the dominant method of interpreting the parables was allegorical. By this method, every detail was treated as having a symbolic meaning. The danger of this approach is that the meanings assigned to the details were often far-fetched and quite unrelated to the time of Jesus and the gospels. For example, Origen, a great church leader and theologian (about AD 182–251), interpreted the victim in the parable of the Good Samaritan (Luke 10:25–37) to be Adam, the inn to which the Good Samaritan took the victim to be the church, and the two denarii that the Good Samaritan left with the innkeeper to be the Father and the Son.[6] With the allegorical method, a parable could be bent to mean almost anything, according to the whim of the interpreter.

A breakthrough in the interpretation of parables occurred in the nineteenth century when a Bible scholar named Adolph Jülicher stated that rather than each detail standing for a meaning, a parable has one main point. This view continues today. As it has continued to be refined by further study, though, some interpreters today would say that a parable may have more than one central point but still a limited number. Even so, this basic understanding of how to interpret parables has been helpful in guarding against simply making the parable mean whatever the interpreter wants it to mean by treating it allegorically.

Another helpful touchstone for interpreting Jesus' parables is to interpret them in light of the culture of that time—both Jesus' time and the time of the first readers of a particular gospel. Thus, by using such an approach, if a parable appears to have allegorical elements, at least the interpreter will see these elements in terms of their meaning in that time rather than erroneously importing modern parallels into the parable. Yet another interpretation key that will be used in this study is to set the parable within the context of the gospel of which it is a part—in this case, the Gospel of Luke.

The Gospel of Luke gives special attention to picturing Jesus breaking down the barriers that separated people and reaching out to all kinds of people. Jesus showed special concern for people whom others considered second-class for one reason or another—such as being poor, being a woman, or not keeping the Jewish traditions. Watch for these special emphases of the Gospel of Luke as you study these parables that are unique to Luke's Gospel.

Ordinarily in these studies, the lessons are clustered into units of two or more lessons. In this study, however, we will simply study the parables unique to Luke's Gospel in the scriptural order in which they appear. All but the first parable to be studied are in the section of Luke known as the "travel narrative," which is in Luke 9:51—19:27. This section of Luke's Gospel is Luke's special section, containing many teachings and incidents that do not appear in the other gospels. This section tells of events and teachings as Jesus made his way toward Jerusalem and the cross. In general, Bible commentators have not found a satisfactory way to outline this section in an overarching, comprehensive way. Since there is nothing approaching consensus on how this section is organized, our imposing a scheme on this section in order to divide the study into units seems unwise, unnecessary, and arbitrary. Thus, we will simply study the parables as they appear in the biblical context.

Parables are meant to challenge our thinking about life and to lead us to think more deeply and creatively than we might otherwise have done. As you study these parables, let them challenge you to look at yourself, your perspective on life, and your commitment to Jesus in a fresh new way. In fact, if you really study these parables, they absolutely will challenge you to do just that in every lesson. If you think you have things all figured out, just study these parables, and you may well find how limited your insights really are.

Note: For many classes, Easter will occur during the time when they engage in this study of the parables in the Gospel of Luke. Since some classes wish to study on Easter a lesson on the resurrection of Jesus, an Easter lesson is included. Classes may study or not study it according to their needs. The Scripture selected for this Easter lesson, Luke 24:13–35, is unique to the Gospel of Luke, as are the parables being studied.

THE GOSPEL OF LUKE: PARABLES JESUS TOLD

Lesson 1	The Two Forgiven Debtors: Showing Gratitude for Forgiveness	Luke 7:36–50
Lesson 2	The Compassionate Samaritan: Acting with Love	Luke 10:25–37
Lesson 3	The Needy Friend Asking for Help: Praying to a Gracious God	Luke 11:5–13
Lesson 4	The Foolish Rich Person: Calculating What's Important in Life	Luke 12:13–21
Lesson 5	The Unfruitful Fig Tree: Recognizing the Need to Repent	Luke 13:1–9
Lesson 6	Banquet Guests and the Host: Relying on God's Grace	Luke 14:7–14
Lesson 7	The Tower Builder and the King: Counting the Cost	Luke 14:25–33
Lesson 8	The Lost Coin and the Father with Two Sons: Rejoicing to Find What Was Lost	Luke 15:8–32
Lesson 9	The Shrewd Manager: Using Resources for the Highest Purpose	Luke 16:1–13

Additional Resources for Studying the Parables in the Gospel of Luke[7]

John Claypool. *Stories Jesus Still Tells: The Parables.* Revised second edition. Cambridge, Massachusetts: Cowley Publications, 2000.

Fred B. Craddock. *Luke.* Interpretation: A Bible Commentary for Teaching and Preaching. Louisville, Kentucky: John Knox Press, 1990.

R. Alan Culpepper, "The Gospel of Luke." *The New Interpreter's Bible.* Volume 9. Nashville: Abingdon Press, 1995.

C. H. Dodd. *The Parables of the Kingdom.* Revised edition. New York: Charles Scribner's Sons, 1961.

Brian L. Harbour. *Jesus (The Storyteller): Relating His Stories to My Story.* Macon, Georgia: Smyth and Helwys, 1999.

Archibald M. Hunter. *Interpreting the Parables.* Philadelphia: The Westminster Press, 1960.

Joachim Jeremias. *The Parables of Jesus.* Second revised edition. New York: Charles Scribner's Sons, 1972.

Peter Rhea Jones. *Studying the Parables of Jesus.* Macon, Georgia: Smyth & Helwys Publishing, Inc., 1999.

Charles H. Talbert. *Reading Luke: A Literary and Theological Commentary.* Revised edition. Macon, Georgia: Smyth & Helwys Publishing, Inc., 2002.

Helmut Thíelícke. *The Waiting Father: The Parables of Jesus.* New York: Harper & Row, Publishers, 1959.

Malcolm Tolbert. "Luke." *The Broadman Bible Commentary.* Volume 9. Nashville: Broadman Press, 1970.

NOTES

1. Unless otherwise indicated, all Scripture quotations in this introduction are from the New Revised Standard Version.
2. The Gospel of John does not feature the use of parables.
3. Archibald M. Hunter, *Interpreting the Parables* (Philadelphia: The Westminster Press, 1960), 122.
4. C. H. Dodd, *The Parables of the Kingdom*, rev. ed. (New York: Charles Scribner's Sons, 1961), 1.
5. Dodd, *Parables*, 5.
6. Peter Rhea Jones, *Studying the Parables in the New Testament* (Macon, Georgia: Smyth and Helwys Publishing, Inc., 1999), 297–298.
7. Listing a book does not imply full agreement by the writers or BAPTISTWAY PRESS® with all of its comments.

Focal Text

Luke 7:36–50

Background

Luke 7:36–50

Main Idea

People serve and love God to the extent that they recognize the greatness of God's forgiveness and receive it.

Question to Explore

To what extent do you recognize the greatness of God's forgiveness of you, and how do you show it?

LESSON ONE The Two Forgiven Debtors

Showing Gratitude for Forgiveness

Study Aim

To evaluate the extent to which I recognize the greatness of God's forgiveness and how I show my gratitude for it

Study and Action Emphases

- Affirm the Bible as our authoritative guide for life and ministry
- Share the gospel with all people
- Develop a growing, vibrant faith
- Include all God's family in decision-making and service
- Value all people as created in the image of God
- Obey and serve Jesus by meeting physical, spiritual, and emotional needs
- Equip people for servant leadership

Quick Read

We serve God either so God will love us or because he already does. When we recognize and experience the greatness of God's forgiveness, we render loving service to him.

Several years ago I participated in a silent retreat, two days of quiet prayer. Our retreat director gave us several articles to read. The first article was by Mike Yaconelli, a well-known Christian columnist. He wrote of his own silent retreat and confessed the status of his soul when it began:

> I spent hours every day doing God's work, but not one second doing soul work. I was consumed by the external and oblivious to the internal. In the darkness of my soul, I was stumbling around and bumping into the symptoms of my soul-lessness—I was busy, superficial, friendless, afraid, and cynical—but I didn't know where all these negative parts of my life were coming from.[1]

Later he heard what he needed:

> In the stillness and solitude, His whispers shouted from my soul, "Michael, I am here. I have been calling you. I have been loving you, but you haven't been listening. Can you hear me, Michael? I love you. I have always loved you. And I have been waiting for you to hear Me say that to you. *But you have been so busy trying to prove to yourself that you are loved that you have not heard me.*" I heard Him, and my slumbering soul was filled with the joy of the prodigal son. My soul was awakened by a loving Father who had been looking and waiting for me.[2]

We serve either to be loved by God or because we already are. Some of us give to receive from God; others receive to give to God and others. We are each in our story and parable this week. When our study is done, we'll know who we are and what to do next.[3]

Luke 7:36–50

36 Now one of the Pharisees invited Jesus to have
dinner with him, so he went to the Pharisee's house and
reclined at the table. 37 When a woman who had lived a
sinful life in that town learned that Jesus was eating at
the Pharisee's house, she brought an alabaster jar of per-
fume, 38 and as she stood behind him at his feet weep-
ing, she began to wet his feet with her tears. Then she
wiped them with her hair, kissed them and poured per-
fume on them.

39 When the Pharisee who had invited him saw this,
he said to himself, "If this man were a prophet, he
would know who is touching him and what kind of
woman she is—that she is a sinner."

40 Jesus answered him, "Simon, I have something to
tell you."

"Tell me, teacher," he said.

41 "Two men owed money to a certain money-
lender. One owed him five hundred denarii, and the
other fifty. 42 Neither of them had the money to pay him
back, so he canceled the debts of both. Now which of
them will love him more?"

43Simon replied, "I suppose the one who had the
bigger debt canceled."

"You have judged correctly," Jesus said.

44Then he turned toward the woman and said to
Simon, "Do you see this woman? I came into your
house. You did not give me any water for my feet, but
she wet my feet with her tears and wiped them with her
hair. 45You did not give me a kiss, but this woman, from
the time I entered, has not stopped kissing my feet.
46You did not put oil on my head, but she has poured
perfume on my feet. 47Therefore, I tell you, her many
sins have been forgiven—for she loved much. But he
who has been forgiven little loves little."

48Then Jesus said to her, "Your sins are forgiven."

49The other guests began to say among themselves,
"Who is this who even forgives sins?"

50Jesus said to the woman, "Your faith has saved
you; go in peace."

Giving to Get (7:36–43)

Jesus had been busy in Galilee, the northern hill country region of Israel. It was a land of flowing and fertile fields, more rural than urban. This was Jesus' home country. Many of its residents had watched him grow up, but few knew who he really was. As Jesus began his ministry here, news of his exploits traveled quickly (Luke 4:14–15). As his ministry unfolded, in Nazareth he revealed his power over enemies (4:30).

In Capernaum he demonstrated his authority over demons, physical disease, physical elements, leprosy, paralysis, the Sabbath, and death (Luke 4—7).

So who was this man? Some thought him a prophet (7:16). John the Baptist's disciples sought his identity (7:18). In our study this week, we will learn the truth: he is God. Jesus chose a most unlikely place and people to reveal that fact to the world.

We serve either to be loved by God or because we already are.

First, meet Jesus' host, Simon the Pharisee. The Pharisees were the elite sect of ancient Israel, never more than 6,000 in number. Their name meant *separated ones*, for they divorced themselves from ordinary life to observe the Jewish law in all its minute detail. They led the opposition to Jesus and would instigate his death. Jesus was not among friends.

Next, let's set the table for the feast. This event may have occurred in Capernaum, where Jesus was well known. This possibility may explain the woman's knowledge of Jesus' presence at Simon's home.

As our text begins, we find that Jesus "reclined at the table" (7:36). A Jew at dinner lay on his left side, supporting himself by his left elbow while he ate with his right hand. His body and feet were stretched out behind him. It was the custom of the day to allow strangers to enter a feast uninvited, especially beggars seeking a gift. Thus the woman in our story came up behind Jesus unannounced.

In a moment we will study her gift and love in detail. For now, let's focus on Simon's response to it. He "said to himself, 'If this man were a prophet, he would know who is touching him and what kind of woman she is—that she is a sinner'" (7:39). The word translated "this man" implies the meaning, *this fellow*, indicating contempt. "If this man were a prophet" translates a Greek expression that assumes that he was not a prophet. A prophet would know "what kind of woman she is"—literally, *from what country she comes*, meant spiritually here. Jesus did know her spiritual country—and Simon's and yours and mine. But the Pharisee was blind to the fact.

The parable . . . corrected both of Simon's mistakes, showing that Jesus did indeed know who this woman was and that Jesus was in fact a prophet and more.

So Jesus enlightened him. "I have something to tell you" (7:40) was a kind way to respond to such a critical spirit. The parable that follows corrected both of Simon's mistakes, showing that Jesus did indeed know who this woman was and that Jesus was in fact a prophet and more.

Jesus' story begins with a "certain moneylender," a professional who made his living lending money at interest. The word is found only here in the New Testament, although it was common in the culture of Jesus' day. One person owed him 500 denarii. The denarius was a Roman silver coin that constituted a workman's daily wage (Matthew 20:2). Two hundred denarii would pay for lunch for 5,000 men and their families (Mark 6:37). So 500 denarii was well more than a year's salary in that day.

The other person in Jesus' parable owed the money-lender fifty denarii, more than a month's salary. The second owed one-tenth the debt of the first.

The contrast was clear: the "sinner" was far more gracious than the Pharisee.

Now came the surprise, the twist that is present in each of Jesus' parables. The professional, the man who made his living by lending money at interest, forgave both debtors—both the principal and the interest owed. It would be grace enough if a friend forgave a debt that exceeded a year's salary, or a month's. For a professional—someone with whom these people had a contractual, legal relationship—to do this is even more surprising. Think of a pawn shop or a loan shark doing this, and you'd have the same shock.

Jesus' parables used surprise to make a spiritual point. He asked (7:42), "Which of them will love him more?" Jesus implied that anyone so forgiven would love the one who had forgiven him or her.

Simon could see where Jesus was going: "I suppose the one who had the bigger debt cancelled." "I suppose" indicates a resentful, reluctant answer that revealed the true condition of his heart. The "woman who had lived a sinful life" (7:37) was grateful to Christ, for she knew her debt had been cancelled. Simon the Pharisee owed a spiritual debt as well, of which he was ignorant and thus liable. Here we find the greatest twist of all. The woman was forgiven, but the Pharisee was guilty.

Simon stands for all religious practitioners who give to get. He performed religious functions so God would look on him with favor. He worked to earn the blessing and prosperity of God. He believed that God would answer his prayers because he had offered them in such religious merit.

So very often so do we. Here's the pointed question: Which of the two was now the greater debtor—the woman known for living as a sinner, or Simon?

Getting to Give (7:44–50)

The other major figure in our text was this woman "who had lived a sinful life in that town" (7:37). The words mean that she was devoted to sin, habitually practicing it. Her sins were not just the occasional or unintended sins of daily life. Rather, she lived intentionally and consistently in sin. The entire town knew her infamous reputation.

We don't know the nature of her sin. But the fact that she wiped Jesus' feet with her hair may indicate that she had been a prostitute, since women bound their hair on their wedding day and never appeared in public with it unbound again. We do know that she was *not* Mary Magdalene or Mary of Bethany, the dear friend of Jesus who later performed a similar act of worship (see the article, "Who Was the Woman Who Anointed Jesus?"). For reasons unexplained in the text, she was grateful beyond words to Jesus. She had been transformed either by the preaching and teaching she had heard from his lips in Capernaum or by a previous personal encounter with him.

Now she showed her gratitude: "She brought an alabaster jar of perfume" (7:37). Alabaster was a soft stone from which flasks or vases were made for the purpose of storing perfume. Women commonly carried such a small flask of perfume around their necks.

Jesus implied that anyone so forgiven would love the one who had forgiven him or her.

She stood behind his outstretched feet, weeping. Men wore sandals, which they left at the door. Thus Jesus was barefooted, and her tears cascaded onto his feet. Despite the shame of letting down her hair in public, she used her hair to wipe his feet. Washing feet was considered the most menial of all tasks. No Jew could be made to do it, not even a Jewish slave.

She then "kissed" Jesus' feet (7:38). The tense means *to kiss repeatedly and fervently*. She also "poured perfume on them" (7:38). Anointing Jesus' feet was the act she came to perform. Everything else was an expression of spontaneous gratitude and love.

Ironically, her actions compensated for Simon's failures. The host of Jesus' day was required to supply water for washing the guest's dirty feet, but

Simon did not (7:44). The host was to give the guest a kiss of greeting, which Simon failed to offer (7:45). The host was to place oil on the head of the guest (see Psalm 23:5; Mark 14:3), which Simon failed to give (Luke 7:46). The contrast was clear: the "sinner" was far more gracious than the Pharisee.

Now we come to the point of the parable and our text: "Her many sins have been forgiven—for she loved much. But he who has been forgiven little loves little" (7:47). "For she loved much" is crucial. It should not be translated or interpreted that she was forgiven *because* she loved much. Rather, she was forgiven and loved much as a *result*. Her love was the product of her forgiveness, not its cause.

Perhaps Luke left the woman unnamed so we each could put our name for hers.

Jesus' promise was conclusive: "Your sins are forgiven" (7:48). The words mean that her sins had been and now were forgiven, and would remain so forever.

This act of forgiveness proved the point of Luke's entire narrative: Jesus was more than a prophet. No prophet in all of Jewish history had ever claimed to forgive sins. This fact explains the reaction of the others present (7:49): "The other guests began to say among themselves, 'Who is this who even forgives sins?'" Earlier the Pharisees considered Jesus guilty of blasphemy for the same reason (5:21). Such a claim to divinity would later lead to Jesus' conviction and crucifixion (22:66–71).

Jesus alone could say to the woman, "Your faith has saved you; go in peace" (7:50). Her faith did not earn her salvation but rather received it. Now she was "saved," delivered, rescued. The tense shows that her salvation was an accomplished fact. Now she could "go in peace." So it can be with us.

Implications for Us

Perhaps Luke left the woman unnamed so we each could put our name for hers. Would you do so now? Have your sins been forgiven? Will you spend eternity in heaven and not hell, in paradise and not punishment, with God and not Satan? When was the last time you thanked God that it is so?

What motivates your studying or teaching this lesson—to be loved by God, or because you *are* loved by God? to be blessed, or because you *are* blessed? to receive the recognition of your class, or to give a grace gift of gratitude to Jesus? Would you allow your words to be your perfume, poured at Jesus' feet, broken and spilled out for your Master in love? Would you offer your life in gratitude and grace?

Simon stands for all religious practitioners who give to get.

In other words, is your name Simon? Or are you more like the woman who came to Jesus? There is no third option.

Who Was the Woman Who Anointed Jesus?

We don't know who the "woman who had lived a sinful life" (7:36) was, but we know who she was not. First, she was not Mary Magdalene, a woman mentioned prior to Jesus' crucifixion only in Luke 8:2. There we learn that "seven demons had come out" of her, an indication of spiritual disease, not necessarily sinful activity.

Neither was she Mary of Bethany. Several passages in the gospels tell of a woman anointing Jesus (Matthew 26:6–13; Mark 14:3–9; John 12:1–8). The Gospel of John names the woman as Mary of Bethany. Matthew, Mark and John locate their event in the last week of Jesus' life, while Luke's story occurred much earlier in Jesus' ministry.

Additionally, Matthew and Mark place their meal at the home of a leper, where a Pharisee would never dine. Mary of Bethany was a moral woman (see Luke 10:39, 42). At her anointing of Jesus, the disciples complained about the amount "wasted" in this act (see John 12:1–8). Luke made no such mention of this issue.

We don't know the identity of the woman, perhaps so that her name can be ours.

Welcome Guests?

The scene in our text must have horrified Simon the Pharisee, given his rigorous moral codes. For this "woman who had lived a sinful life" even to be in his house was an offense (Luke 7:37). Too, for Jesus to allow her to touch him was even worse, since no women touched men in public.

Imagine you invited your pastor to your home for lunch after church this Sunday, only for the occasion to be interrupted by a prostitute from the street who entered your home and acted toward him as the woman in the Scripture text did. How would you respond to such an event?

Questions

1. Luke included our text in his Gospel to show that Jesus was more than a prophet or religious leader, but rather that he was the Son of God. What contemporary evidence for this fact is most compelling to today's society?

2. Why do you suppose Simon invited Jesus to his home? Are any of his possible motives still popular among religious people today? Why?

3. What would have motivated the woman to her action of such courage and sacrifice?

4. What are the "worst" sins for which you have been forgiven? the latest? How have you responded to God's grace?

5. The woman modeled a loving commitment made in the presence of great adversity. Who might be "Simon the Pharisee" for you? Where might his house be located this week?

NOTES

1. Cited in James C. Denison, *Life on the Brickpile: Answers to Suffering from the Letters of Revelation* (Macon, Georgia: Mercer University Press, 1997), 108.
2. Denison, 118 (italics added).
3. Unless otherwise indicated, all Scripture quotations in lessons 1–9 are from the New International Version.

Focal Text

Luke 10:25–37

Background

Luke 10:25–37

Main Idea

Genuine faith in God leads a person to reach out in generous loving concern to people in need.

Question to Explore

To what extent and to whom are you a neighbor?

LESSON TWO

The Compassionate Samaritan

Acting with Love

Study Aim

To evaluate the extent to which my life mirrors the behavior of the Good Samaritan

Study and Action Emphases

- Affirm the Bible as our authoritative guide for life and ministry
- Develop a growing, vibrant faith
- Include all God's family in decision-making and service
- Value all people as created in the image of God
- Obey and serve Jesus by meeting physical, spiritual, and emotional needs
- Equip people for servant leadership

Quick Read

When we realize how unconditionally Jesus loves us, we will reach out to those in need with Jesus' compassion and grace.

The microwave oven has changed our lives so much that sociologists now call us the "microwave society." Cooking popcorn once meant getting out the pan, putting in the oil, stirring in the seeds, and waiting five or ten minutes. Today popcorn comes in microwave bags—and we get impatient that it takes two minutes to cook.

Some restaurants now have entire rooms for cell-phone users, so people can eat and make phone calls and thus save time. "Sink Eaters Anonymous" is an actual support group for people who are so busy they eat their meals standing over the kitchen sink. The value of time has clearly surpassed the value of money in our society.

In this Bible study lesson we come squarely against the issue of time, priorities, and values. Which comes first: people or projects? relationships or responsibilities? souls or success?

Luke 10:25–37

25On one occasion an expert in the law stood up to
test Jesus. "Teacher," he asked, "what must I do to
inherit eternal life?"
26"What is written in the Law?" he replied. "How
do you read it?"
27He answered: "'Love the Lord your God with all
your heart and with all your soul and with all your

strength and with all your mind'; and, 'Love your neigh-
bor as yourself.'"

28"You have answered correctly," Jesus replied. "Do
this and you will live."

29But he wanted to justify himself, so he asked
Jesus, "And who is my neighbor?"

30In reply Jesus said: "A man was going down from
Jerusalem to Jericho, when he fell into the hands of rob-
bers. They stripped him of his clothes, beat him and
went away, leaving him half dead. 31A priest happened
to be going down the same road, and when he saw the
man, he passed by on the other side. 32So too, a Levite,
when he came to the place and saw him, passed by on
the other side. 33But a Samaritan, as he traveled, came
where the man was; and when he saw him, he took pity
on him. 34He went to him and bandaged his wounds,
pouring on oil and wine. Then he put the man on his
own donkey, took him to an inn and took care of him.
35The next day he took out two silver coins and gave
them to the innkeeper. 'Look after him,' he said, 'and
when I return, I will reimburse you for any extra expense
you may have.'

36"Which of these three do you think was a neigh-
bor to the man who fell into the hands of robbers?"

37The expert in the law replied, "The one who had
mercy on him."

Jesus told him, "Go and do likewise."

Seeking Life (10:25–29)

One of the most famous stories in all of literature begins with the central question of ancient Judaism (Luke 10:25): "What must I do to inherit eternal life?" On this occasion, however, the question said more about the person who asked it than the one who would answer it.

Jesus was only months away from the cross. Since last week's parable in Luke 7:36–50, he had taught his disciples to sow the seed of the gospel and display its light as his brothers (8:1–21). He had calmed a storm and healed a demoniac, a dead girl, and a sick woman (8:22–56). He had sent the Twelve into ministry, fed 5,000 families, accepted Peter's declaration of his Messiahship, showed his disciples his transfigured glory, healed a demon-possessed boy, and called his disciples into servant leadership (9:1–62). He had commissioned seventy-two followers for their mission (10:1–24). In the face of such expanded ministry, his enemies had gathered strength and conviction in their strategies against him.

Which comes first: people or projects? relationships or responsibilities? souls or success?

So "an expert in the law stood up to test Jesus" (10:25). This "expert" was a Jewish scribe, a professional religious scholar.

Perhaps the setting was a synagogue, where scholars were sitting together in discussion of the

Scriptures. The scribe asked his question to "test" Jesus (10:25). The word meant *to expose weakness or heresy*. Jesus used this word against Satan: "Do not put the Lord your God to the *test*" (4:12, italics for emphasis).

The man's question revealed his heart (10:25, italics for emphasis): "What must I *do* to inherit eternal life?" The verb indicates that the lawyer thought there was something that could be done once and for all to guarantee inheritance in heaven.

Jews in Jesus' day thought they could observe the law, keep the commandments, do the rituals, and thus deserve a place in God's kingdom. Most Americans agree. Most of us think that as long as we live "good" lives and believe in God, we will go to heaven. We see church and morality as things to "do" to earn a place in paradise. We're wrong.

> *Whether from religious or personal motives, the practical consequence was that the dying man was left to die.*

Jesus exposed the man's heart. He replied to his question with his own (10:26): "What is written in the Law?" Jesus would show the man that no one could keep the Law sufficiently to inherit eternal life. Jesus would begin with whatever part of the Law the lawyer affirmed first.

The lawyer quoted Deuteronomy 6.5: "Love the Lord your God with all your heart and with all your soul and with all your strength." Then he added Leviticus 19.18: "Love your neighbor as yourself."

Jesus commended his answer: “Do this and you shall live” (Luke 10:28). But the problem is that we can’t do it. We cannot keep these commandments. One slip is failure.

Somehow the scholar knew he could not meet this standard. He “wanted to justify himself,” to vindicate himself legally. He knew he could not love God with all his heart, soul, and strength. So he seized on the second of his commandments (10:29): “And who is my neighbor?”

Keeping Life (10:30–32)

Ancient Jewish religious leaders regarded only their fellow countrymen as their neighbors. The Jews hated Gentiles, so much so that some considered it illegal to help a Gentile woman in childbirth, for this would merely bring another Gentile into the world. Undoubtedly our scribe had been seeking to love his Jewish neighbors. Now Jesus showed him that he had only begun to love *all* his neighbors.

When last did you stop to care for someone at cost to yourself?

You have heard Jesus’ story all your life. I’ll add a few historical details so we can hear it as Jesus’ first audience did. A “man” was “going down” from Jerusalem to Jericho. Jesus didn’t specify that the man was a Jew, although the fact that he was leaving Jerusalem leads us to assume that he was. The road went "down" quickly—Jerusalem is 2,500 feet above sea level, while Jericho sits 770 feet below it. The road drops 3,300 feet in just 18 miles.

On the road the traveler was assaulted by robbers. They took his possessions and clothes, beat him, and left him. It was no surprise to Jesus' audience that robbers would assault a man on this road (see article, "A Good Samaritan on the Jericho Road"). Those, however, who would help him and those who would not were a surprise indeed.

First came a priest. Jericho was preeminently a city of priests, home to many priests and Levites. About half of the priestly orders in Israel lived in Jericho.

The priest saw the injured man but "passed by on the other side" (10:31). He literally *stepped over to the opposite side of the road*. Why did he not stop to help?

The hurting are not helped by our attitude, only by our actions.

He may have had a religious motive. Numbers 19:11 specifies, "Whoever touches the dead body of anyone will be unclean for seven days." If this priest were on his way to his temple responsibilities and touched this apparently dead person, he could not do his duty.

He likely had a personal motive as well. Robbers would often make one of their number lie alongside the road as though injured. When a traveler stopped to help, the other robbers would attack him. This could be a ploy, a sign that other robbers were in the immediate area. Whether from religious or personal motives, the practical consequence was that the dying man was left to die.

All was not lost. A Levite came along next. Levites were non-Aaronic descendants of the tribe of Levi. By Jesus' day they had assumed secondary roles in the worship and life of the Jewish people. This man "saw him," perhaps indicating that he drew even closer than did the priest. The result, though, was the same. He "passed by on the other side" (10:32).

Prove you love God by loving your neighbor.

When last did you stop to care for someone at cost to yourself? Are we so different?

Sharing Life (10:33–37)

Next came our hero, the "Good Samaritan." No one in Jesus' day would have called any person by this oxymoron. It was ironic that a foreigner, a man not included in the Jewish legal definition of a neighbor, would show himself neighbor to this hurting man. It was even more ironic that the foreigner was a Samaritan, a person the Jews considered to be a half-breed. When Jesus spoke to the Samaritan woman at Jacob's well, she was surprised, because "Jews do not associate with Samaritans" (John 4:9).

No Jew traveling from Jerusalem to Jericho would expect help from this maligned person. Jesus' audience likely would have assumed the Samaritan would finish the job started by the bandits when he "came where the man was" (Luke 10:33). But no: "he took pity on him." Perhaps the priest or Levite felt similar pity, but the injured man never knew it. The hurting are not helped by our attitude, only by our actions.

So the Samaritan "went to him," risking injury to himself. Perhaps robbers were still in the area. He "bandaged his wounds," risking religious uncleanness. He literally *bound up* his wounds, a technical medical term for wrapping a physical injury. He probably had to use his own clothing to make these bandages, since the injured man was stripped naked by the robbers and the Samaritan would have had no reason to bring bandages on his journey.

The Samaritan *poured on* (a technical medical term for treating the injury) oil and wine. The oil softened the wound, while the wine acted as an antiseptic. This was typical medical treatment.

Then the Samaritan placed the injured man on his own donkey, exposing himself further to assault by bandits. He brought him to an "inn," a large place for receiving travelers on this busy road. He "took care of him" personally (10:34). The next day he gave the innkeeper "two silver coins" (10:35), two denarii. This amount was two days' pay in that day. The Samaritan promised to pay any further debts the man incurred, likely indicating that the innkeeper knew and trusted the Samaritan.

Now came the question to which Jesus had been leading his audience all along (10:36): "Which of these three do you think was a neighbor to the man who fell into the hands of robbers?" Which of these three loved his neighbor as himself? Which did the most to "inherit eternal life"? The lawyer could not bring himself to say that it was a Samaritan. He simply said, "The one who had mercy on him" (10:37).

He got to the top, but there was nothing there.

Jesus responded with twin commandments: "Go and do likewise" (10:37). Go—don't wait for hurting souls to find you. Do—care for them. Prove your faith by your works. Prove you love God by loving your neighbor. Only if you do this perfectly can you "inherit eternal life."

No one can do this perfectly, though, of course. Romans 3:20 is plain: "No one will be declared righteous in his sight by observing the law; rather, through the law we become conscious of sin." We cannot help and care perfectly enough to warrant inclusion in God's perfect heaven. We must appeal to the grace of the One who helps our hurting souls, for we can never earn his mercy. Eternal life must be given, or it will never be received.

On another level, however, Jesus' story challenges us. Once we have received the grace of God, we must give it. To grow in faith, we must share the faith. We must breathe out to breathe in. We must empty our hands to fill them. It has been well said that the difference between law and grace is that law says, *Do this and live*, but grace says, *Live and do this*.

Robert McFarlane was President Reagan's National Security Advisor, a twenty-year veteran of the Marine Corps, and an architect of the Iran-contra plan for selling arms to Iran and secretly and illegally sharing the proceeds with rebels in Nicaragua. When his plan failed, Mr. McFarlane resigned his position and later attempted suicide.

I heard him speak a few years ago at a National Prayer Breakfast. He described the incredible power he had achieved, the ladder to success he had climbed. But then he told us with tears in his eyes that it was nothing. He got to the top, but there was nothing there. Only after he fell off that ladder did he discover that it was leaning against the wrong wall—that life consists of loving God and loving people. Nothing else.

Only when we love our neighbor do we truly love our Lord.

Have you made this discovery yet? You cannot get to heaven by helping people. But if you are going there, you must help others join you. This is the only proof that we love Jesus: when we love each other (John 13:35). Only when we love our neighbor do we truly love our Lord.

On your road to Jericho today, you'll meet someone who has been robbed and beaten by life. You'll have many reasons to pass by on the other side. You will have only one reason to stop. Choose wisely.

A Good Samaritan on the Jericho Road

The road from Jerusalem to Jericho, with its twists, crags, and rocky shadows, was an ideal place for bandits to hide. Herod the Great dismissed thousands of men who had been employed in building the temple in Jerusalem. Many turned to highway robbery, many of them to this very highway.

It was no surprise that the man in Jesus' parable would be assaulted here. But his rescuer was a great shock. When Assyria captured the ten northern tribes of Israel in 722 BC, they left some Israelites behind in the land. Some of those who were left intermarried with Gentiles (see 2 Kings 17:24). They were a race of "half breeds" in Jewish eyes, and the area in which they lived was known as Samaria. Their Jewish neighbors would know no "Good Samaritans."

Who Will Help?

A seminary professor of ethics divided fifteen students into three groups. The first was given fifteen minutes to cross the campus, with a grade penalty if they were late. The second group was given forty-five minutes, and the third was given three hours.

By prior arrangement, three students met them along the way. One held his head, moaning in great pain. The second pretended to be unconscious. The third acted out a seizure.

How many ethics students stopped to help? Of the first group, not one. Of the second, only two. Of the third, all five.

In which group are you?

Questions

1. How are we tempted today to refuse human need for religious reasons?

2. How are we tempted to refuse compassion out of personal security?

3. Who would be a "Samaritan" to your culture or church? Would you accept such a person's help? Why or why not?

4. When last did you offer sacrificial help to someone in need?

Focal Text

Luke 11:5–13

Background

Luke 11:1–13

Main Idea

We can pray with assurance of God's desire to answer our prayers and grant us blessings, especially the greatest blessing, God's presence in the Holy Spirit.

Question to Explore

Can we trust God to answer prayer?

LESSON THREE

The Needy Friend Asking for Help

Praying to a Gracious God

Study Aim

To describe the understanding of prayer and the nature of God that arises from Jesus' teachings in this passage

Study and Action Emphases

- Affirm the Bible as our authoritative guide for life and ministry
- Develop a growing, vibrant faith
- Equip people for servant leadership

Quick Read

We can go to God in prayer, not in our goodness but in God's grace, as children who are loved by their Father.

Have you ever lost your keys? I used to do so regularly, until my wife gave me a "key basket" and trained me in its use. There's nothing quite like the joy of running through the house, late for work, looking for keys that are in hiding. You cannot borrow someone else's keys; you can't just go buy a new set or make one up. It has to be the right keys. With them, doors are easy to open. Without them, they're impossible.

In this study we will explore the single most important key to the throne room of God. Jesus' disciples voiced the question of many human hearts: "Lord, teach us to pray" (Luke 11:1). After giving them the Model Prayer (11:2–4) with its template for our conversation with God, Jesus spoke to the motive behind the method. If our hearts are not right, our words will not be effective. If we don't pray in the right spirit, we cannot commune fully with the Holy Spirit.

In my pastoral experience, the issue of this study has been misunderstood more than any other element of prayer. Let's discover the wrong and right ways to approach Almighty God. Nothing is more important to the abundant life Jesus offers you today.

Luke 11:5–13

5Then he said to them, "Suppose one of you has a
friend, and he goes to him at midnight and says,
'Friend, lend me three loaves of bread, 6because a friend

of mine on a journey has come to me, and I have noth-
ing to set before him.'
7"Then the one inside answers, 'Don't bother me.
The door is already locked, and my children are with me
in bed. I can't get up and give you anything.' 8I tell you,
though he will not get up and give him the bread
because he is his friend, yet because of the man's bold-
ness he will get up and give him as much as he needs.
9"So I say to you: Ask and it will be given to you;
seek and you will find; knock and the door will be
opened to you. 10For everyone who asks receives; he
who seeks finds; and to him who knocks, the door will
be opened.
11"Which of you fathers, if your son asks for a fish,
will give him a snake instead? 12Or if he asks for an egg,
will give him a scorpion? 13If you then, though you are
evil, know how to give good gifts to your children, how
much more will your Father in heaven give the Holy
Spirit to those who ask him!"

Knocking at Midnight (11:5–8)

Jesus' parable begins with a problem. A man has a friend who comes to him at midnight with a strange request: "Friend, lend me three loaves of bread, because a friend of mine on a journey has come to me, and I have nothing to set before him" (11:5–6).

The friend arrived at midnight, because people traveled at night to avoid the heat of the day. His host had "nothing to set before him." People typically baked only enough bread for the day's needs, since they had no way to preserve it for the future. When the day was done, none was left. Hospitality was a sacred obligation, though, as it still is in the Middle East. Even though the man's late arrival seemingly rendered his host innocent of blame, the culture nonetheless required that he feed his guest appropriately. Thus the problem the man now shared with his neighbor.

In my pastoral experience, the issue of this study has been misunderstood more than any other element of prayer.

He asked for three loaves of bread. Apparently their village was so small that it had no market, or at least none open at this hour. He asked him to "lend" the bread, not to lend on interest but to give. (The word translated "lend" is used only here in the New Testament.)

The father's response seems abrupt and unkind to us, but it was completely understandable in Jesus' culture. "Don't bother me," he said through the locked door (11:7). Literally the expression is, *Stop troubling me*. Why? Because the door was already locked, a completed action. People in that culture seldom locked their door, as they had little of value to protect from theft. They locked the door only when they wished not to be disturbed by their neighbors. A locked door was the same thing as hanging the "do not disturb" sign on your hotel room or hospital door.

To make matters worse, his children were with him in bed. The typical home was only one room, where the family and animals all stayed for the night. The family section was a wooden floor, the back third of the structure. The animals were given the dirt floor that separated the family from the one door of the house.

Thus the father told his neighbor, "I can't get up and give you anything" (11:7). To rise meant waking the family and the animals. The man and his family would lose the evening's sleep before the hard day of manual labor that would face them in the morning.

So everything about the neighbor's request was wrong. Thus what follows is the surprise of the parable: "I tell you, though he will not get up and give him the bread because he is his friend, yet because of the man's boldness he will get up and give him as much as he needs" (11:8). The word translated "boldness" indicates a lack of feeling of shame (the only instance of this Greek word in the New Testament). He would have preferred to sleep, but his neighbor's shameless knocking caused him to meet his need. Is this how God hears our prayers, our "knocking at midnight"?

Banging on God's Door (11:9–13)

The first way many understand our parable is that we must earn the right to be answered by God. In this view, "because of the man's boldness" means that we must convince God of our merit before God will meet our need.

This view of God is ancient. For instance, one of the Greek gods said to Prometheus, the divine figure who was bound by Zeus for giving fire to mortals: "Many a groan and many a lamentation you shall utter, but they shall not serve you. For the mind of Zeus is hard to soften with prayer."[1] Many people still believe we must beg God before God will hear and help us.

. . . We are to ask God for God's help, not because we deserve it but because we do not, not out of our goodness but out of God's grace.

A second misinterpretation is similar: we can force God to answer our prayers if we ask in enough faith. If we pray in the right words, the right faith, the right religious merit, God *must* answer our prayer and meet our need. If God has not done so, the fault is ours.

Let's see whether either approach squares with the word of God.

Jesus gave us the key to this parable in the commentary that follows it. He set up two contrasts. First, no father would give his child a snake instead of a fish. Some fish in the Sea of Galilee were like long sardines. They looked much like the snakes that lived in the reeds and rushes along the shoreline.

Second, no father would give his child a scorpion instead of an egg. Scorpions in that region were light in color, so as to blend in with the desert and rocks of

Palestine. They rolled into balls for self-protection, looking like an egg.

We are "evil" by nature, not just by conduct (11:13). Even so, we would give good gifts to our children, never snakes for fish or scorpions for eggs. Wouldn't you?

Now comes the key (11:13): "How much more will your Father in heaven give the Holy Spirit to those who ask him!" "How much more" points us to Jesus' teaching technique, common among the rabbis. Called *the lesser to the greater*, it compared the human to the divine, a lesser characteristic to a greater (see article, "The Lesser to the Greater"). If no parent would give his child less than the child asked, how much more would our Heavenly Father give us what we need.

He would have preferred to sleep, but his neighbor's shameless knocking caused him to meet his need.

Now let's take this technique back into Jesus' parable. If a man locks his door, telling the village he is not to be disturbed, and he has fallen asleep with his family and animals, he has every right to refuse his neighbor's request for midnight bread. The man, however, meets his neighbor's need anyway, because his friend continues to ask in faith that he will. If such a man would answer such a request, how much more will our Father in heaven answer our requests made in faith.

In other words, we are to ask God for God's help, not because we deserve it but because we do not, not out of our goodness but out of God's grace. When we do, God gives us our need and even God's Holy Spirit, God's greatest gift.

Jesus taught us the same principle in a different way: "I will do whatever you ask in my name, so that the Son may bring glory to the Father. You may ask me for anything in my name, and I will do it" (John 14:13–14). To pray in Jesus' "name" is to draw on Jesus' account, to sign Jesus' name to our check. When we do, God meets our need not out of our merit but out of God's Son's merit. His Son's death paid for our sins; in Jesus' name they are forgiven. His Son rose from death to life; in Jesus' name, so will we. When we pray in Jesus' name, we receive all that Jesus has earned the right to give.

As long as we are God's children and pray in God's grace, we receive all that we need in God's will.

Dr. R. A. Torrey, a leading evangelistic leader and author of the late nineteenth and early twentieth centuries, told of a time he was speaking in Melbourne, Australia, at a business leaders' meeting. A man asked why God had not answered his prayers. He said he had been a Presbyterian for thirty years and a leader in his church. Yet God did not answer his prayers. He couldn't understand why.

Dr. Torrey explained that the man thought

> that God is under obligation to answer his prayer. He is really praying in his own name, and God will not hear our prayers when we

approach Him in that way. We must, if we would have God answer our prayers, give up any thought that we have any claims upon God. Not one of us deserves anything from God. If we got what we deserved, every last one of us would spend eternity in hell. But Jesus Christ has great claims on God, and we should go to God in our prayers not on the ground of any goodness in ourselves, but on the ground of Jesus Christ's claims.[2]

Expecting God's Answer

So we can do as Jesus instructed: "Ask and it will be given to you; seek and you will find; knock and the door will be opened to you" (11:9). "Ask," "seek" and "knock" are all in the present tense and are continuous actions. As we continue to ask, we are heard. When we continue knocking as did the neighbor, we receive. Jesus' promise is unconditional: "Everyone who asks receives." As long as we are God's children and pray in God's grace, we receive all that we need in God's will.

> *. . . God meets our need not out of our merit but out of God's Son's merit.*

Dr. Torrey also told of an event that occurred during the Civil War. A father and mother were living in Columbus, Ohio. They had an only son, and he was the joy of their hearts. Soon after the outbreak of the war he came home one day and said to his parents, "I have enlisted in the army." Of course, they were greatly concerned about their son, but they loved their country and were willing to make the sacrifice of giving their son to go to the war and fight for his country. He wrote home regularly. One day, though, at the regular time, no letter came.

Days passed, and no letter. Weeks passed. Then one day a letter came from the United States government that told them that there had been a great battle and their son was among those killed.

The light went out in that home. Days and weeks, months and years, passed by. The war came to an end. One morning as they were sitting at the breakfast table the maid came in. She said, "There is a poor, ragged fellow at the door and he wants to speak to you. But I knew you did not wish to speak to a man like him, and he handed me this note and asked me to put it in your hand."

> *There is nothing in heaven or on earth that is too good for us, as long as we ask in Jesus' name.*

She put in the hands of the father a soiled and crumpled piece of paper. The father opened it. When he glanced at it his eyes fell upon the writing, and he recognizing the writing of his son.

The note said:

> Dear Father and Mother, I have been shot and have only a short time to live, and I am writing you this last farewell note. As I write

> there is kneeling beside me my most intimate friend in the company, and when the war is over he will bring you this note, and when he does be kind to him for Charlie's sake. Your son Charles.[3]

There was nothing in that house that was too good for that young man, for his request was made in their son's name. There is nothing in heaven or on earth that is too good for us, as long as we ask in Jesus' name.

Who is your Friend at midnight (11:5)? What do you need from God today? Go to God, not in your goodness but in God's grace. Go as a child who knows the care of a loving Father. Is God waiting for you right now?

The Lesser to the Greater

A common rabbinic teaching technique in Jesus' day was the lesser to the greater. We find this practice explicitly in today's text at Luke 11:13, and underlying the parable of verses 5–8. You will see it later when we study Luke 18:1–8, the parable of the unfit judge. Both parables at first appear to portray God as unwilling to meet our needs. In fact, the opposite is true. A man already asleep with his family, and even worse, a person of disreputable and selfish character, would both answer a persistent request. How much more would a Father who never sleeps, a holy God whose nature is love, answer our prayers?

We see this principle in positive parables as well. If a father would greet his prodigal son with joy, how much more would our Father in heaven welcome his wayward children? If a hated Samaritan would help a person in need, how much more would our loving Lord help our hurt? Our Teacher leads us from our fallen world to our heavenly Father—lesser to greater, indeed.

To Think About

Charles Spurgeon, the outstanding British Baptist preacher and leader of the nineteenth century, told about two men who fell into the river that flows into Niagara Falls. Those on the shore floated a rope to them. One man grabbed it. The other saw a log floating by and grabbed hold of it instead. Both believed they would be saved, and both held the object of their faith with equal commitment. One was rescued, and the other was lost.[4]

How do you think Spurgeon's story might relate to Jesus' parable?

Questions

1. Is there an unanswered prayer in your life today? How should you apply Jesus' parable to it?

2. Why does Jesus instruct us to "ask," meaning *to keep on asking*? Why is not a single request enough? What is the benefit of continued intercession?

3. If a little girl asks her parent for something and is refused, how will she interpret the decision? What is more likely the real reason for the parent's answer?

4. How might you be tempted to pray in your own "name"? How would Jesus' parable apply to your motives for prayer?

NOTES

1. Aeschylus, *Prometheus Bound*, Great Books of the Western World, ed. Mortimer J. Adler (Chicago: Encyclopedia Britannica, Inc., 1990), 40.
2. R. A. Torrey, *The Power of Prayer and the Prayer of Power* (Grand Rapids, Michigan: Zondervan, 1971 [1924], 106–107.
3. Torrey, 110–111.
4. Charles Spurgeon, *Words of Wisdom for Daily Life* (Pasadena, Texas: Pilgrim Publications, 1973), 13–14.

Focal Text

Luke 12:13–21

Background

Luke 12:13–34

Main Idea

Placing priority on material things rather than on God leaves one unprepared for the coming judgment.

Question to Explore

How is my emphasis on material things affecting my life?

LESSON FOUR

The Foolish Rich Person

Calculating What's Important in Life

Study Aim

To evaluate my emphasis on material things in light of Jesus' teachings in this passage

Study and Action Emphases

- Affirm the Bible as our authoritative guide for life and ministry
- Develop a growing, vibrant faith
- Encourage healthy families
- Obey and serve Jesus by meeting physical, spiritual, and emotional needs
- Equip people for servant leadership

Quick Read

We are prepared for the coming judgment only when we use our material possessions to glorify God and build God's kingdom on earth.

Ruth, a single mother in Chicago, began buying $5 worth of Illinois lottery tickets every week. She needed these periodic "doses of hope" to counter her occasional feelings of depression. Then the miracle happened. Ruth won $22 million. She was beside herself with joy. She quit her job of wrapping gifts at Neiman-Marcus and bought an eighteen-room house, an expensive wardrobe, and a Jaguar. She sent her twin sons to private school. Strangely, however, as the next year went by, her mood became more and more depressed. By the end of that year, her expensive new therapist diagnosed her as having a case of chronic depression.[1]

Dr. Martin E. P. Seligman is the former president of the American Psychological Association and the author of twenty books in his field. His research indicates that once a person has the basic necessities of life, added money adds little or no happiness.[2] He concludes: "Materialism seems to be counterproductive: at all levels of real income, people who value money more than other goals are less satisfied with their income and with their lives as a whole. . . ." He finishes his sentence, "although precisely why is a mystery."[3] There was no mystery to Jesus, as we'll learn in this study.

Would you like to discover a life purpose that transcends your next paycheck? Would you like to know joyful significance that the stock market or the morning newspaper cannot take from you? Let's discover the best definition of success, before it's too late.

Luke 12:13–21

13 Someone in the crowd said to him, "Teacher, tell
my brother to divide the inheritance with me."
14 Jesus replied, "Man, who appointed me a judge
or an arbiter between you?" 15 Then he said to them,
"Watch out! Be on your guard against all kinds of greed;
a man's life does not consist in the abundance of his
possessions."
16 And he told them this parable: "The ground of a
certain rich man produced a good crop. 17 He thought
to himself, 'What shall I do? I have no place to store my
crops.'
18 "Then he said, 'This is what I'll do. I will tear
down my barns and build bigger ones, and there I will
store all my grain and my goods. 19 And I'll say to
myself, "You have plenty of good things laid up for
many years. Take life easy; eat, drink and be merry."'
20 "But God said to him, 'You fool! This very night
your life will be demanded from you. Then who will get
what you have prepared for yourself?'
21 "This is how it will be with anyone who stores up
things for himself but is not rich toward God."

Don't Give In to Greed (12:13–15)

Four major *isms* define our age.

- Secular postmodernism says, *Whatever you believe is true for you. There are no absolute truths or objective ethics. You can believe and do as you wish, as long as you don't hurt me.*

- Individualism says, *You are the measure of significance. Possessions or principles are valuable to the degree that they benefit you personally.*
- Consumerism says, *Your happiness comes first. Everything and everyone is a means to your ends, tools in your fulfillment and ambition.*
- Materialism says, *What you see is all there is. The only reality that matters is material. Money is just green paper, except that it buys the possessions and power that will meet your consumer needs, benefit you personally, and fulfill your subjective values.*

We think these notions are new, but they're not. Twenty centuries ago a man in a crowd expressed them all in a single sentence. Jesus had been teaching the crowds about evil spirits, warning the people of their sins, disputing with the legal authorities, and exhorting people to follow him by faith (Luke 11:14—12:12).

As Jesus made clear, prosperity is no guarantee of godliness.

Now "someone in the crowd said to him, 'Teacher, tell my brother to divide the inheritance with me'" (12:13). Luke didn't name the speaker; the speaker can be every person in every age. "Teacher," he began. The word means *rabbi* or *religious speaker*. It was a common title for the religious leaders of the day. In no sense did the man identify Jesus as Lord or

God. He wanted Jesus' instruction, not Jesus' authority. He wanted Jesus to conform to his beliefs and to his request.

"Tell my brother," he continued. Solve my problem. "Tell" is imperative; he was ordering Jesus. His command was individualistic: do what I ask, meet my needs.

Tell him "to divide the inheritance with me." His imperative is consumerist materialism: give me the finances I want. The Jewish law specified that the older brother was to receive two-thirds of the estate, the younger the remaining one-third (Deuteronomy 21:17). Perhaps the older brother had inherited the estate and refused to give one-third to the younger.

We must refuse the temptation of greed, the belief that we are what we have, drive, or wear, or how we look.

Jesus exposed his theology (Luke 12:14): "Man, who appointed me a judge or an arbiter between you?" "Man" was a common form of address, in no sense unkind. *Sir,* we might say. "Arbiter" was a legal term for one who decides between two parties in a lawsuit. In essence, our Lord said to the voice from the crowd, *If I am not your Lord and God, I am not your judge or arbiter. If I'm only your rabbi, I have no authority in your life. I'm not just your teacher, but your Lord.*

Isn't it still common to approach Jesus as that man did? We treat Jesus as the solver of our problems and provider of our wants, a genie in our bottle. If we live in the right ways and pray the right prayers, God will bless our ambitions and provide for our every need. Or so conventional wisdom seems to say. Will you ask that man's question of God this week?

Next Jesus spoke to the man's individualistic, consumerist materialism. "Watch out!"—a strong expression of warning. "Be on your guard"—a present-tense command to constant vigilance, for this enemy is always on the attack. Guard "against all kinds of greed," every form of covetousness. Such coveting violates the tenth commandment (see Deuteronomy 5:21). Coveting is idolatry in God's eyes (see Colossians 3:5).

Why must we be so warned against greed? For this simple reason, the central principle of our study: "A man's life does not consist in the abundance of his possessions" (Luke 12:15). We must refuse the temptation of greed, the belief that we are what we have, drive, or wear, or how we look. We are more than we can see or possess.

We are more than we can see or possess.

The word of God repeatedly warns us against greed (Mark 7:22; Romans 1:29; Ephesians 4:19; 2 Peter 2:3). Ephesians 5:3 summarizes: "Among you there must not be even a hint of sexual immorality, or of any kind of impurity, or of greed, because these are improper for God's holy people." Too, 1 Timothy 6:10 is clear: "The love of money is a root of all kinds of evil. Some people, eager for money, have wandered from the faith and pierced themselves with many griefs."

The Bible does not condemn the material, but it condemns materialism. Not money but the "love of money" is the "root of all kinds of evil" (see article, "What God Thinks of the Material").

Someone asked one of the world's wealthiest men how much money was enough. His reply: "Just a little more."

Be Ready Today for God (12:16–20)

Jesus knew that the crowd would hear him with skepticism. Every culture to that point in history defined reality and success in material terms. The greater a person's holdings, the higher a king's throne, the more successful he was. So our Lord told them a parable that defied every part of their materialist theology.

The Bible does not condemn the material, but it condemns materialism.

He began, "The ground of a certain rich man produced a good crop" (Luke 12:16). Jesus was explicit. The man did not produce this crop; the ground that the Lord God made produced the crop. The farmer was the recipient of this blessing, not its cause.

But he didn't know it: "He thought to himself, 'What shall I do? I have no place to store my crops'" (12:17). Here is the major premise of his thought process: *Life consists in the abundance of possessions, and so I need more room to possess more.*

Thus he set forth his minor premise: "This is what I'll do. I will tear down my barns and build bigger ones, and there I will store all my grain and my goods" (12:18). Count the number of personal pronouns and possessives in that verse, and you'll have a window to the man's soul.

Here is his conclusion: "I'll say to myself, 'You have plenty of good things laid up for many years'" (12:18). In other words, he would *have it made*. Now he could "take life easy" (12:18). "Take life easy" is in the continuous Greek tense that means *rest and continually keep on resting*. With "eat, drink and be merry," the wealthy farmer quoted a common threefold formula (see Ecclesiastes 2:24; 3:13; 5:18; 8:15). The prophet Isaiah cited the Lord's condemnation of such a lifestyle (Isaiah 22:13; see also 1 Corinthians 15:32).

Remember continually that what you cannot give away you don't possess—it possesses you.

To the popular Jewish mind, though, the farmer was right. Prosperity was the sign of God's blessing; adversity signaled God's judgment. The psalmist said, "Men praise you when you prosper" (Psalm 49:18). The psalmist also said two verses later, though: "A man who has riches without understanding is like the beasts that perish" (Ps. 49:20). As Jesus made clear, prosperity is no guarantee of godliness.

So "God said to him, 'You fool!'" (Luke 12:20). "Fool" in the Bible means a person who is without reason or sense, one who is reckless and immoral. Why was the rich farmer such a person? Because "this very night your life will be demanded from you" (12:20). The Greek literally can be translated, *They are demanding your soul of you*. The Jews typically used "they" to refer to God without speaking his name. Jesus meant that God would come calling for his soul in judgment that very night. Jesus continued with this question (12:20): "Then who will get what you have prepared for yourself?"

Death comes to us all, typically when we do not expect its arrival. Proverbs 27:1 is still good advice: "Do not boast about tomorrow, for you do not know what a day may bring forth." So, "Let another praise you, and not your own mouth; someone else, and not your own lips" (Proverbs 27:2).

When our lives are over, the only property we will have will be the clothes, casket, and ground in which we are buried. An old proverb notes that there are no pockets in a burial shroud. I once asked a mortician whether he ever placed anything in the pockets of those he buried. He laughed at the question. Someone pointed out that we never find a U-Haul trailer attached to a hearse.

No possessions can exempt us from the call and judgment of God. King Belshazzar was the most powerful man in the world on the night the "handwriting on the wall" pronounced his doom and his kingdom fell (Daniel 5:3–31). You can think of political and business leaders of recent years who have fallen into disrepute and disgrace. We must be ready every day to meet God. Today we're one day closer to Christ's return than we have been in all of human history.

Be Rich Toward God (12:21)

Here is Jesus' conclusion of the matter: "This is how it will be with anyone who stores up things for himself but is not rich toward God" (Luke 12:21). The wealth of the world will do us no good in eternity. If we are not "rich toward God," we are not rich at all. So, how do we attain this status?

If we are not "rich toward God," we are not rich at all.

First, join God's family. Be certain that you have made Jesus your Lord and Savior. Some may think that because they give time and money to their church they belong to Christ, having paid their "dues" to God. We give, though, because we have a relationship with God, not to earn that relationship.

Second, live for God. Remember the source of your personal worth: you are loved by the Lord of the universe (Isaiah 30:18). Use all you possess, every dollar and every moment, to extend God's kingdom on earth. Give your tithe to him through your church, and use what you keep of God's creation for God's glory.

Third, lead your family to trust God with their resources and ambitions. It is never too soon to begin teaching your children that one's "life does not consist in the abundance of his possessions" (Luke 12:15). This is a counter-cultural message you will need to reinforce all through their lives. Remember continually that what you cannot give away you don't possess—it possesses you.

I once heard Anne Graham Lotz, the daughter of Billy Graham, say, "Gold must not matter much to God—he uses it for pavement in heaven." He would like us to use ours to help people go there, don't you think?

Peter shrugged and said, "I did the best I could with what you sent."

A contemporary story pictures a wealthy man being led by Peter to his place in heaven. To the tycoon's shock, his eternal dwelling was a run-down shack. "But I lived in a great estate on earth!" the man protested.

Peter shrugged and said, "I did the best I could with what you sent."

A tourist in Israel stopped to visit with a famous rabbi. He voiced his surprise at the great teacher's meager possessions: a simple room with a bed, desk, and chair. The rabbi looked the tourist over and said, "I see that you don't have many possessions with you today."

The tourist replied, "But I'm just passing through."

The rabbi smiled and said, "So am I."

What God Thinks of the Material

Today's text highlights the difference between the material and materialism. The Judeo-Christian tradition values greatly the material world. When God finished his creating work, he "saw all that he had made, and it was very good" (Genesis 1:31). Even though the fall corrupted God's creation (Romans 8:19–22), the material is still useful to God. Jesus was fully human and fully God.

Greek theology viewed the material differently. According to the Orphic cult (six centuries before Christ), the soul is good, and the body is evil. The point of life is to liberate our souls from the prison house of the flesh. This theology heavily influenced Plato, and Plato in turn influenced the Western world. Even today we speak of the secular as evil, the spiritual as good. The Bible knows no such distinction.

God's word affirms the material, but it warns against materialism. Materialism places supreme value in material possessions and reality. Money is not the root of all evil, but loving it is. So, value God's creation, but use it to honor God.

What Really Matters?

Major Arthur Peuchen booked a first-class stateroom on the *Titanic* for its voyage in 1912. There he placed an ornate tin box containing $200,000 in bonds and

$100,000 in stock. When the shipwreck came, the major changed quickly from his tuxedo into two pairs of long underwear and heavy clothes. He looked at his tin box. Then he stuffed three oranges into his pockets and slammed the door of his stateroom behind him, leaving the box to the ocean depths.[4]

If a fire came to your home tonight, what objects would you rescue first? What is their financial worth? Why are they so valuable to you?

Questions

1. The ground produced the crop that the farmer took as his own. How much of what you possess is the result of your labor? How much comes directly from the creative work of God?

2. In what ways do people tear down barns and build bigger ones in today's economy and culture?

3. Jesus warned us that our lives will be demanded of us suddenly. Whose recent death illustrates his admonition?

4. Is there any dimension of your life that you would not surrender to God if asked? Your job? Your plans for your family? Your intended future?

NOTES

1. Martin E. P. Seligman, *Authentic Happiness* (New York: Free Press, 2002), 48.
2. Seligman, 53.
3. Seligman, 55.
4. Steve Farrar, *Finishing Strong* (Sisters, Oregon: Multnomah Books, 1995), 89.

Focal Text

Luke 13:1–9

Background

Luke 13:1–9

Main Idea

Jesus calls people to accept God's gracious offer of repentance while they still have the opportunity.

Question to Explore

In light of God's grace, do we really need to repent?

LESSON FIVE The Unfruitful Fig Tree

Recognizing the Need to Repent

Study Aim

To relate God's grace and God's demand for repentance to my life

Study and Action Emphases

- Affirm the Bible as our authoritative guide for life and ministry
- Share the gospel with all people
- Develop a growing, vibrant faith

Quick Read

None of us knows when we will face the judgment of God, and so we must accept God's gracious offer of repentance while there is still opportunity.

An elderly saint was near death and made a strange request of her pastor: "When my casket is opened at the funeral, and all my friends come by for a last look, I want them to see me ready to be buried with a dessert fork in my right hand." She explained to her puzzled minister, "I want you to tell the congregation: you know what it means when they clear the dishes from a big meal and someone says, 'Keep your fork.' You know that something good is coming—maybe a piece of apple pie or chocolate cake. Pastor, I want to be buried with a dessert fork in my hand. It will be my way of saying, 'The best is yet to come.'"

And so it was. Everyone who saw her body in the casket saw her final witness. For her, death and judgment were not disaster but dessert.

No question confuses Americans more than the judgment. A recent survey revealed that 79% of us believe that Mother Teresa is in heaven. But 87% are convinced that they will go to heaven themselves.[1] Recent polls indicate that only 4% of Americans are afraid they might face the judgment of God and spend eternity in hell.[2]

Yet the Bible is clear and blunt, stating that "man is destined to die once and after that to face judgment" (Hebrews 9:27). What does the Bible say on the one subject no one can avoid? How can you prepare for the day you will stand before Almighty God?

Luke 13:1–9

1 Now there were some present at that time who
told Jesus about the Galileans whose blood Pilate had
mixed with their sacrifices. 2 Jesus answered, "Do you
think that these Galileans were worse sinners than all the
other Galileans because they suffered this way? 3 I tell
you, no! But unless you repent, you too will all perish.
4 Or those eighteen who died when the tower in Siloam
fell on them—do you think they were more guilty than
all the others living in Jerusalem? 5 I tell you, no! But
unless you repent, you too will all perish."

6 Then he told this parable: "A man had a fig tree,
planted in his vineyard, and he went to look for fruit on
it, but did not find any. 7 So he said to the man who
took care of the vineyard, 'For three years now I've been
coming to look for fruit on this fig tree and haven't
found any. Cut it down! Why should it use up the soil?'

8 "'Sir,' the man replied, 'leave it alone for one more
year, and I'll dig around it and fertilize it. 9 If it bears fruit
next year, fine! If not, then cut it down.'"

Is Suffering Always Due to Sin? (13:1–3)

A preacher warned the congregation, "Members of this church, each of you will stand one day before God in judgment."

A man on the second row began laughing. Surprised, the preacher repeated the warning with greater force. The man began laughing harder.

Shocked, the preacher shouted again: "Members of this church, each of you will stand before God in judgment." The man laughed still louder. The pastor stopped his sermon and asked the man why he was laughing.

The man grinned and said, "I'm not a member of this church." Like that man, the crowds in our text were not exempt from the message about judgment, although they didn't know it.

Jesus had taught his disciples not to worry about their present needs but trust them to the Father, ready always for their Master to come (Luke 12:22–59). Now some who heard his words "told Jesus about the Galileans whose blood Pilate had mixed with their sacrifices" (Luke 13:1). They were shocked at his response.

No question confuses Americans more than the judgment.

History does not record the event to which they referred, although it was most certainly consistent with what we know of Pilate's behavior toward the Jews. During his ten years in office, his troops killed a group of Samaritans climbing Mount Gerizim; he introduced Roman idols into Jerusalem and sparked a riot; he seized temple treasury funds to build his own aqueduct.

Here is the likely explanation for the event told to Jesus. Galileans were known to be far more rebellious toward Rome than their neighbors to the south. Perhaps some at a feast in Jerusalem had begun an insurrection. Pilate's soldiers would have executed them on the spot, even though they were in the midst of temple sacrifice. In this way Pilate "mixed" their blood "with their sacrifices."

People coming from Jerusalem brought news of the tragedy to Jesus. Perhaps they expected Jesus to respond to Pilate's atrocity by condemning the pagan governor. More likely, they cited this event as proof of sins committed by those who were executed. Jesus' reply indicates that those telling the news were taking the latter approach. Thus Jesus asked (13:2), "Do you think that these Galileans were worse sinners than all the other Galileans because they suffered this way?"

Conventional wisdom was clear that suffering was always God's punishment for sin.

Here we come face to face with one of the most persistent heresies in ancient Jewish theology, that suffering is always proof of sin. We find this belief as early as Job 4:7: "Who, being innocent, has ever perished? Where were the upright ever destroyed?" Job's friends repeated their theological conclusion: "When your children sinned against him, he gave them over to the penalty of their sin" (Job 8:4); "Surely God does not reject a blameless man or strengthen the hands of evildoers" (Job 8:20).

Conventional wisdom was clear that suffering was always God's punishment for sin. If a man was sick, a woman was childless, or a family was impoverished, they were considered to be under the judgment of

God. A wealthy person was certified as one blessed by God; a suffering person was guilty of something.

Jesus' disciples were thinking in exactly these terms when they saw a man blind from birth and asked our Lord (John 9:2), "Rabbi, who sinned, this man or his parents, that he was born blind?" They could think of no third option. But Jesus could: "Neither this man nor his parents sinned . . . but this happened so that the work of God might be displayed in his life" (John 9:3).

Here we face the question of God's righteousness in the face of the suffering and evil of life. Christians believe that God is all loving, so that God would want to end all suffering. We believe that God is all powerful, so that God could end all suffering. Yet suffering persists. Thus, one logical explanation for suffering is that it is the judgment of God. Of course, sometimes it is. The Canaanites were driven from their land by Joshua in part because of their idolatrous sinfulness. The children of Israel wandered beforehand in the wilderness for forty years because of their unbelief. As punishment for their sin, the ten northern tribes were lost to Assyria, and the two southern tribes were imprisoned by Babylon.

Sometimes our suffering is our fault, but not always.

Sometimes our suffering is our fault, but not always. If conventional wisdom were always true, the disciples' martyrdoms were not for faithfulness but sin.

Job's sufferings were his fault. Too, Jesus' crucifixion was not the sacrifice of the innocent Son of God but righteous punishment by the religious authorities. Please beware of attributing all suffering to sin. Often such theology only makes suffering worse (see article, "The Issue of *Theodicy*").

In our text Jesus makes this point clear (Luke 13:2): "Do you think that these Galileans were worse sinners than all the other Galileans because they suffered this way?" Here is his answer: "I tell you, no!" (13:3). The Galileans' execution at the hands of Pilate was evidence of Pilate's sin, not theirs.

To this point the inquirers were interested in theological conversation and speculation. But Jesus always turned theology to practice: "But unless you repent, you too will all perish" (13:3). The Galileans' deaths were not the result of their sins, but they served to warn this crowd to repent of their own.

There will be a "final exam."

Is Disaster Always God's Decree? (13:4–5)

The crowd could still misinterpret. Perhaps the Galileans did not die as a result of their sin but Pilate's evil. What, though, of those who perish from natural calamity? Surely such disasters, without the extenuating circumstance of human agency, are proof of God's direct hand in judgment. Thus, God may not cause drunk driving, but God surely creates tornadoes and earthquakes.

Jesus closed this theological loophole (13:4): "Or those eighteen who died when the tower in Siloam fell on them—do you think they were more guilty than all the others living in Jerusalem?"

Siloam was a pool in the southeastern corner of Jerusalem. The tower in question may have been an independent structure or one connected to the wall of the city. We have no independent historical reference to this tragedy, but faulty architecture and frequent seismic events in the region made such catastrophes not uncommon. So eighteen people, in the vicinity of the pool or perhaps bathing there, perished.

. . . We are judged by God on the basis of our obedience to God's purpose for our lives.

Here was proof to the typical Jewish mind of God's hand and judgment at work. Surely their sins were the reason for their deaths. Again Jesus shocked his listeners (13:5): "I tell you, no!" Again Jesus made speculation practical: "But unless you repent, you too will all perish" (13:5).

Jesus' teaching can be summarized briefly. No event proves the judgment of God. Our trials and travails may be evidence of God's displeasure, or Satan's, or the world's. No one is immune from difficulties. If Jesus' best friend would experience exile on Patmos and Jesus' other followers would be executed for their faith, no one is guaranteed a life without pain or persecution. No one, however, has the right to interpret such suffering by others as sin.

So, keeping in mind this teaching of Jesus, how do you know whether your struggles are God's punishment? Start by asking God. As you do, recognize first that none of us will be able to plead ignorance about God's judgment: "We must all appear before the judgment seat of Christ, that each one may receive what is due him for the things done while in the body, whether good or bad" (2 Corinthians 5:10). In the meanwhile, realize that God wants you to know his will even more than you want to know it. He is a loving Father, one who disciplines his children only after warning them and only when he must.

Make Jonathan Edwards' resolution yours: "Resolved, to live with all my might while I do live. Resolved, that I will live so as I shall wish I had done when I come to die." Start today.

How Do We Prepare for Judgment? (13:6–9)

There will be a "final exam." What will be on it? How do we get ready? Jesus' parable answers our question. It begins: "A man had a fig tree, planted in his vineyard" (13:6). The crowd thought immediately of Israel, as the vineyard was symbolic of their nation (see Isaiah 5:1–7).

A fig tree has only one purpose: bearing figs. The farmer's fig tree, though, had no figs. The fig tree was only taking soil and water from productive plants. The farmer had been coming for three years to look for fruit from it (13:7). He had been more than patient. Now it was time to cut the fruitless tree down.

The vinedresser asked one more chance for the tree. He would dig for irrigation and fertilize for growth (13:8). If the tree bore fruit, they would keep it; "If not, cut it down" (13:9).

We must not misinterpret the elements of Jesus' parable. The three years are not symbolic of Jesus' three years of ministry, or the three Persons of the Trinity. The vinedresser is not the compassionate Christ defending sinful humanity before his wrathful Father. Rather, "God so loved the world that he gave his one and only Son" (John 3:16). The Lord of the universe is your Father in heaven. Here's how God feels about you: "The Lord longs to be gracious to you; he rises to show you compassion" (Isaiah 30:18).

You have been given spiritual gifts to be used for ministry in God's kingdom on earth.

The point of Jesus' parable is simple: we are judged by God on the basis of our obedience to God's purpose for our lives. No circumstances of suffering prove disobedience, whether they come from Pilate's hand or from nature. Obedience does not earn God's grace. Rather, it positions us to receive what God already wants to give. Grace is the basis for the judgment of God.

You have been given spiritual gifts to be used for ministry in God's kingdom on earth. Your life has a central purpose and calling. You will be held accountable by your Creator for your use of his creation. To be ready for God's judgment, stay faithful. Bear the "figs" for which you were made. Stay obedient to the last word you heard from God.

Mother Teresa was in New York City to dedicate a new orphanage. A reporter asked her how she would measure the success of the enterprise. The story is that she smiled, looked into the television lights, and said, "I don't believe our Lord ever spoke of success. He spoke only of faithfulness in love."

Are you faithful to the purpose of God? Faithful with every dimension of your life, time, resources, abilities? Your eternal reward is tied to your present obedience to the will and purpose of God.

The Issue of *Theodicy*

Theodicy combines Greek words to mean *the justice of God in the face of evil and suffering*. Four such approaches to this perennial issue have been helpful in Christian theology.

First is the *free-will theodicy*: God gave us freedom of will so we could choose to worship him. When we misuse this freedom, the consequences are not God's fault but ours. This lesson shows that this approach is sometimes relevant but sometimes inappropriate and even damaging. Just ask Job.

Second is the *soul-building* model: God permits or even causes some suffering in order to grow us spiritually, as Paul's "thorn in the flesh" illustrates (2 Cor. 12:7–10).

A third approach is the *future hope* model: suffering we cannot understand at present will one day be explained and validated (see Romans 8:18).

Last is the *present help* approach: even when we cannot understand why we are suffering, we know God hurts with us and will help us through (see Isaiah 43:1–5).

Whatever the reason for our pain, our Father loves us. This is the promise of God.

A Powerful Note

Once after I had preached a Sunday morning sermon on judgment, that evening a dear member of my church told me that she and her husband had spent time in prayer that afternoon, making sure they were right with God. On Monday morning, she died suddenly. Tuesday I received a note from her in the mail, sent the previous Sunday. I read her note in her memorial service on Wednesday.

If you knew that tomorrow was your last day, what would you do to prepare today? We don't know that tomorrow is the last day. But we don't know that it is not.

Questions

1. Why are most Americans so certain they will be in heaven when they die? What can you do to help people understand the facts of the gospel?

2. It's been said that we compare our "insides" with other people's "outsides," our motives with their actions. Are you likely to associate the suffering of others with sin? Are you less likely to view your own suffering in this way? Why?

3. Some critics of America interpreted the tragedy of September 11, 2001, as God's judgment against our nation. How do Jesus' words and parable relate to this issue?

4. What kind of "fig" are you most responsible for producing? How faithful have you been this week to your purpose?

NOTES

1. *Context*, ed. Martin Marty (May 1, 1999): 8.
2. See James Patterson and Peter Kim, *The Day America Told the Truth* (New York: Prentice-Hall Press, 1991), 204.

Focal Text

Luke 14:7–14

Background

Luke 14:1–14

Main Idea

Following Jesus means reversing our self-seeking ways of acquiring approval, honor, and recognition.

Question to Explore

What does "success" mean to you?

LESSON SIX

Banquet Guests and the Host

Relying on God's Grace

Study Aim

To identify the kind of "success" Jesus rejects and the kind Jesus affirms in these parables and describe ways to apply Jesus' message

Study and Action Emphases

- Affirm the Bible as our authoritative guide for life and ministry
- Share the gospel with all people
- Develop a growing, vibrant faith
- Include all God's family in decision-making and service
- Value all people as created in the image of God
- Obey and serve Jesus by meeting physical, spiritual, and emotional needs
- Equip people for servant leadership

Quick Read

Christians should renounce worldly methods of seeking what humans consider success and strive to allow God to create in and through them the real success of service in God's kingdom. This kind of success comes through humility and not by exalting self.

Arthur obviously was attempting to impress everyone with his vast intelligence. He repeatedly demonstrated his knowledge of words in various languages. He shared his understanding of various nations and lands. He strained toward his idea of success—to be accepted and recognized as of superior intelligence.

One group member said to another, "Arthur is going all out to impress everyone."

"That is true," answered another. "And he is impressing them. The trouble is he is not impressing them positively of his intelligence but negatively of his pride and desire to appear smart."

Many people try to reach their ideals of success by human, self-seeking means. They seek wealth, approval, honor, power, and/or recognition by human efforts. In a striking parable, Jesus taught that seeking success on the human level most often results in missing the true success of serving Jesus and others.

What is your ideal for success? Some consider money success. For others it is prestige, power, recognition, or appreciation. Real success is simply doing the will of Jesus and serving others. Seeking the highest place for selfish reasons results in falling to the lowest valleys.

Luke 14:7–14

7When he noticed how the guests picked the places
of honor at the table, he told them this parable: 8"When

someone invites you to a wedding feast, do not take the
place of honor, for a person more distinguished than
you may have been invited. 9If so, the host who invited
both of you will come and say to you, 'Give this man
your seat.' Then, humiliated, you will have to take the
least important place. 10But when you are invited, take
the lowest place, so that when your host comes, he will
say to you, 'Friend, move up to a better place.' Then
you will be honored in the presence of all your fellow
guests. 11For everyone who exalts himself will be hum-
bled, and he who humbles himself will be exalted."

12Then Jesus said to his host, "When you give a
luncheon or dinner, do not invite your friends, your
brothers or relatives, or your rich neighbors; if you do,
they may invite you back and so you will be repaid.
13But when you give a banquet, invite the poor, the
crippled, the lame, the blind, 14and you will be blessed.
Although they cannot repay you, you will be repaid at
the resurrection of the righteous."

The Setting of the Parable (14:1–6)

A cluster of the teachings of Jesus comes from the context of a meal in the home of a prominent Pharisee. As Jesus continued on his journey to Jerusalem, he had experienced increasing opposition from and conflict with the Pharisees. This section of Luke's Gospel reveals the key themes of criticism of the Pharisees for their pride and hypocrisy as well as

Jesus' affirmation of God's love for the outcast, powerless, and needy.

Since he had underlined the necessity of repentance in the parable of the fig tree (Luke 13:1–9), Jesus had faced further conflict with Jewish leaders. He had been challenged because of his healing of the crippled woman on the Sabbath (13:10–17), had delivered the parables of the mustard seed and the yeast (13:18–21), had warned of the narrow door into God's kingdom (13:22–30), and had revealed his great love and longing for Jerusalem (13:31–35).

Many people try to reach their ideals of success by human, self-seeking means.

Surprisingly, Jesus accepted an invitation to eat a Sabbath meal in a Pharisee's home. Jesus' previous experience at a meal in a Pharisee's house had resulted in hostility (11:37–54). As that occasion had allowed significant teaching opportunities, Jesus received like opportunities in this situation.

Luke recorded that the Pharisees were carefully watching Jesus to see whether he would violate any of their many rules. A person, most likely not a guest, entered and approached Jesus. He may have been planted by the Pharisees to see whether Jesus would heal him on the Sabbath. The man was suffering from dropsy, a disease medically known as edema that results in an excessive accumulation of fluid in tissue spaces or in the body cavity, causing both pain and swelling. In most cases it is the symptom of other serious conditions.

Using a method the Pharisees often employed, Jesus asked a question either answer to which might prove embarrassing to the Pharisees. He asked whether healing on the Sabbath was lawful. If the Pharisees answered *yes*, they would take sides in the on-going debate within their own party. If they answered *no*, they would reveal a dismal lack of compassion. They said nothing.

Jesus took hold of the man, cured him, and sent him away. Jesus then turned to the Pharisees and experts in the law. He asked which of them, if a son or an ox fell into a pit or waterhole, would not rescue him immediately, without any hesitation. With these words, Jesus entered a long debate among Jewish leaders about efforts that were permissible on the Sabbath. Deuteronomy 5:14 set out the law on Sabbath work, but the Jewish people had added many prohibitions. The rabbinic writings taught many and different ways of helping livestock on the Sabbath. These authorities on the Jewish law had said that one could rescue a person on the Sabbath but must not use a rope or ladder. The Jews had many traditions that spelled out what was prohibited and what was allowed. In the event of his healing of the crippled woman on the Sabbath (Luke 13:10–17), Jesus had pointed out the hypocrisy of taking extreme measures to protect one's property while objecting to an act of human compassion. Perhaps the Pharisees

What is your ideal for success?

knew of this exchange and therefore held their words (14:6).

These events led up to the exact setting of the parable. Jesus took notice of the people who had been invited to the meal as they struggled and scrambled to secure the places of highest honor at the table. He then pointed to the value of true humility over against the reward of seeking recognition by worldly effort (14:7). Detailed study of the resulting parable shows Jesus' deep understanding of human personality.

Finishing Last by Pushing for First (14:7–9)

The meal in the home of the chief Pharisee was a Sabbath meal, but Jesus used the picture of a wedding feast, a much more formal occasion, for the parable. At a wedding feast, the host would seat each guest carefully, according to the social ranking and prestige. Those allowed to recline on the couches nearest the host would be seen as those receiving the greatest honor.

Real success is simply doing the will of Jesus and serving others.

Jesus advised the people not to seek recognition and renown by scrambling for the most honored places. The host might require the "place-seeker" to move from the place of higher honor to a lower place. Since other places would have been taken, the one demoted would find himself in the lowest, least dignified, of spaces. In Jewish life, as in most other societies, the public shame of moving from the highest place to the last in the presence of others would be a great humiliation.

Jesus did not teach that one would refrain from taking the highest space simply in order to avoid embarrassment. He taught that when people reach for the human trappings of success or honor, they often bring on themselves the eminent danger of falling into dishonor. Humans often value and therefore seek wealth, power, respect, prestige, and honor through the appearances of these values. Intrusive people render themselves open to the most open of rebuffs. Jesus taught against the pride that incites the desire for the highest places and the employment of the utmost efforts, and the lowest means, to secure them.

Jesus underlined the importance of humility.

Reaching High by Starting Low (14:10)

Jesus underlined the importance of humility. He advised a person, when invited to an occasion, to voluntarily take the lowest, least honored place. Then, if the host invites him or her to the higher place, the one lifted to this higher position would have honor, glory, consideration, or respect in the eyes of the fellow guests.

Jesus did not here project another way to win or secure success. This teaching represents no "health and wealth gospel." We are not to humble ourselves *so that* we will be lifted to a higher place. We are to accept our place in God's kingdom *so that* we will please him. We will not be content simply to wrap ourselves in the coverings of honor, respect, and success. We will commit to the Lord and the Lord's way of life, and the Lord will bring to us the real success of service.

Finding Success the Jesus Way (14:11–14)

People too often seek success in appearances. Jesus teaches about true success and assures us that this success is attained only through humility and never by self-aggrandizement. Jesus declared that everyone who exalts himself will be humbled, and everyone who humbles himself will be exalted. These truths are not compatible with our contemporary judgments. Our accepted valuations reject the paradoxes of the Beatitudes in which Jesus proclaimed the true way to life's best (Matthew 5:3–10).

People too often seek success in appearances.

Modern people seek success by gaining attention, fame, power, and earthly honor. The watchword of many people is that it does not matter what they say about you as long as they are talking about you. Furthermore, people have the notion that life owes them good times, safe harbors, and abundant resources. We gain all these by standing up for ourselves, winning every competition, gaining every advantage, pushing for every promotion, and establishing our superiority at every level.

Jesus said that real success, though, is doing the will of God and finding ways to serve others because of God's love within us (Matt. 22:34–40). Jesus further teaches that the way to this success is humility. Humility is not cowardice, self-depreciation, or lack of enthusiasm. Humility is seeing ourselves as God sees us, accepting God's will for our lives, and allowing God to use us as God sees fit.

Humility is a river fed by two streams. The first is a sense of indebtedness for what God has provided us. All we have is from God. The concept of the "self-made" person is as distasteful as it is inaccurate. Understanding the meaning of the cross of Christ drives us to say with the hymn writer that we must count all our gains as only loss and pour contempt on all our pride.[1]

Humility is seeing ourselves as God sees us, accepting God's will for our lives, and allowing God to use us as God sees fit.

The other stream into the river of humility is the reverence that produces a deep sense of need. One observing the beauty of one of God's sunsets realizes that no human can capture such magnificence. Humility that sees the contrast between God's excellence and human frailty results in a sense of need and elicits the practice of prayer.

Placing self first and demanding exceptional treatment for oneself falls far short of genuine success. Service to others as the response to God's love for us in Jesus Christ is the way to real success. To walk in this beautiful way demands we begin with humility.

So great was Jesus' desire to impress this message of service through humility that he continued the story to give other advice. He said that if people intended to provide a luncheon or dinner, they should invite the poor, the needy, and the powerless who could never repay the invitation. The well-to-do, who might reciprocate with an invitation, should not be the invitees. Humility drives people to serve rather than seek ways to gain service.

Service to others as the response to God's love for us in Jesus Christ is the way to real success.

The central teaching of this parable is simply that those who seek to raise themselves to places of highest honor and respect will fail to reach the highest place of honor—approval by God.

Meals, Banquets, and Social Status in Biblical Times

Meals served important functions in the biblical world beyond just eating. They constituted social occasions in that one usually would eat only with people in his or her own social class. Furthermore, the host revealed the social position of the guests by their placement at the meal. Among the Jews, scrupulous Pharisees would not eat at the home of common Israelites (people of the land) since the Pharisee could not be certain that the food was ceremonially clean or that it had been properly tithed.

Jews normally ate two meals a day—a mid-morning meal and a mid-afternoon meal. On the Sabbath, the Sabbath meal became a third time of eating. The Pharisees had detailed regulations as to the manner of washing before the meal. These regulations are not found in the Old Testament but were added by the Pharisees. Jesus' failure to observe all these regulations aroused conflict with the Pharisees (Luke 11:37–42).

The Sabbath meal and banquets were more formal and involved reclining on couches—the placement of which revealed the esteem with which one was held by the host. Jesus' use of the term for "banquet" in Luke 14:13 makes his image of inviting the social outcasts even more striking.

Questions

1. What is your measure of success? You can probably find the answer to the question by considering what you pursue most avidly.

2. Do you ever seek to gain recognition by maintaining association with those of high profile? Do you sometimes seek to be seen as one of high prestige? Why?

3. What wrappings of high status do people today sometimes seek to use? What does this parable say about these actions?

4. How would you compare and contrast the life based on humility to a life based on the pursuit of fame, honor, power, or wealth?

NOTES

1. "When I Survey the Wondrous Cross," Words, Isaac Watts, 1707.

Focal Text

Luke 14:25–33

Background

Luke 14:25–35

Main Idea

Following Jesus calls for such a radical change in how one lives that counting the cost is both wise and necessary.

Question to Explore

How much of your life are you willing to devote to following Jesus?

LESSON SEVEN

The Tower Builder and the King

Counting the Cost

Study Aim

To evaluate the extent to which I am willing to be Jesus' disciple in light of the radical discipleship Jesus demanded

Study and Action Emphases

- Affirm the Bible as our authoritative guide for life and ministry
- Share the gospel with all people
- Develop a growing, vibrant faith
- Encourage healthy families

Quick Read

Disciples of Christ should recognize the difficulties and trials of the Christian life so that they will remain faithful in spite of temptations.

George decided to join the army. "After all," he said, "It sounds like camping out and deer hunting." So off to basic training he went. To his shock, basic training proved different from camping out and deer hunting. After a few miserable days, George went home.

Very soon two military police pulled up to the front porch where George sat drinking tea. They asked why he was not in camp and doing basic training, George answered, "You know, that basic training was not what I thought it would be. I wasn't having any fun. Go back and tell the sergeant that I decided to quit."

Needless to say, George didn't quit. The problem was that he had not realized what the journey involved before he began the trip. When the going got difficult, he backed out.

Jesus was concerned that all who were considering following him would fully realize the costs and conditions. He explained clearly and concisely with two insightful stories the necessity of anticipating the costs, understanding the requirements, and committing to the life of discipleship. These stories accurately impress the Master's call to count the cost and commit to the plan.

Luke 14:25–33

25 Large crowds were traveling with Jesus, and
turning to them he said: 26 "If anyone comes to me

and does not hate his father and mother, his wife and children, his brothers and sisters—yes, even his own life—he cannot be my disciple. [27]And anyone who does not carry his cross and follow me cannot be my disciple.

[28]"Suppose one of you wants to build a tower. Will he not first sit down and estimate the cost to see if he has enough money to complete it? [29]For if he lays the foundation and is not able to finish it, everyone who sees it will ridicule him, [30]saying, 'This fellow began to build and was not able to finish.'

[31]"Or suppose a king is about to go to war against another king. Will he not first sit down and consider whether he is able with ten thousand men to oppose the one coming against him with twenty thousand? [32]If he is not able, he will send a delegation while the other is still a long way off and will ask for terms of peace. [33]In the same way, any of you who does not give up everything he has cannot be my disciple.

The Setting of the Sayings (14:25)

These stories were given following Jesus' experience in the house of the Pharisee (Luke 14:1–24). There he had been watched carefully to see whether he would defy the Sabbath tradition and heal the man with dropsy. He had received less than a congenial response (14:6). He had set forth an ideal that many in the house were unwilling to follow.

As Jesus left the house, a crowd was waiting and began to follow him. These were the last months of Jesus' earthly ministry. Many came to him—some out of excitement at hearing his teachings and miracles, some out of hope for healing or gain, but some out of sincere desire to consider following his way of life. Knowing that some were in the process of deciding to follow him or turn back, Jesus suddenly turned and spoke, setting out the conditions of following him.

Discipleship Demands Counting the Cost (14:26–27)

The winsome Jesus had drawn the crowds to himself and his message. The winnowing Jesus would separate out of the crowd those truly determined to become followers. He would sift out the real followers by setting forth clearly and strikingly the conditions demanded of those who would become his disciples. Jesus sought to separate those who came along simply out of excitement or desire for gain and to retain those sincerely desiring and intending to become his followers.

To his shock, basic training proved different from camping out and deer hunting.

Any person who becomes a genuine follower or disciple will of necessity come to love Christ supremely and unconditionally. A disciple will love

Jesus and his mission more than family or even his or her own life (14:26). Jesus had emphasized this teaching before (9:23). No one should attempt to follow Jesus without understanding the full import of discipleship and its full cost.

Jesus obviously used the idea of "hate" as a Jewish hyperbole since he in other teachings emphasized loving even our enemies (6:27, 35). Yet Jesus went beyond simple hyperbole and announced a profound truth in the word "hate." He expressed the fact that following him required separation from all other objects of love should these objects interfere with dedication to him. Even family, with its importance in the Jewish culture, was not to deter one from following faithfully the call and direction of Jesus.

Jesus was concerned that all who were considering following him would fully realize the costs and conditions of such following.

Following Jesus requires a complete and undivided devotion. In requiring that one "hate" his closest family, Jesus meant more than *love them less*. He taught that should our dearest relatives prove to be obstacles to our following him and carrying out his will for our lives, then the loving relationships must be set aside.

Jesus, therefore, used the concept of "hate" in this verse to cement the idea that the necessary devotion to him and God's plan would be so intense that love of family by comparison would seem as "hate."

Hebrew and Greek terms for *hate* often had the meaning of rejecting something in favor of a greater love. One who deemed to follow Jesus must come willingly to such commitment.

According to Jesus, a disciple would follow Jesus' goals, intentions, plans, and ways of living. In effect, Jesus laid down the condition of undivided devotion and all-consuming dedication to him for anyone who truly desired to become his follower.

Discipleship, as well as hating one's own family, goes even further and requires hating one's own "life" (14:26). Jesus used the term "life" here to mean not only physical existence, but also the desires, passions, and impulses—both good and evil. Hating one's life involves controlling these impulses and directing them to good ends.

Jesus sought to separate those who came along simply out of excitement or desire for gain and to retain those sincerely desiring and intending to become his followers.

Jesus taught that discipleship involves dying to self. Dying to self follows the analogy of the seed. Only if the seed falls into the ground and dies can it produce the plant that brings the harvest. Likewise, only one who hates his or her life to the extent that he or she voluntarily invests in God's kingdom can bring forth fruit for Christ (see John 12: 20–33).

The process of hating one's life, said Jesus, may well result in suffering and sacrifice and must be based on willingness to suffer and sacrifice. Jesus taught that anyone who did not take up his or her cross and follow him could not be his disciple (14:27). The Roman prisoner, bound for crucifixion, was forced to carry the horizontal beam of the cross on which he was to be nailed at the place of execution. Jesus was referring to this custom in teaching that discipleship involved a daily willingness to accept any and every demand for serving God.

No one should attempt to follow Jesus without understanding the full import of discipleship and its full cost.

Thus Jesus set forth the radical nature of Christian discipleship. He called people to no easy pursuit. He indicated that only as a person became willing to assume such a devotion and dedication could he or she become a disciple (14:27). Jesus impressed on the crowd the conditions of discipleship so that the people would consider the demands of following him and enter into this life with total knowledge of what it involves.

The Necessity of Counting the Cost (14:28–32)

Jesus knew that one who attempted to follow him in discipleship without thoroughly understanding and appreciating the cost would in all probability fall when difficulties, demands, and persecutions arose. He delivered two striking stories to impress the necessity of counting the cost of discipleship. Both stories relate to the common and natural prudence that a person in the world should exercise before beginning a work of importance. How much more foresight should be taken in relation to spiritual matters? These words were intended to convey the significant lesson of the importance of counting the cost.

Jesus first illustrated the necessity of counting the cost by referring to one who desired to build a "tower" (14:28–30). The word refers to a "tower" that would serve as protective fortification for cities, private homes, land, or vineyards. A "tower" was usually a fortified structure of some height that enabled the watchman to view in every direction. Before beginning such a structure, the prudent builder would make certain he or she had enough resources to complete the job. Pilate had begun building an aqueduct that, due to lack of funds, was left incomplete. Perhaps Jesus was alluding to this example.

Following Jesus requires a complete and undivided devotion.

Jesus warned that the building project that points to the sky and yet ends in an unfinished stub is a target of ridicule. But so is an extinguished enthusiasm! To begin to walk with Jesus and then to fall back will bring scorn on the person and on the cause of Christ. The disciple, then, should count the cost and appreciate the demands of building a life on the blueprint of the Sermon on the Mount. The disciple must preview the persecutions and temptations to fall away and be prepared to stand.

Second, Jesus illustrated the necessity of counting the cost of discipleship by referring to the king who was to engage an enemy on the battlefield (14:31–32). The wise general would make certain he had resources enough to prevail. If he did not, prudence would call for making peace—that is, for asking for terms for peace.

In the first illustration the price of failing to count the cost would be ridicule. In the second, the price would be defeat. The illustrations do not teach that we should never begin or that we should always seek terms of surrender rather than striving. The central teaching of the stories is that of the importance of counting the cost of discipleship so as to both begin and remain faithful in the journey. A person should understand well the conditions of discipleship, fully recognize the difficulty, and courageously embark on the lifestyle of Jesus.

According to Jesus, a disciple would follow Jesus' goals, intentions, plans, and ways of living.

The Imperative of Remaining True (14:33–35)

Jesus challenged the hearers (and us as well) to understand the conditions and embark on the life to which disciples are called. Jesus did not suggest we behave exactly as the people in the parables. Rather, every person should come to Jesus whatever the cost but also should be aware of the cost when he or she commits to discipleship.

The imperative of accepting Jesus' discipleship is simply that one cannot be his disciple without this total and decisive commitment. Twice the Master had taught that apart from a definite and complete commitment to his way of life one could not become his disciple (14:26–27). Now, in verse 33, Jesus said that unless one gives up all possessions, he or she cannot be Jesus' disciple. Only to the degree that we totally commit our lives and possessions to Christ can we become his disciples and be used effectively.

A person should understand well the conditions of discipleship, fully recognize the difficulty, and courageously embark on the lifestyle of Jesus.

Jesus illustrated the principle with salt. Salt is good—that is, has many uses. Flavoring and preserving were the most important functions of salt, but salt could be used for other matters as well. What if, Jesus asked, salt lost it saltiness? Could it be made salty again? Jesus obviously expected the negative answer. He continued, salt that is no longer salty is not good for flavoring, for fertilizing, or even for killing weeds on the manure pile.

With these words Jesus warned against beginning discipleship without understanding the full conditions. He taught that we should count the cost, commit, and begin the path of discipleship while remembering that to begin and fall back is to be fruitless (John 15:6). One who began and then fell from discipleship would have no function, as salt that lost its saltiness could produce no good end.

Jesus called his listeners, and he calls us, to recognize clearly the extreme and radical conditions of discipleship, to accept decisively the responsibilities of discipleship—the cross—and to undertake unreservedly the path of discipleship. He promised the empowering of the Holy Spirit in this effort (John 14:15–17; Luke 24:49). Only by following this plan can anyone become Jesus' disciple.

Salt in the Biblical World

Salt was important in the biblical world. It was used for flavoring, preserving, cleansing, fertilizing, killing weeds, and serving as a catalyst in certain kinds of ovens. Salt was often put on manure piles as it killed weeds and slowed the fermentation process.

In saying "salt is good" (Luke 14:34), Jesus used the word for *beneficial* or *productive*, not the word for *moral*. He used it illustratively three times. Jesus said that his followers were the salt of the earth (Matthew 5:13) and that his followers would have salt within themselves (Mark 9:50), meaning that his followers would share salt and eat together in peace. In Luke 14:34, Jesus used salt to mean that those who do not commit and remain faithful cannot function in his kingdom.

Actually, sodium chloride (table salt) as a chemical cannot lose its saltiness. Jesus probably referred to the kind of salt that people gathered from around the Dead Sea. This salt, heavily mixed with other chemicals, when diluted with water could lose the sodium chloride and leave mostly impurities—hence, losing its ability to function as salt.

Jesus said that salt that loses its saltiness could not produce any of the important functions of salt. Outward religion without the inner meaning of commitment to Jesus is worthless and will be cast out as having no function.

Questions

1. Have you ever felt that some of the requirements of following Jesus were too hard or too demanding? What does this lesson indicate about these requirements?

2. Do you think the radical demands of discipleship are for every Christian or only for those called into career service—such as missionaries, pastors, or other church staff people?

3. Since the conditions of discipleship are so strenuous, how can Christians be certain that they can live up to these conditions?

4. What in your life would need to change if you followed the call of Jesus into discipleship? Are you willing to follow Jesus even it means giving up this matter?

Focal Text

Luke 15:8–32

Background

Luke 15:1–32

Main Idea

When we recognize God's grace in our lives, we join in the celebration as God welcomes people back, regardless of who they are and what they have done.

Question to Explore

Do you share the joy of God's welcoming all people who return to him? Why not?

LESSON EIGHT

The Lost Coin and the Father with Two Sons

Rejoicing to Find What Was Lost

Study Aim

To accept God's grace in my life and identify ways I will join in joyfully sharing it with all other people

Study and Action Emphases

- Affirm the Bible as our authoritative guide for life and ministry
- Share the gospel with all people
- Develop a growing, vibrant faith
- Include all God's family in decision-making and service
- Value all people as created in the image of God
- Encourage healthy families

Quick Read

God greatly values, diligently seeks, and joyfully finds the lost. God does not look at nationality, status in life, place in history, or worldly importance of those he seeks. God invites all Christians to join in the search, the finding, and the joy.

The young couple was distressed by the loss of a diamond ring. The ring was not of tremendous monetary value, but it had been the property of the young wife's grandmother, her mother, and now her. As the third-generation owner, she understandably felt the loss most intensely!

A happy ending ensued. The ring was found through an intense hunt by a group of neighborhood people. The finding produced great joy, not only because the treasured ring was regained, but also due to the experience of having friends join the search.

Our lesson concerns parables about losing, seeking, and finding. Jesus told us how much God loves and desires to find those who are separated from him and God's great joy when one of the separated is found—that is, returned to him. Jesus invites us to join both in the search and in the joy of finding. The parables of the lost sheep, the lost coin, and the lost son express the love of seeking and the joy of finding.

Background of the Parables (15:1–7)

These parables arose out of an encounter between Jesus and the Pharisees and teachers of the law (scribes). The immediate circumstances of the parables related to the grumbling of these Jewish leaders. These leaders were enraged that Jesus was associating with people they held as unfit for relationship. Jesus was associating with tax collectors and "sinners" (15:1). The Jewish leaders rejected these people.

Tax collectors routinely were despised both for their reputation of extortion and for their complicity with the hated Romans. The Romans used local authorities to impose taxes on almost everything. The Romans leased the right to collect taxes to individuals who then took a measure for themselves. Since the tax charges were seldom controlled, the system was open to great abuse and corruption. "Sinners" were people, usually of the lower classes, who did not follow the rigorous religious regimen of the Pharisees.

The focus of the Pharisees' anger stemmed from their contemptuous, self-serving, self-righteous, and self-exalting spirit. They pointed to the fact that Jesus not only associated with the tax collectors and sinners but actually ate with them—something no Pharisee would consider. The words "welcomes sinners" indicate that Jesus accepted these into close comradeship, relationship, and fellowship (15:1–2).

Jesus explained his willingness to welcome the distressed and sinful through these stories of the intense love God holds for all. God loves all people, regardless of who they are, the families from which they come, the evil acts they have performed, or the weaknesses to which they are subject. Perhaps we would better title these parables the Found Sheep, the Found Coin, and the Found Son or even better, the Accepting Father.

Luke 15:8–32

8"Or suppose a woman has ten silver coins and
loses one. Does she not light a lamp, sweep the house
and search carefully until she finds it? 9And when she
finds it, she calls her friends and neighbors together and
says, 'Rejoice with me; I have found my lost coin.' 10In
the same way, I tell you, there is rejoicing in the pres-
ence of the angels of God over one sinner who
repents."

11Jesus continued: "There was a man who had two
sons. 12The younger one said to his father, 'Father, give
me my share of the estate.' So he divided his property
between them.

13"Not long after that, the younger son got
together all he had, set off for a distant country and
there squandered his wealth in wild living. 14After he
had spent everything, there was a severe famine in that
whole country, and he began to be in need. 15So he
went and hired himself out to a citizen of that country,
who sent him to his fields to feed pigs. 16He longed to
fill his stomach with the pods that the pigs were eating,
but no one gave him anything.

17"When he came to his senses, he said, 'How
many of my father's hired men have food to spare, and
here I am starving to death! 18I will set out and go back
to my father and say to him: Father, I have sinned
against heaven and against you. 19I am no longer wor-
thy to be called your son; make me like one of your
hired men.' 20So he got up and went to his father.

"But while he was still a long way off, his father saw
him and was filled with compassion for him; he ran to
his son, threw his arms around him and kissed him.

[21] "The son said to him, 'Father, I have sinned
against heaven and against you. I am no longer worthy
to be called your son.'

[22] "But the father said to his servants, 'Quick! Bring
the best robe and put it on him. Put a ring on his finger
and sandals on his feet. [23] Bring the fattened calf and kill
it. Let's have a feast and celebrate. [24] For this son of
mine was dead and is alive again; he was lost and is
found.' So they began to celebrate.

[25] "Meanwhile, the older son was in the field. When
he came near the house, he heard music and dancing.
[26] So he called one of the servants and asked him what
was going on. [27] 'Your brother has come,' he replied,
'and your father has killed the fattened calf because he
has him back safe and sound.'

[28] "The older brother became angry and refused to
go in. So his father went out and pleaded with him.
[29] But he answered his father, 'Look! All these years I've
been slaving for you and never disobeyed your orders.
Yet you never gave me even a young goat so I could cel-
ebrate with my friends. [30] But when this son of yours
who has squandered your property with prostitutes
comes home, you kill the fattened calf for him!'

[31] "'My son,' the father said, 'you are always with
me, and everything I have is yours. [32] But we had to cel-
ebrate and be glad, because this brother of yours was
dead and is alive again; he was lost and is found.'"

The God Who Seeks the Lost (15:8–12)

After the parable of the shepherd searching for the one lost sheep and the joy of the shepherd and his friends upon finding it, Jesus moved to the story of the woman who found her lost coin. He suggested that a woman who had ten silver coins and lost one would search diligently for the lost coin. The "coin" was the Greek *drachma*, worth around a day's wages (thus similar in value to a *denarius*). To a working person it would assume large significance.

Jesus invites us to join both in the search and in the joy of finding.

The significance of the coin is variously interpreted. I think more is involved than the simple loss of one piece of money. The coin might have been part of the frontlet worn by women to indicate their betrothal or their marriage relationship. Regardless of the monetary value, the coin would be meaningful to the woman. Or the coin may have represented part of her bridal price and have been intended for her care in case of unforeseen circumstances. Or it might have been the last part of her temple tax. In any event the coin was very precious to her.

The story's emphasis relates to the intensity of her search, the thoroughness of her methods, and the joy of her success. The woman seemingly laid aside all other tasks and sought carefully until she found it. Lighting a lamp and sweeping the house underline the thoroughness of the search. Jesus expressed the joy of finding by adding that friends would join the woman in the celebration. The fact that the finding of the lost would bring joy in the presence of angels has the same meaning as joy in heaven in the previous parable (15:7, 10).

God's love leads him to seek the lost intensely, diligently, relentlessly, carefully, and compassionately and rejoice at their finding. God invites all Christians to join in both the search for and the celebration of the finding of the lost.

God's love leads him to seek the lost intensely, diligently, relentlessly, carefully, and compassionately and rejoice at their finding.

The Loving and Accepting God (15:11–24)

The father, upon the demand of his younger son, divided the property between his two sons (15:11–12). Both the demand and the action were unusual. Inheritance by Jewish law was not distributed until after the father's death. To ask for the inheritance early would be like stating to the father that the son wished he were dead.

The *Misnah* (rabbinic comments on the Jewish law) did allow a father to divide his property before his death. The right to dispose of the wealth, however, did not pass to the heirs until the father's death. What is unusual is that this son demanded, received, and squandered his part of the inheritance. Jesus' listeners would be horrified that the son would ask for the inheritance and demand power over it immediately. Furthermore, Jews considered the loss of family wealth to Gentiles as a grievous offense and a ground for excommunication.

Driven by self-centered pride and desire, the son sold his land, called in any loans, and turned his other property into cash (15:13). Setting off for a distant country, where he expected no restraints, the errant son "squandered" his wealth—a word meaning *throwing one's possessions to the wind.* The son used up his money in "wild living." The Greek word for "wild" is composed of the word *save* with an *a* as a prefix, thus reversing the meaning. The younger son's way of living did not contribute to saving. He wasted his money. The result was destitution.

He determined to return to his father, confess his sinfulness, and beg to be accepted again.

The depletion of the son's money, a famine in the land, and the resulting dire circumstances drove him to hire himself to a Gentile. The Gentile sent him to feed the swine (15:14–16). The son's freedom from restraint in the father's home had turned to slavery to sin. The disgrace of tending swine would be felt acutely by Jews, who abhorred pigs.

The son's condition continued to decline. His hunger made him want to fill his stomach with the "pods" that were fed to pigs. These "pods" were used for animal food and eaten only by very poor people. The young man had fallen to the lowest state—working for a Gentile, tending pigs, and longing to eat their disreputable food.

The young man "came to his senses," that is, to a full realization of what had caused his grievous situation (15:17). These words reveal the first step in repentance—the discovery that one's failure, despair, misery, and helplessness stem directly from turning away from God to the "pleasures" of the world. One stands only a short step from contrite return to God when he or she realizes that the reason for one's tragic situation is rebellion against God.

While the son was at a distance, the father ran, embraced the son, and broke into the son's confession to express the forgiveness of willing acceptance.

The young man took the next and imperative step in repentance. He determined to return to his father, confess his sinfulness, and beg to be accepted again. He realized his sin was not only against his father and his culture, but also against God (15:21).

Repentance and conversion involve turning from sin and to God. The experience includes recognizing sinfulness, confessing the wrong, accepting the responsibility, placing oneself in the hands of God through faith, and believing in God's promised acceptance.

Acting on his decision, the son arose and journeyed to the father. He demonstrated more than a flash of remorse or a depression caused by need. He turned from the rejection of God and involvement in sinful living. With his confession ready the son approached the father's house. The father seemingly had been waiting and watching in hope that the son would return. While the son was at a distance, the father ran, embraced the son, and broke into the son's confession to express the forgiveness of willing acceptance.

Repentance and conversion involve turning from sin and to God.

The father commanded the servants to bring a robe, a ring, and sandals. These items represented full reinstatement into the family. The "best robe" may have been the father's own. The robe symbolized honor and authority (15:22). The ring may have been the signet ring that signified membership and authority in the family. Sandals distinguished between sons and servants. The son was reinstated to his place in the family.

The father commanded the preparation of a feast involving the "fattened calf," that is, the calf that was being fed in preparation for a special event. The fact that the father called for a calf rather than a goat or sheep indicated that he intended on inviting the entire community. The father desired to reconcile the son with the entire community. The family, the friends, and the entire community joined in the celebration of joy at the return of the wayward son.

The parable contains many applications, including these:

- First and foremost, God is willing and desirous of accepting all repentant sinners. The depth of sin and the harshness of the rebellion are swept away by the God who accepts repentant people.
- Those whom God accepts are brought fully and completely into the family of God and placed in conditions of sonship.
- God's acceptance is ready, but human repentance marks the way for God to implement forgiveness.
- Repentance includes ceasing from sin, confessing that sin is rebellion against God, and turning to God.
- God expects and invites all Christians to participate in intense, careful, and diligent search for the lost.
- The return of the repentant sinner to God leads to joy and thanksgiving at the wonderful new status the Lord has given.

The Failure of the Unconcerned (15:25–32)

Jesus did not end the story with the joyous celebration of the sinful son's return. He denounced self-righteousness and unconcern in his account of the elder son. The elder son, laboring in the fields, returned home to hear the celebration. A servant answered his question and told him the celebration was because of his brother's return. Rather than rejoice at this news, the elder son expressed anger, jealousy, self-righteousness, and unconcern (15:25–28). So great was his anger, the elder son refused to join the celebration. He thereby greatly insulted both the father and the community.

The father left the celebration to entreat the elder son to come in. The elder son demonstrated his jealousy and self-righteousness, saying that he had served and obeyed but never received a celebration. The younger son, who had rebelled and wasted the family wealth, was given the banquet. The elder son revealed disrespect and dishonor toward his father as he failed to use the honorific title, *father* (15:28–30).

Envy and lovelessness indicate a heart far different from the heart of the seeking, accepting God.

The father indicated his deep feelings for the elder son by using the tender expression, *child* (translated "my son" by NIV). The father pointed out that the elder son was always with him and that he still possessed all the father had. The father affirmed his impartial love, eternal appreciation, and continuing concern for the elder son.

The elder son was as great a sinner as the prodigal. Self-righteousness constitutes sin as much as unrighteousness does. In fact, it often produces even more serious consequences. Envy and lovelessness indicate a heart far different from the heart of the seeking, accepting God. Many people have been driven back to the "distant country" (15:13) by the lovelessness, envy, and self-righteousness that was manifested by the elder brother. Religious exclusiveness blocks missionary effort.

In all probability, Jesus had in mind the Jewish people in general and the Pharisees in particular as he added the story of the elder brother. God called the Jewish people, Israel, to be his missionaries to spread his message to all peoples. God intended Israel to reflect his love, concern, and desire for all. Like the elder son, Israel demonstrated the sins of ungratefulness, self-righteousness, lovelessness, and a lack of missionary consciousness. Jesus taught that in spite of these sins, the seeking and accepting God still loved and desired Israel—including the Pharisees—and longed for their return.

Religious exclusiveness blocks missionary effort.

This latter portion of the parable contains significant applications, including these:

- Self-righteousness, lovelessness, envy, and exclusiveness are as sinful as the more spectacular sins of the flesh and often even more harmful.
- Even the proud, arrogant, self-righteous, and envious remain in the heart of the loving and seeking God.
- Christians everywhere should accept their responsibilities and opportunities to be messengers of God's love and light to all peoples and share in God's worldwide missionary objective (Matthew 28:18–20).
- Christians should welcome into God's family all those who come by faith.

God's Universal Commission and the Sin of Exclusiveness

God's universal commission calls for making disciples of all the peoples of the world (Matthew 28:18–20). Exclusiveness is the mistaken notion that God is concerned about only a certain group or nation. This mistake often leads to self-righteousness and contempt for other people. Those committed to pleasing God will accept the commission, commit to its demands, and avoid exclusiveness.

God created Israel to become a blessing for all nations (Genesis 12:1–3), to be a "light for the Gentiles" (Isaiah 49:6), and to take the message of God's love to people (2 Corinthians 5:11–20). Israel had forgotten these purposes and had become radically exclusive. They thought God's love was for them alone. The result of this exclusiveness was self-righteousness, lack of concern for others, and feelings of hatred and contempt for others.

Questions

1. Have you at some time felt that those who recently have come to Christ and church membership should have less rights in the church in comparison to those who have served long and with great sacrifice? Is this feeling proper?

2. Does the social status of the lost person have anything to do with your willingness or determination to witness to that person?

3. What evidences of self-righteousness and lovelessness do you see in your life? How do you think these sinful conditions might be overcome?

Focal Text

Luke 16:1–13

Background

Luke 16:1–15

Main Idea

Christians should use their money and other resources wisely, so as to provide for eternal purposes.

Question to Explore

What relation does how you use your money and other resources have to eternity?

LESSON NINE

The Shrewd Manager

Using Resources for the Highest Purpose

Study Aim

To identify ways of using my money and other resources wisely so as to provide for eternal purposes

Study and Action Emphases

- Affirm the Bible as our authoritative guide for life and ministry
- Share the gospel with all people
- Develop a growing, vibrant faith
- Obey and serve Jesus by meeting physical, spiritual, and emotional needs
- Equip people for servant leadership

Quick Read

Christians should employ every proper business practice and financial tactic that helps them use material resources for eternal purposes. Possessions should never be used merely for what appears to be earthly success.

I invited a businessperson to address my seminary class on Christian Ethics. In his presentation, the man said that if he received a traffic citation he would get it fixed as this would cost far less than the fine, take less time from him than attending court, and not affect his automobile insurance rate. To my relief, the students questioned the ethics of his suggestion, expressing the conviction that using questionable means to escape punishment for an obvious offense violated biblical guidelines for Christian behavior. What do you think?

But wait, in the parable about the shrewd manager, some think that Jesus was praising or at least approving behavior that sounds like the businessman's suggestion. Was Jesus suggesting that believers use unethical or improper business tactics in order to ensure themselves profits, material security, or safety in this world? If so, this parable would indeed present a problem!

As we will see as we examine this parable, Jesus was teaching one central and important lesson—that Christians should use their material possessions to provide for eternal purposes. Jesus did not suggest using shrewd business practices for the purpose of increasing wealth or ensuring financial security. He used the dishonest, shrewd manager as a positive illustration of using wise practices but emphasized that the proper reason for using effective business strategies was not financial gain or earthly security. Jesus taught that Christians should use all resources, all earthly gifts of wealth and opportunity, for the attainment of the high purposes of eternal gain, not for earthly aims.

Luke 16:1–13

1 Jesus told his disciples: "There was a rich man
whose manager was accused of wasting his possessions.
2 So he called him in and asked him, 'What is this I hear
about you? Give an account of your management,
because you cannot be manager any longer.'
3 "The manager said to himself, 'What shall I do
now? My master is taking away my job. I'm not strong
enough to dig, and I'm ashamed to beg—4 I know what
I'll do so that, when I lose my job here, people will wel-
come me into their houses.'
5 "So he called in each one of his master's debtors.
He asked the first, 'How much do you owe my master?'
6 "'Eight hundred gallons of olive oil,' he replied.
"The manager told him, 'Take your bill, sit down
quickly, and make it four hundred.'
7 "Then he asked the second, 'And how much do
you owe?'
"'A thousand bushels of wheat,' he replied.
"He told him, 'Take your bill and make it eight hundred.'
8 "The master commended the dishonest manager
because he had acted shrewdly. For the people of this
world are more shrewd in dealing with their own kind
than are the people of the light. 9 I tell you, use

worldly wealth to gain friends for yourselves, so that
when it is gone, you will be welcomed into eternal
dwellings.
10"Whoever can be trusted with very little can also
be trusted with much, and whoever is dishonest with
very little will also be dishonest with much. 11So if you
have not been trustworthy in handling worldly wealth,
who will trust you with true riches? 12And if you have
not been trustworthy with someone else's property, who
will give you property of your own?
13"No servant can serve two masters. Either he will
hate the one and love the other, or he will be devoted
to the one and despise the other. You cannot serve both
God and Money."

The Perplexing Parable

Proper understanding of the parable demands adequate attention to the background. According to Luke, Jesus gave this parable as Jesus continued the journey to Jerusalem. In addition to the disciples (Luke 16:1), Jesus' listeners included "the Pharisees, who were lovers of money" (16:14). In the previous chapter, Jesus had told the parables of the lost sheep, the lost coin, and the lost son, which described God's great love and compassion for all people.

Now Jesus turned to advice about how to use material resources. He taught the importance of using material wealth properly. The importance of correctly evaluating and using material resources is seen in the fact that Luke 16 begins with this parable about the shrewd manager and ends with the account of Lazarus, the six brothers, and the imperative of helping the needy (16:19–31, which will be studied in the next lesson).

This parable is often characterized as one of the most perplexing! After all, a superficial reading might indicate that Jesus condoned the evil practice of two men. One was the shrewd manager who misused the resources trusted to him and then covered up the misdeed with other questionable acts. The second was the "master" (owner, landlord) who commended the manager's act (16:8). Practicing and condoning sinful behavior and failing to stand against unethical practices constitute unfaithfulness to God and a sinful condition. Little wonder the parable has given pause to many interpreters over the years and received diverse interpretations.

Was Jesus suggesting that believers use unethical or improper business tactics in order to ensure themselves profits, material security, or safety in this world?

Perplexity to Clarity (16:1–9)

Perplexity gives way to clarity when the parable is correctly understood. The story is straightforward. A "rich man," most likely a large landholder, employed a "manager" or steward to oversee the collection of what was due from his land. Such was an often repeated custom in Galilee. The rich landlord employed an estate manager to oversee the collections from the tenant farmers of the land. The tenants were responsible for paying a portion of the increase of the fields to the landlord. The manager was responsible for conducting this business faithfully and honestly. Managers had significant financial and administrative authority.

Jesus taught that Christians should use all resources, all earthly gifts of wealth and opportunity, for the attainment of the high purposes of eternal gain, not for earthly aims.

The landlord received information that the manager was "wasting his possessions," that is, mismanaging his property (16:1). The word translated "wasting" may suggest that the manager was squandering the landlord's income on himself. The landlord demanded an accounting of the manager's oversight of the business. Obviously the manager knew the accounts were not in order. The landlord even announced that the manager had lost his position (16:2).

Realizing that he could not dissuade the master from dismissing him, the manager assessed his position. A life of luxury had made him unfit for manual labor, and his pride prohibited him from begging. Begging was considered a shameful life.

The manager fixed upon a scheme to escape the circumstance he himself had caused (16:3–4). His plan, although ingenious, was thoroughly unprincipled and dishonest. It was no less than stealing. He determined to defraud the landlord once more to his own advantage. He would ensure that those who were in debt to the landlord would "welcome me into their houses," that is, take him in or give him a place in their endeavors when his position was closed (16:4). He would seek gratitude and goodwill from the debtors in exchange for his ruse.

Calling each of the debtors, he inquired what they owed the landlord. Jesus gave two examples of what transpired (16:5–7). The first debtor indicated a debt of 100 *bath* of olive oil, or 800 gallons (since a *bath* equaled about 8 gallons). The manager returned his "bill" and told him to write 50 *bath*, or 400 gallons. According to the value in that day, the amount of money saved would have equaled around 1000 *denarii* or three years' wages for a daily laborer. The second debtor owed 100 *cors*, or 1000 bushels, of wheat and was told to write 80 *cors*. Since a *cor* was about 10 bushels, the savings to this man would have amounted to 2500 *denarii* or eight years' wages for a laborer. The reduction to the debtors was no small sum.

The manager's scheme was an example of prudent, shrewd, well-considered use of material resources for the promotion of a future important end.

The landlord commended the dishonest manager's actions (16:8). The commendation came not from Jesus but from the owner of the land. The landlord's commendation indicates that the manager had worked "shrewdly" or cleverly, with shrewd business sense. The manager had at once escaped detection in regard to his mismanagement and also secured the goodwill of friends who would aid him in his time of need. He had faced the obvious situation without buoying himself with delusive hopes. This action involved smartness, which was exactly what an Oriental landlord would admire, even though the landlord saw through it. The manager's scheme was an example of prudent, shrewd, well-considered use of material resources for the promotion of a future important end.

. . . Followers of Jesus should use their material gifts of wealth and opportunity for heavenly rather than earthly aims.

Jesus now added a commentary on the action, pointing to a reason the manager had acted shrewdly. He was a person "of this world" (NIV, or "age," NASB, NRSV). Jesus said that the manager and others "of this world" often behave more astutely with "their own kind" (NIV, NASB) or "their own generation" (NRSV) in relation to their own age than do those who see the eternal viewpoint.

The manager and the landlord, as people of their own generation and understanding, responded through limited outlooks. They comprehended only that which was tied to the present time period and understood nothing beyond the physical realities. On the other hand, the people of light see beyond the present, earthly realities. They thus are to place upon today the measures of eternity. The people of this world may act shrewdly in reference to this world and its values, but the people of light are to act shrewdly with regard to eternity.

Jesus turned to a dramatic application of his parable (16:9). Jesus instructed that his followers should make friends for themselves by the proper use of material possessions so that when these material resources fail (as they will), these proper uses of wealth will result in welcome to an eternal home or reward. Jesus counseled his followers to win friends by the proper and wise use of "worldly wealth" (16:9). The phrase "worldly wealth" does not indicate that the wealth was gained dishonestly, but simply that wealth often becomes unrighteous because of how people assess it wrongly and use it improperly. The actual word *mammon* in the Greek text is the Syriac or Aramaic word for money. It can mean as well all material possessions.

Christians should seek ways to use their material possessions for eternal purposes rather than simply for earthly matters.

Jesus advised using material possessions so that when they are gone, "they"—referring to the "friends"—will welcome you into eternal benefits (16:9). Thus, the central message of this parable is that followers of Jesus should use their material gifts of wealth and opportunity for heavenly rather than earthly aims.

Principles from the Parable (16:10–13)

Remaining faithful to the interpretive guide of finding one main teaching in parables, we can grasp these two direct principles in Jesus' words in verses 10–13:

- First, Jesus taught that people who are faithful with small matters will also be dependable with larger trusts. Only those who prove trustworthy will receive opportunity to serve through the management of more important matters (16:10–12).
- Second, Jesus taught that one must commit totally to serve God and not attempt to serve both God and gold (16:13).

Applications to Life

The parable provides helpful and imperative applications or directives for Christian living, including these:

- Wealth and possessions constitute vast spiritual dangers for those who are lovers of money (see 16:14–15).
- Christians should seek ways to use their material possessions for eternal purposes rather than simply for earthly matters.
- Christians should employ for eternal purposes principles that come from the business and professional world of using money, material possessions, and opportunities.

- Christians should use resourceful zeal in responding to need.
- Christians should respond to the demands of reality with appropriate foresight.
- Christian assessment of the world and the events in the world should be based not on the narrow view of earthly matters but on the true view of eternity.
- Christians should view themselves as stewards of their possessions, and they should view these material possessions from the perspective of eternity. Love of money should be set aside in lieu of the biblical love for others, which demands a proper use of what God has entrusted to us.
- Christians should accept no teaching or suggestion for behavior that contradicts what we know of God's will through the revelation of the words, actions, and spirit of Jesus Christ.

. . . Jesus was teaching one central and important lesson—that Christians should use their material possessions to provide for eternal purposes.

Testing Our Interpretations

How can we be certain that Jesus did not advise following the example of the dishonest and deceptive tactics of the manager or the acceptance and praise of wrongdoing by the landlord? The Bible remains the perfect guide to all belief and practice. It never teaches anything that is incorrect or suggests any conduct that is improper. God's truth is revealed most fully in the life, words, actions, and spirit of Jesus Christ.

When faced with an uncertainty about any interpretation, we can test this interpretation by matching it against the teachings of the entire Bible and by comparing it with the words and spirit of Jesus. This truth indicates the importance of the statement, "The criterion by which the Bible is to be interpreted is Jesus Christ."[1] This test assures that Jesus neither condoned nor advised sinful actions. Such behavior would fail the test of comparison with the spirit of Jesus.

Questions

1. How often are you guilty of viewing your money, possessions, or opportunities as belonging to you rather than as being a trust from God?

2. How can you use your possessions and resources more wisely so as to allow them to be used for eternal purposes?

3. What methods from the business world are proper for Christians? What methods are not proper for Christians?

NOTES

1. Article 1, 1963 statement, "The Baptist Faith and Message."

Focal Text

Luke 16:19–31

Background

Luke 16:19–31

Main Idea

Failing to engage in actively helping people in need results in God's judgment.

Question to Explore

Is helping people in need unimportant, optional, or essential?

LESSON TEN

Lazarus and the Six Brothers

Helping People in Need

Study Aim

To draw conclusions for my life from comparing my actions to those of the rich man

Study and Action Emphases

- Affirm the Bible as our authoritative guide for life and ministry
- Share the gospel with all people
- Develop a growing, vibrant faith
- Value all people as created in the image of God
- Obey and serve Jesus by meeting physical, spiritual, and emotional needs
- Equip people for servant leadership

Quick Read

In spite of our culture's obsession with wealth as a measure of the successful life, God's truth reveals the greater significance of the servant life, directed in this world to those around us in need.

Have you ever noticed how differently most of us behave in the presence of people of prominence and wealth? We generally insist that we judge people more on character than on status. Still, when a prominent politician, entertainer, sports personality, or business executive comes around, we begin to feel that we are in the presence of success. Most of us are in varying degrees of admiration of such people. It affects our behavior more than we want to admit. Such behavior reveals that we have much to learn from the Son of God. He has much better insight into the measure of a successful person.

Contained in this parable is a story filled with irony and seeming contradiction. It flies in the face of popular ideas of success and failure, and it affirms in many ways the entire gospel message Jesus lived and taught. The parable is a stinging indictment on indifference. It calls us to serious involvement in a world of human need that surrounds us where we live and work each day. Remember that a parable was intended to strike like an arrow at the heart of the hearer, forcing us to rethink assumptions that may have gone without reflection for a lifetime.

If Luke intended to present a witness to Jesus in which the Lord challenged the walls that separate people, then this one surely hits at the heart of a common barrier. Let this parable speak with special force to a culture characterized by both great affluence and appalling poverty. Our culture has seen a growing gap between the *haves* and the *have-nots*, not unlike the great divide that existed in Jesus' day.

Do not look on this parable as a detailed description of the after-life. See instead a powerful instruction about the responsibilities of God's people in this life. This world is our land of opportunity for service and ministry in the spirit of Jesus. Here is our mission field in which we obey or ignore the will of God for our lives. It is in this life that we will demonstrate our character and our true value systems.

Luke 16:19–31

19"There was a rich man who was dressed in pur-
ple and fine linen and who feasted sumptuously every
day. 20And at his gate lay a poor man named Lazarus,
covered with sores, 21who longed to satisfy his hunger
with what fell from the rich man's table; even the dogs
would come and lick his sores. 22The poor man died
and was carried away by the angels to be with Abra-
ham. The rich man also died and was buried. 23In
Hades, where he was being tormented, he looked up
and saw Abraham far away with Lazarus by his side.
24He called out, 'Father Abraham, have mercy on me,
and send Lazarus to dip the tip of his finger in water and
cool my tongue; for I am in agony in these flames.'
25But Abraham said, 'Child, remember that during your
lifetime you received your good things, and Lazarus in
like manner evil things; but now he is comforted here,

and you are in agony. 26Besides all this, between you
and us a great chasm has been fixed, so that those who
might want to pass from here to you cannot do so, and
no one can cross from there to us.' 27He said, 'Then,
father, I beg you to send him to my father's house—
28for I have five brothers—that he may warn them, so
that they will not also come into this place of torment.'
29Abraham replied, 'They have Moses and the prophets;
they should listen to them.' 30He said, 'No, father Abra-
ham; but if someone goes to them from the dead, they
will repent.' 31He said to him, 'If they do not listen to
Moses and the prophets, neither will they be convinced
even if someone rises from the dead.'"

The Poverty of Wealth and the Wealth of Poverty (16:19–21)

Luke 16 begins and ends with parables that deal with wealth. The first, dealing with the shrewd manager, was the subject in the previous session. Jesus realized even in that ancient cultural setting how easily we are misled by the love and pursuit of wealth and how we are made insensitive to the world around us by its seductive powers.

This parable is set against a popular notion of Jesus' day. Many of the religious leaders taught that riches were a sign of God's blessing and that poverty was an indication of God's judgment. They looked at wealth as the reward for righteous living. In an earlier verse, we are told that "the Pharisees, who were lovers of money, heard all this, and they ridiculed him" (16:14).[1]

As they ridiculed Jesus, they revealed that they had missed the insight of Jesus that riches are but a trust in the hands of people to be used for the service of others. To use possessions in any other way can only reveal that they, rather than God, have become our lord. This is nothing less than idolatry.

Have you ever noticed how differently most of us behave in the presence of people of prominence and wealth?

It is difficult to imagine two more dissimilar people than the two described in these verses. One was in every measure of the day a "rich man," displaying all the evidence of wealth. He was dressed in costly purple, with undergarments of finest linen. He dined on the most excellent foods and wines available, served by others who responded to his call.

His friends, neighbors, and even the religious leaders would have spoken of him as being blessed. He was successful, popular, envied, and imitated by others, no doubt. He seemed to have it all. To top it all off, he was kind enough to have the leftover from his splendid feasts taken to the poor people out by the gate of the city.

On the other hand, there was Lazarus, poor to the extreme, sick with a despicable disease that left him repulsive to others. Indeed, they might become unclean if they touched him. His only attendants were the dogs who came and licked his sores. Dogs, by the way, were considered unclean animals, underscoring the isolation of this outcast from his community. For food, he was dependent on what the rich man considered useless.

Lazarus was the kind of person most decent people would have avoided seeing if at all possible. He would be considered cursed, suffering for some unnamed sin, and, in the minds of most, obviously receiving the just punishment from God. One could imagine the local leaders discussing how to move him out of their midst so that ordinary people would not have to see any more of this.

Lazarus was the kind of person most decent people would have avoided seeing if at all possible.

As Jesus told this parable, we can envision a growing sense of discomfort from his hearers. What could Jesus possibly say about their lives by this story that sounded so appropriate to this point? After all, their most trusted leaders and friends had assured them that prosperity was a sign of blessing and suffering was a clear indication of sin.

Death—the Common Place of Meeting (16:22–26)

We may well be insulated from the sufferers of this world during this lifetime. We can build walls of wealth and privilege that effectively keep others away from our presence. However, there is one place where we must all stand together. The great equalizer is the experience of death. In death, poor Lazarus was attended by angels and taken to sit alongside Abraham, the great patriarch. The rich man was simply buried by those assigned such a task. The message of the parable unfolds in this setting.

In death the realities of life are revealed. Death is the common experience of all people, since we all will die one day. The rich man cried out for Lazarus to come and serve his needs. He had been accustomed to that kind of attention in life and no doubt expected the same in death. The point is made here, however, that after death it is too late to repair the misspent life.

. . . Their most trusted leaders and friends had assured them that prosperity was a sign of blessing and suffering was a clear indication of sin.

We do not necessarily see the rich man as a wicked fellow. After all, he allowed Lazarus to wait at his gate. Too, the food that "fell from his table" may well have been the leftovers of his banquet table.

The rich man, however, had never really seen this poor man with enough clarity to minister to his need. He had never discovered the truth that Jesus lived and taught that the greatest among us will be the servants of all (see Matthew 23:11).

The Truth Already Revealed (16:27–31)

The man of wealth, his true poverty now revealed, pleaded for Abraham to send someone to warn his five surviving brothers of the peril of their ways. The patriarch reminded him that he and they had had the insights and wisdom of the Old Testament Scriptures, filled with ample reminders of their responsibility. Further warnings, even from one who returned from the dead, would not likely change their insensitivity.

The God of all creation has looked on his world with love, and that love has led him to consider all people as worthy of his redemptive grace.

Through the voice of Abraham, Jesus drove home the point that we all have ample warning about truth. No sign or wonder, even from one who has died, is needed to add to what God has already revealed through God's word. One can only wonder whether Jesus did not here speak words that portended his own death and resurrection. Even the presence of the risen Lord was not enough to convince many of the eternal truth of Jesus' message.

We are reminded here of Paul's words to the Romans of the way in which God has made himself known to all from the beginning of time. "Ever since the creation of the world his eternal power and divine nature, invisible though they are, have been understood and seen through the things he has made. So they are without excuse" (Romans 1:20).

Applications

Someone has said that the opposite of love is not hate but indifference. The God of all creation has looked on his world with love, and that love has led him to consider all people as worthy of his redemptive grace.

Compare that to the contemporary attitude of many toward people, especially those who are different from them in some way. These "different" people may be poor, lonely, homeless, or in prison. They may be of a different economic status, racial group, or religious orientation. We don't hate them. We just ignore them. We tell demeaning jokes about them and laugh at the cartoons that portray them as deserving of their plight. We keep them separated so that we do not have to see them or feel their hurts or consider ourselves to have responsibility for ministering to their need.

In death the realities of life are revealed.

This parable strikes clearly at our tendency to ignore the plight of those around us who are trapped in prisons of poverty, disease, and isolation. We know such people exist, but they often seem far removed from our daily experiences. It is easy in our culture to keep such people out of sight and out of mind and to dismiss their plight as being signs of laziness or indifference.

Some years ago our local congregation, located in a comfortable and affluent suburb, began participating in an area program to provide overnight shelter to homeless people from the inner city. It was not easy for us to open our doors, much less our hearts, to these people who seemed so different from our normal contacts. Most of us had never met a homeless person. We had seen some begging on street corners and read in the paper of their problems. However, as we entered into the ministry, sat and talked with some of these guests, and learned of their struggles and pain, it became a ministry our church eagerly accepted. Some members have caught such a vision of the problem that they have organized to attack the causes and are attempting to help some people be freed from the cycle of poverty and homelessness.

This parable strikes clearly at our tendency to ignore the plight of those around us who are trapped in prisons of poverty, disease, and isolation.

It is difficult to read this parable and not be reminded of the powerful message of Jesus found in Matthew's Gospel. Speaking of the final judgment, Jesus told the familiar story about those who had helped people in need and those who hadn't. Those who had helped said, "'Lord, when was it that we saw you hungry or thirsty or a stranger or naked or sick or in prison, and did not take care of you?' Then he will answer them, 'Truly I tell you, just as you did not do it to one of the least of these, you did not do it to me'" (Matthew 25:44–45).

A well-meaning pastor once shared his convictions about how to build a strong and growing church.

His strategy, he unapologetically told me, was to go after the wealthy and prominent people in the community. He believed that if you could get them into the church, they would attract people of lesser means who would come out of admiration and envy of the wealthy.

Compare that to the methodology of Jesus. Jesus seemed to spend far more of his ministry with the poor, the outcasts, the sick and needy, and the people marginalized by society. To be sure, prominent people followed Jesus. They were drawn, though, not by envy of Jesus' success, but by Jesus' love and grace, and by the authority with which Jesus spoke to the issues of life.

We don't hate them. We just ignore them.

Albert Schweitzer

This parable so caught the attention of Dr. Albert Schweitzer that it sent him to spend his life in a crude jungle hospital in Africa. Schweitzer was widely known and respected as a theologian, organist, and musicologist. When he read this parable, he concluded that impoverished Africa was a beggar lying at the gates of prosperous Europe. He could not escape the conviction of responsibility to go and make a difference.

After being trained in medicine and surgery, in 1913 he went to Africa as a missionary. He devoted much of the rest of his life to humanitarian ministries to some of the neediest of earth's people.

Questions

1. What groups of people do you see who are most in need in your community?

2. What obstacles present themselves that keep us from seeing the needy people around us? What can we do to help break down those barriers?

3. If you attempt to overcome those barriers, can you think of potential resistance you might expect to encounter, either within yourself or from others?

4. What experiences have you had in ministries to people of need in your local community, in your state, or in other countries? What are some of the lessons you learned about the people to whom you ministered?

NOTES

1. Unless otherwise indicated, all Scripture quotations in lessons 10–13 and the Easter lesson are from the New Revised Standard Version.

Focal Text

Luke 17:7–10

Background

Luke 17:1–10

Main Idea

Humble gratitude for God's grace that results in obedient service to God is our only proper response to God.

Question to Explore

What do you think God owes you for your acts of goodness and kindness?

LESSON ELEVEN The Unrewarded Servant

Recognizing that God Owes Us Nothing

Study Aim

To discover what this parable teaches about a relationship with God and explain why fulfilling our responsibilities to God does not put God in our debt

Study and Action Emphases

- Affirm the Bible as our authoritative guide for life and ministry
- Share the gospel with all people
- Develop a growing, vibrant faith
- Equip people for servant leadership

Quick Read

If God is the Lord of us all and we are God's servants on this earth, then we will find our highest joy in life in serving our Master, not in satisfying our wants and desires.

He was genuinely puzzled by the turn of events. This active churchman, generous giver of his money and time, lay in his hospital bed with a confusion arising from the report his surgeon had delivered about the malignant tumor in his body. It would mean further surgery, chemotherapy, and a lengthy period of recovery. To his wife and the pastor who had arrived he poured out his bewilderment. "I just don't understand! After all I have done for God and for our church, how could God allow this to happen to me?"

His questioning was understandable, and over the course of the months he would gain new perspective. His questioning, however, revealed a common misunderstanding many of us harbor about our assumed reward for our Christian service. Too often we find ourselves feeling that we have somehow done enough good and resisted enough evil to obligate God to provide for our wishes.

Using a social reality of his day, namely that of the relationship of slaves and their masters, our Lord spoke about the relationship of a disciple and the Master. This brief parable, which appears only in Luke's Gospel, is not on most people's list of favorite parables. Indeed, it sounds almost harsh to our ears, accustomed as we are to a kind of religious commitment that has in it little demand or responsibility.

In beginning it must be said that this parable, as is true of all of them, is not the whole truth of the nature of God and God's ways with people. Note that this passage is directed to disciples (17:1). It is meaningful in helping us understand what it means to be a disciple and the spirit with which we should relate to our heavenly Father.

Luke 17 opens with a warning about causing another to stumble. Jesus knew that we would all face more than our share of things that might lead us to some sin, but the disciple must never be the source of confusion or disillusionment for those seeking to find and follow their Lord. What follows in our focal text is an illustration of the kind of arrogance or pride that could well become an impediment to another's understanding of the way of Jesus.

Luke 17:7–10

7"Who among you would say to your slave who has
just come in from plowing or tending sheep in the field,
'Come here at once and take your place at the table'?
8Would you not rather say to him, 'Prepare supper for
me, put on your apron and serve me while I eat and
drink; later you may eat and drink'? 9Do you thank the
slave for doing what was commanded? 10So you also,
when you have done all that you were ordered to do,
say, 'We are worthless slaves; we have done only what
we ought to have done!'"

The Reality of Slaves and Their Masters (17:7)

Jesus was neither condemning nor condoning the institution of slavery in this brief parable. Slavery was everywhere in the culture of that day. Here Jesus merely used this common reality to illustrate something of the nature of our relationship to the Creator. Many words and examples in the life of our Lord demonstrate the inherent evil of slavery. In this parable we are helped to see something of our duty toward our God.

It is, once again, important to remember the nature of parables. They are teachings phrased in practices taken from the fabric of society, intended to drive home one major point. They must be seen in this light and not as allegories in which each element of the parable is taken as a specific teaching separate from the rest.

". . . After all I have done for God and for our church, how could God allow this to happen to me?"

The existence of slavery in Jesus' day was an obvious fact of life. From ancient times, Israel and the surrounding cultures that formed the ancient Near East practiced forms of slavery. Captives of war, as well as traffic in human beings from one nation to another, served to supply a group of slaves in every nation. In addition, in some Middle Eastern nations, the sale of children, particularly in difficult economic times, was fairly common, although there is no evidence of this among the Jews. The Old Testament law codes spoke about the treatment of those who sold themselves into slavery when they could find no other way of survival.

Slaves were treated as a commodity. They could be bought and sold, used as a pledge against a debt, and inherited from one generation to the next. As such, slaves had few rights and privileges, serving at the whim of their master.

Too often we find ourselves feeling that we have somehow done enough good and resisted enough evil to obligate God to provide for our wishes.

In applying this insight to our Christian walk we can see a vital lesson in our attitude toward the Almighty. We have all heard the casual talk of celebrities and ordinary folk alike who speak of God in terms more appropriate for a golfing partner or bridge club mate. God as "the man upstairs" is not compatible with the awe and reverence with which Scripture speaks of God's holy nature.

Recall the experience of Isaiah in that memorable experience in the temple in which he sensed his call to prophetic service. Having glimpsed something of the wonder of the Creator, he cried out (Isaiah 6:3b–5),

> "Holy, holy, holy is the LORD of hosts; the whole earth is full of his glory." The pivots on the thresholds shook at the voices of those who called, and the house filled with smoke. And I said: "Woe is me! I am lost, for I am a

> man of unclean lips, and I live among a people of unclean lips; yet my eyes have seen the King, the LORD of hosts!"

That is hardly the response of one who feels the Holy God is little more than a "cosmic pal." It is the confession of one who has glimpsed the awesome majesty of God and is keenly aware of his own frailty and imperfection.

Further, this comparison of masters and slaves might well help us see the folly of our feelings of self-pity. Many is the time we have been tempted to lapse into a mood of "me against the world," feeling that we have been overworked and under-appreciated.

God as "the man upstairs" is not compatible with the awe and reverence with which Scripture speaks of God's holy nature.

Remember the old verse, "Man works from sun to sun, but woman's work is never done"? After an exhausting day of work, taxiing the kids to games and groups, shopping and cooking and cleaning, a wife and mother may often feel the pain of that demanding, endless responsibility, but she gladly (at least most of the time!) accepts it as the role of one who holds the title "Mother."

A soldier in the field may be sorely tested by the elements, by hunger and thirst, by threats of the enemy, and by the fear and anxiety of war, but it is the nature of the soldier's task to be steadfast to the last breath.

The soldier does it, not to earn honors and awards, but out of duty, patriotism, and honor. To do less would be to discredit the vow of devotion to country.

In like manner, the Christian labors for the Lord with no regard for reward and no demand for recognition. Sacrificial service and devotion to Christ are the very essence of the believer's relationship to the Master. Jesus set us the clear example by his tireless devotion to fulfilling his purpose. His invitation to all who would be his disciples was that they "deny themselves and take up their cross and follow me" (Matthew 16:24).

Sacrificial service and devotion to Christ are the very essence of the believer's relationship to the Master.

The Error of a Compartmentalized Religion (17:8–9)

We often divide our lives into neatly separated compartments, giving some of them to God and vainly attempting to keep other portions of our living for our own pursuits. No slave in Jesus' day had such luxury. Coming in from a wearisome day in the fields or guarding the sheep, no slave could plead that he had put in his full day and was now entitled to the evening off. He would instead come in, gird on the servant's apron, and prepare to help with the supper preparation.

Could anything less be expected from those who had committed themselves to the sovereignty of God in God's kingdom? To do less would be to deny God's Lordship. There is no way in which a serious disciple can ever say, *I am now off duty from my Christian life*, any more than we could imagine Jesus saying, *I am now off duty as God's Son for the afternoon while I take my rest.* Such a statement from Jesus would be absurd given Jesus' tireless sacrifice for those who were in need of God's redemptive truth. To render such ministry was Jesus' very nature.

Christian service is not based on seeking merit for God's blessing.

In thinking of this parable, we should not miss the point that Jesus was only asking us to follow his example of service. His reminder to his disciples about greatness in God's kingdom is worth remembering here, "Whoever wishes to be first among you must be your slave; just as the Son of Man came not to be served but to serve, and to give his life a ransom for many" (Matthew 20:28). He was asking his disciples to do what he did in his life.

"We Have Done Only What We Ought to Have Done" (17:10)

A dear friend passed away not long ago. As I stood in the line at the funeral home, waiting to speak to the family, I heard many in the line repeating one statement. It went something like this: *If anyone is going to get to heaven, she surely is. Just think of all the wonderful things she did for her church!*

It was an understandable comment. She had been a pillar of the church for decades. Countless people had learned choral music through her teaching. Her choirs were known far and wide for their quality of performance. She was widely read in the Christian faith, and she shared her wisdom with many. But is this what earns one a place in heaven?

Not long ago a remarkable event occurred in our area. A man driving a delivery truck noticed smoke coming from a house in the neighborhood as he drove past. Stopping, he realized that there might be someone inside. With little thought for his safety, he rushed in to attempt a rescue. He emerged with one apparently lifeless person he had found inside. Then he was himself rushed into a rescue truck that had arrived. The man had suffered serious burns over much of his body and would spend the next months in treatment and rehabilitation. The remarkable part of this story is that when the city sought to honor his heroism, he downplayed it, saying that anyone might have done the same if in his position. He saw it as the normal response of one person to another who was in peril.

If we accept Jesus as Lord, the Master of our lives, then what we do in service to others is done in the spirit of grateful obedience.

If we accept Jesus as Lord, the Master of our lives, then what we do in service to others is done in the spirit of grateful obedience. We have lived out the implications of a faith response to Jesus as Lord. We serve God by serving others. As Jesus taught, "We have done only what we ought to have done" (17:10).

Amazing Grace

The biblical reality that transforms this parable from harsh demand to reverent relationship is the wonder and amazing truth of grace. Far from being revealed in the New Testament as a cruel taskmaster, God is shown in Jesus far more often as Loving Father and Giver of grace.

. . . Christian service comes out of humble gratitude that God has permitted us to be his sons and daughters.

In this particular parable, Jesus was not saying that masters ought to have treated slaves as this one did, but he was using a common practice in that culture to help clarify his point. The one major point of this parable is clearly that God owes us nothing in return for our works of goodness and mercy but that God blesses us instead because in God's grace God loves us freely.

We should remember Paul's great affirmation to the Ephesians when he wrote, "For by grace you have been saved through faith, and this is not your own doing; it is the gift of God—not the result of works, so that no one may boast" (Ephesians 2:8–9). Christian service is not based on seeking merit for God's blessing. Rather, Christian service comes out of humble gratitude that God has permitted us to be his sons and daughters.

In Christian discipleship there is no place for prideful boasting about achievements. We can only stand in amazement at the grace of God, the unmerited favor of the Almighty, and declare, "We have done only what we ought to have done" (Luke 17:10).

Slaves

Several words in the Greek language are translated into the English versions of our Bibles as "servant" or "slave."

- Among the words used in the New Testament is the word *diakonos,* meaning "servant" and from which we get the title of "deacon." The *diakonos* was a servant who ministered to the needs of others.
- Another New Testament word is *misthios,* which described a hired servant who worked for daily wages (see Luke 15:17, 19, lesson eight).
- The word used in Luke 16:13, studied in lesson nine, is *oiketes,* which referred specifically to a household servant. An *oiketes* might or might not be a slave.
- The word Jesus used in this parable in Luke 17:7–11 is *doulos,* which refers to a slave. A slave was considered the property of the master, drew his meaning from the master, and lived to do the wishes of the master. He or she lived under

the obligation to obey and to work for the benefit of the master. With this strong idea Jesus spoke of the relationship of a disciple to God.

Applying the Parable

If we are to take the message of this parable into our lives, we will need to discipline ourselves in a number of ways. Consider these:

- Study the ways in which Scripture portrays the sovereignty of God over the creation and all that is in it.
- Reflect on the relationship of the creature (humanity) to the sovereign God.
- Practice the spirit of humility in relationship to other people.
- Look for opportunities to apply the servant principle in some way each day.
- Praise and worship God faithfully as the Giver of amazing grace.

Questions

1. Someone has said the message of this parable is that God is not here to meet our needs but rather we are here to meet God's needs. Do you agree or disagree with that assertion? Why?

2. In what ways do you feel God is like the master in the parable? In what ways do you feel God is different?

3. In Mark 10:44, Jesus taught, "And whoever wishes to be first among you must be slave of all." What do you feel it means to be a "slave" to others?

4. List some of the ministries your church provides to the community around you and to the world beyond. In what other ways do you feel you, your class, or your church might do more in ministering in the name of Christ?

Focal Text

Luke 18:1–8

Background

Luke 17:20—18:8

Main Idea

Placing emphasis on prayer provides encouragement for remaining faithful and not losing heart in facing life's challenges.

Question to Explore

When the Son of Man comes, will he find that you have faith?

LESSON TWELVE

The Widow and the Unfit Judge

Praying and Not Losing Heart

Study Aim

To identify how greater attention to prayer could encourage us to grow in our faith

Study and Action Emphases

- Affirm the Bible as our authoritative guide for life and ministry
- Share the gospel with all people
- Develop a growing, vibrant faith
- Value all people as created in the image of God
- Obey and serve Jesus by meeting physical, spiritual, and emotional needs

Quick Read

To people who face the temptation to give up too soon in prayer, Jesus urged persistence and patience. Using two interesting characters from ancient culture, Jesus appealed to his disciples to press on in seeking God's guidance.

It happens almost every evening. Just as we settle down for our evening meal the phone rings. It is not one of the children calling. Neither is it a call from a special friend. More and more calls are coming into our homes in which one answers the phone to be greeted by a recorded message assuring us of a rare opportunity for easy gain. Most of us react to these messages with a quick hang-up of the receiver! Who wants to respond to an impersonal, fleeting contact by a recorded message? Certainly not at dinner time!

On the other hand, most of us can recall experiences through the years when the persistent encouragement of a trusted friend succeeded in getting us to a doctor, take care of some needed purchase, write a will, or attend to some other important responsibility. A determined reminder by that special person, growing out of a relationship cultivated through the years, led us to do what we knew in our heart was the right thing. That kind of persistence earns our undying gratitude.

The Gospel of Luke relates two familiar parables (the good Samaritan and the rich man and Lazarus) that clearly relate to our treatment of people around us who are in distress. Chapter 18 introduces to us insights from the mind and heart of Jesus about our attitudes and behavior in relationship to God.

This parable, complete with its rogue judge and a doggedly determined widow, is at once filled with humor and at the same time serious, life-changing truth. Anticipating the difficulty and discouragement that would surely come to the earliest Christian congregations, Jesus offered here words of exhortation to faithfulness in prayer that ultimately would bring results.

The meaning of this parable seems to be related to the preceding passages of Luke 17 that speak of the coming "days of the Son of Man" (see 17:22, 24, 26, 30). In response to a question put to Jesus by the Pharisees as to when the kingdom of God was coming (17:20), Jesus offered insights. Religious leaders in those days often debated the kinds of signs or wonders that would introduce the golden age. Their imaginations ran wild with bizarre expectations. Jesus warned against seeking such signs, since the kingdom of God would come in unexpected ways and according to God's timing. Indeed, there was a sense in which God's kingdom was already in their midst (see 17:21).

The scene in chapter 18 shifts from the discourse on the coming of the kingdom of God to the issue of readiness for its coming. Luke recorded this parable as directed not to the Pharisees but to the disciples. The Gospel of Luke introduces it in 18:1 with an editorial comment that explains the parable's purpose.

Many scholars see the resemblance of this parable to the parable of the unrelenting visitor in Luke 11:5–9 (see lesson three). In both, the emphasis is on bold and persistent praying in the face of great need.

Luke 18:1–8

1Then Jesus told them a parable about their need to
pray always and not to lose heart. 2He said, "In a certain
city there was a judge who neither feared God nor had
respect for people. 3In that city there was a widow who
kept coming to him and saying, 'Grant me justice
against my opponent.' 4For a while he refused; but later
he said to himself, 'Though I have no fear of God and no
respect for anyone, 5yet because this widow keeps both-
ering me, I will grant her justice, so that she may not
wear me out by continually coming.'" 6And the Lord
said, "Listen to what the unjust judge says. 7And will not
God grant justice to his chosen ones who cry to him day
and night? Will he delay long in helping them? 8I tell
you, he will quickly grant justice to them. And yet, when
the Son of Man comes, will he find faith on earth?"

The Characters (18:1–3)

The parable revolves around a scene that might have unfolded in a local law court of the day. The two characters were the judge and the plaintiff who appealed for help in settling some issue, likely one of a financial nature.

Not much is known about the administration of justice on the village level at that time in history. This parable seems to show that it was in the hands of a single judge, perhaps an elder of the village, who delivered the verdict in matters of local concern. In such a position of responsibility, judges were always faced with the temptation of bribes for favorable outcomes.

In Hebrew life, the judge was intended to serve not only as an unbiased handler of all the evidence, but also as a zealous defender of those who had no other defender to stand up for them. This would surely include such people as widows, orphans, foreigners, and the poor.

Old Testament history reveals God as One who cares for the afflicted, the oppressed, and the powerless.

Old Testament history reveals God as One who cares for the afflicted, the oppressed, and the powerless. A Hebrew judge should be one who recognized this character of Yahweh. A judge should see that he must protect the rights and respect the plight of all for whom he served as a judge.

In the parable, the judge is clearly unfit for this kind of service since he "neither feared God nor had respect for people" (18:2). As such he was hardly in a position to represent the compassion of God for the needs of a powerless individual, or to demonstrate the justice God desires for people. The judge is not presented here as a picture of the nature of God. The judge's unfit character serves only to underscore "how much more" God would act in the right manner (see Luke 11:13; Matthew 7:11). In all likelihood he was not a Jewish judge, but one of the notorious magistrates appointed either by Herod or the Romans.

The plight of widows was particularly difficult in that ancient culture. Women typically were considered the property of husbands and found their significance in the successes of the men. Losing one's husband left a widow with little status in her community. Further, she would be deprived of the support of her husband's labor. She might not even inherit his estate since typically that would go to his sons or brothers.

In the parable, we see a widow who had no one to intercede for her and no money with which to pay a bribe had she been so inclined. She was in a position in which her only technique was persistence and a forceful presentation of her case. The only things she had going for her was an unswerving determination that her cause was just and an unending persistence. Surely the widow here serves as symbol of all who were poor and defenseless in her culture.

How easily we tire of our prayers and lapse into self-pity, protesting that God has not honored or answered our appeals.

It must be remembered that the parables have one primary thrust, and we must not bog down in endless efforts to identify all the characters in the parable. The central message lies not in the characters but in the necessity for persistence in our praying.

How easily we tire of our prayers and lapse into self-pity, protesting that God has not honored or answered our appeals. Jesus must have known that difficult days were ahead for the little band of disciples. They would need deep commitment to the cause of Christ, and persistence in the face of temptation to give up.

The Verdict (18:4–5)

It must have been tempting for those disciples who first heard this story to let their minds drift to the injustice they had seen given out by merciless Roman judges or corrupt local officials. But this would be to miss the point. Parables call for quick reactions and insights that drive home a point. The Gospel of Luke has already called our attention to those who need to take this parable to heart. It is those who are tempted to give up, to lose the courage to keep on in the face of opposition, misunderstanding, and resistance.

Persistent, faithful, earnest prayer was very much a part of Jesus' life.

Pay attention to the verdict in the parable, Jesus might well have said to them and be saying to us (18:6). In this parable, even unjust judges who had little respect for people and none for the ways of God, still responded to the persistence of a powerless widow. How much more will the loving and gracious God of creation respond to the persistence of God's people!

Do not miss the stated verdict, "I will grant her justice" (18:5). It is not always easy for the poor and those with little power to gain justice in the best of systems. In the ancient Near East it could be even more difficult. In this parable, though, the widow gained justice, or vindication, even from a heartless judge.

Jesus Applies the Truth (18:6–8)

Twice more Jesus repeated the verdict. God will "grant justice" (18:7). Again, God "will quickly grant justice" (18:8). It is worth noting here that Jesus avoided the temptation that afflicts many of us when we do not receive what we consider to be justice. Vindictiveness easily creeps in, and revenge becomes our motive. In applying the truth contained in the parable, Jesus pointed out that it is God who will vindicate God's people. Vengeance belongs to God, who sees all things clearly, and not to revenge-seekers, who want only to sooth their bruised egos.

One can imagine generations of believers down through the centuries since these words were uttered who have drawn courage to keep on seeking God's justice.

One can imagine generations of believers down through the centuries since these words were uttered who have drawn courage to keep on seeking God's justice. As the first century came to a close, resistance to the Christian way and persecution of those who openly declared their faith filled many with fear and apprehension. Some fell away and refused to be identified with Christ. Thousands, however, heeded the spirit of this parable and prayed without ceasing for God's justice. Many suffered and some died for their faith, but all were vindicated by the gracious hand of God.

In the face of baffling diseases, many have prayed for cures to be discovered that could deliver us. Some of those prayers have been answered in marvelous ways. Those of us who were children in the 1950s remember the fear that swept the nation during the summers as outbreaks of polio struck down many with its paralysis and even death. Swimming pools closed, and many public gatherings were cancelled as the disease spread. People prayed for new treatments for those suffering from polio and for cures to be found that could prevent it. Not all those who prayed lived to see their prayers answered, but we celebrate today their vision and commitment. In God's time, God vindicated their prayerful aims.

The parable urges us to put our unswerving trust in the power of God to give what we truly need and to demonstrate that trust with the same determined persistence as this desperate widow.

Today millions pray for peace in our fractured world or for economic justice for impoverished masses. Others have just given up praying or hoping for such idealistic goals. Does this parable not call us to keep on praying, and not to lose heart, even though we do not see answers as we wish? In God's time, God will bring justice.

This parable is a powerful contrast to the kind of justice rendered by unworthy judges who give in rather than put up with pesky widows, over against the gracious and merciful justice of God. The parable urges us to put our unswerving trust in the power of God to give what we truly need and to demonstrate that trust with the same determined persistence as this desperate widow.

We are called to be faithful in prayer, always hopeful and confident that the heavenly Father will give us the strength, courage, and endurance to deal with whatever life brings us.

One is reminded of the insights about prayer of Luke 11:13, "If you then, who are evil, know how to give good gifts to your children, how much more will the heavenly Father give the Holy Spirit to those who ask him!" So it is with this parable. We are called to be faithful in prayer, always hopeful and confident that the heavenly Father will give us the strength, courage, and endurance to deal with whatever life brings us.

The parable, drawn from a cultural experience Jesus may well have witnessed, is also a portrait of Jesus' own prayer life. Time and again in Scripture we see Jesus turn aside from his activities to spend time in prayer. There were occasions when Jesus spent nights alone in prayer. Persistent, faithful, earnest prayer was very much a part of Jesus' life. Out of that experience Jesus urges his followers to do the same in the face of trying times and discouraging experiences when they see no answers to their praying.

Don't miss the concluding question with which the parable ends. "And yet, when the Son of Man comes, will he find faith on earth?" (18:7). Thus the questions for us might well be, *What does the Son of Man see in our lives now? Does he find faith in us now? Does he find us praying with the tenacity of a desperate widow or drifting off into indifference and neglect?*

Ministry to Widows

One of the beautiful aspects of the Old Testament is its sensitivity to those who are powerless and in great need. The plight of widows is addressed clearly in the Old Testament. There the Scriptures show that God viewed widows with particular compassion (see Deuteronomy 10:17–18; Psalms 68:5; 146:9). In light of God's attitude toward widows, we can conclude that God's people should have a similar attitude. This apparently was not always the case in actual practice.

Acts 6:1 introduces us to an early ministry issue of the church with respect to widows. Apparently this assistance to the needs of such women was a part of the understanding of Jesus' disciples from the beginning. Pointed instruction on a ministry to widows is found in the Epistle of James: "Religion that is pure and undefiled before God, the Father, is this: to care for orphans and widows in their distress, and to keep oneself unstained by the world" (James 1:27).

Perseverance

A small congregation in a semi-rural area found itself with a dilemma. Population in the county was shrinking. Employment opportunities were limited. There were few prospects for the church. Membership dropped with every death and with every young person who moved to the city to live and work.

How would the church survive? Should they close their church, merge with another congregation, or find other answers? What would you suggest to help such a church keep the faith and not give up?

Questions

1. Why do you feel Jesus spoke about praying with persistence? Does it have to do with changing God or with changing the one who prays?

2. Have you had an experience in which your prayers were answered, but only after months or even years of praying persistently for that outcome? Would you share your experience with your Bible study group?

3. Have you known people who demonstrated the indomitable spirit of persistence in the face of seeming injustice? What do you think gave them the determination to press on in seeking justice?

4. What is the difference between *justice* and *vengeance*? What effect does each of those qualities have on relationships?

5. To what extent is prayer a kind of partnership of people with God? Explain your answer.

Focal Text

Luke 18:9–14

Background

Luke 18:9–14

Main Idea

An authentic relationship with God is based on asking for God's mercy, not on engaging in self-justification and considering oneself better than others before God.

Question to Explore

On what is a genuine relationship with God based?

LESSON THIRTEEN

Relating Authentically to God

Study Aim

To evaluate the authenticity of our relationship with God and respond with humility

Study and Action Emphases

- Affirm the Bible as our authoritative guide for life and ministry
- Share the gospel with all people
- Develop a growing, vibrant faith
- Value all people as created in the image of God
- Equip people for servant leadership

Quick Read

Jesus used the example of two unlike groups of people in that day—Pharisees and tax collectors—to teach the qualities of attitude and action that God considers valid in judging our lives.

You have probably heard a person say of another, "He is so heavenly-minded that he is of no earthly good." Is it possible to be religious and yet totally miss the mark in the eyes of God? The answer presented in this familiar parable may help us arrive at a proper conclusion.

The Gospel of Luke interprets the purpose of this parable in verse 9 when it identifies the audience to whom it is addressed. This parable was directed to ". . . some who trusted in themselves that they were righteous and regarded others with contempt" (Luke 18:9).

We cannot limit the impact of Jesus' words to one group, such as the Pharisees. All of us must struggle against pride and self-righteousness. These are among the most destructive character flaws for those who seek to follow Jesus.

Luke 18:9–14

9 He also told this parable to some who trusted in
themselves that they were righteous and regarded oth-
ers with contempt: 10 "Two men went up to the temple
to pray, one a Pharisee and the other a tax collector.
11 The Pharisee, standing by himself, was praying thus,
'God, I thank you that I am not like other people:
thieves, rogues, adulterers, or even like this tax collector.
12 I fast twice a week; I give a tenth of all my income.'
13 But the tax collector, standing far off, would not even

look up to heaven, but was beating his breast and say-
ing, 'God, be merciful to me, a sinner!' 14I tell you, this
man went down to his home justified rather than the
other; for all who exalt themselves will be humbled, but
all who humble themselves will be exalted."

Two Men Went to Pray (18:9–10)

So many of the teachings of Jesus fly in the face of conventional wisdom. Much of what Jesus taught and did with his life seemed designed to challenge popular beliefs and push people to see in fresh new ways. Surely this familiar parable fits these descriptions. Commonly accepted ways of judging the success or failure of another are demonstrated to be flawed.

Two men of Jewish society, representing two entirely different attitudes toward themselves, others, and God, went to the temple for prayer. It was common for those of Jerusalem to go to the courts of the temple area to pray. That is the setting of the parable. Devout Jews prayed at set hours of the day. The temple would be an appealing place for those who could manage to be there at the times of prayer. Sometimes their motives might prove to be faulty, however, as Jesus illustrated in the story.

"Pharisee" and "tax collector" represented opposites in the Jewish mind. The Pharisee of the parable exemplified the very highest morals and ceremonial regulations of Judaism. This movement within

Judaism was devoted to observing the Torah, the law, and maintaining purity of religious life. Its adherents were in so many ways exemplary in their manner of life. Honest, helpful, and religious, they set an example that would likely shame even the most devout among us.

On the other hand, there is the tax gatherer. His values reflected all that offended the best sensibilities of ordinary people. He was obviously a Jew since he was going to the temple to pray, but he was a Jew who had hired himself out to a conquering nation. These men paid Rome in advance for the right to collect tolls, tariffs, and customs fees. They then added amounts for their own profit. Many grew rich at the expense of their kinsmen. It is easy to see how they came to be looked upon with such scorn as traitors to their Jewish heritage.

All of us must struggle against pride and self-righteousness.

The story of Jesus and the tax man, Zacchaeus, illustrates the scheme followed by those engaged in this trade (Luke 19:2–10). Having come down from the tree and shared a meal with the Master, Zacchaeus set out to give his wealth to the poor and to repay fourfold all those who had been cheated.

In our parable, both men went up to the temple to pray. No more unlikely worshipers ever found themselves in the place of prayer together than these two! One was a respected and exemplary leader who would have been a welcome participant in any gathering for prayer. The other was a renegade outcast who would have been unwelcome and considered unclean by most of those who witnessed this event.

Two Prayers, One Conclusion (18:11–14)

The Gospel of Luke takes care in recounting the parable to present both the posture of the two men and the content of their prayers.

The Pharisee prayed, "standing by himself," in keeping with his sense of separateness. Note that there is some difference in the translation of this phrase. The NIV renders it, "The Pharisee stood up and prayed about himself" (18:11). At any rate he seemed quite comfortable with his standing before God and prayed to himself and those standing near as much as he did to his Creator.

So many of the teachings of Jesus fly in the face of conventional wisdom.

The Pharisee's prayer is largely phrased in the first person, recalling his distinction from the "thieves, rogues, adulterers, or even like this tax collector" (18:11). He apparently followed the Pharisees' practice of fasting on Mondays and Thursdays, market days when the maximum number of people would see their looks of suffering. Matthew 6:16–18 records Jesus' words of caution, "Whenever you fast, do not look dismal, like the hypocrites, for they disfigure their faces so as to show others that they are fasting." The Pharisee further boasted of his tithes and in his prayer asked for nothing, apparently assuming that he had done quite enough to earn the favor of his God.

The tax collector, on the other hand, seemed to be a man tormented by his failure. He took his place "standing far off," likely not wanting to be recognized as one of the despised tax men (18:13). His stance seems to indicate that he took himself to a far corner of the outer temple court. There he would be removed from the Pharisee, the holy place, and the other worshipers. He would not lift his eyes toward heaven. Instead, he beat upon his breast as a sign of remorse and grief. In his prayer, he boasted of nothing. He knew there was not much to hold up as exemplary as he considered his sorry past. All he could do was ask the mercy of God, casting himself on the love and grace of a God he had done little to embrace.

Is it possible to be religious and yet totally miss the mark in the eyes of God?

So far the parable would have been understood perfectly by those who heard the story. Most hearers would have nodded agreeably with the assumptions of the Pharisee. They would have chuckled quietly at the audacity of the tax collector. Jesus was not through, however, and the Master's conclusion is what makes this parable so powerful. Speaking of the tax collector, Jesus dropped the bombshell, "I tell you, this man went down to his home justified rather than the other" (18:14).

One can imagine the crowd growing strangely silent at that point, some drifting away and other puzzling as to what this could mean. The hearers might have asked themselves and one another, *What is wrong with the Pharisee's prayer and life?* While Jesus did not explain his answer, we see the flaws in a religious life that was so impressed with itself that it could look only with contempt on others. The Pharisee's life was one of rules without compassion, of legal obligations with no room for grace. Such was not acceptable to God.

How smug we can be in assuming that we are prepared for God's judgment because of our active religious life, busy church schedules, and knowledge of religious lingo.

By way of contrast, the tax collector's humility, brokenness, and honest confession of dependence on God's mercy revealed Jesus' basis for declaring his life to be justified in the sight of God. Indeed, what Jesus was saying was something as old as the prophets of the Old Testament. They knew that God was looking for inward reverence and trust rather than outward show (see Micah 6:6–8).

The term "justified," along with the term "righteous" from the same root, is a key concept of biblical faith (see Luke 18:9, 14). Used primarily by Paul in the New Testament, "justify" means to treat one as righteous. Paul voiced the understanding in Romans 3:10 that "there is no one who is righteous, not even one." Thus, the New Testament message of the gospel offers the way to righteousness through a faith relationship to Christ. Romans 3:21–26 describes this righteousness, or justification, that comes from God and is not based on human goodness.

A trusting relationship with God that acknowledges our sin and trusts God's grace is the doorway to truly being justified.

In the parable, Jesus again voiced the insight that God is not interested in a kind of righteousness that consists only of efforts at good behavior. A trusting relationship with God that acknowledges our sin and trusts God's grace is the doorway to being justified. In this light, the tax collector went to his home having been justified by God, not by the judgment of the Pharisees and their legalistic approach.

Applications of the Truth (18:14)

This is one of those stories that appears easy to grasp at first glance. We find ourselves sitting on the sidelines cheering for a poor, repentant sinner and jeering at a pompous and proud boaster. That seems neat and appropriate until we see the conclusion Jesus drew. Jesus looked all humanity in the eye and clearly stated, "All who exalt themselves will be humbled, but all who humble themselves will be exalted" (18:14).

With those challenging words the purpose of the parable becomes clearer. While we see the pride of the Pharisee and the humility of the tax man, it is all of us to whom this parable is sent. It is a powerful statement about our approach to the throne of God's grace. How smug we can be in assuming that we are prepared for God's judgment because of our active religious life, busy church schedules, and knowledge of religious lingo. We secretly feel that God is quite fortunate to have us on his side.

Putting our trust in our own goodness is a sure way to be blinded to the biblical road that leads toward a right relationship to God.

The parable, however, calls all of us to a serious examination of ourselves and to a humble and contrite approach to God. The testimony of the Apostle Paul is, "For by grace you have been saved through faith, and this is not your own doing; it is the gift of God" (Ephesians 2:8).

The parable surely speaks to our attitude toward others, as well. There comes to mind too many days when we have practiced pride and boasting for our achievements and religious correctness. There are those days when we have looked down on some fallen sinner and quietly felt smug and complacent because we have not fallen victim to that sin. We have been blind to the grievous failures and flaws in our character while judging the missteps of another.

Jesus' attitude toward the most offensive of sinners should speak to our circumstances. He did not heap condemnation on them. They needed compassion and a relationship to God. Jesus opened the door to both.

Have you noticed how some Christians seem to have tunnel vision as they attack certain sins and immoralities? They preach powerful sermons, organize others for action, and lead groups to pass resolutions condemning those sins. If a person does not come to the same conclusions about their particular cause, that person will be considered wrong and will be avoided or excluded. Their discernment of the sin may be correct, but their pride and arrogance stifles their credibility.

Could it be that we need to be aware of the old axiom, *We preach (or teach) most what we most need to hear?* Rather than looking for those who are guilty of certain sins so that we might condemn them, perhaps a more appropriate response in light of this parable would be to repeat, *There but for the grace of God go I.*

We secretly feel that God is quite fortunate to have us on his side.

Our world is filled with those whose arrogance may win them a wide audience on talk shows and in their books and articles, but arrogance is no virtue! The Apostle Paul wrote about the fruit of the Spirit, which reveals a totally different approach to life. Having written about various degrading traits, he declared that "the fruit of the Spirit is love, joy, peace, patience, kindness, generosity, faithfulness, gentleness, and self-control" (Galatians 5:22–23).

Putting our trust in our own goodness is a sure way to be blinded to the biblical road that leads toward a right relationship to God. It is through humility, confession, and faith in God's grace that one finds a life-changing relationship that leads to everlasting life. In this trusting relationship with God lies the key to authentic religious experience.

Pharisee

Often mentioned in Scripture, the term *Pharisee* is derived from a Hebrew word that means *separated one*. Driven by a determination to maintain purity of Jewish life, Pharisees devoted themselves to God through the study of the Torah and sought purity in every area of life. Guided by a multitude of interpretations of the law in matters of ritual, food, and daily life, they maintained separation from others lest they compromise their purity.

Applying the Parable

To apply the parable in your daily walk:

- Take time to listen to your prayers and notice what you hear
- Make personal confession a part of your personal prayers daily
- Practice humility, not superiority, toward those whom you see as sinful

- Look for ways each day to practice the kind of mercy God demonstrated to the tax collector
- Explore ways to express your joy in your relationship to God

Questions

1. Reflecting on the character of the Pharisee, what do you think was the basic flaw of character that robbed his prayer of acceptance?

2. As you reflect on the tax collector in the parable, what was the primary quality in his life and prayer that made him acceptable to God?

3. What do you feel can help a Christian avoid the pride and arrogance of the Pharisee while maintaining a commitment to high standards of belief and behavior?

4. What insights into the nature of prayer do you gain from this parable?

Focal Text

Luke 24:13–35

Background

Luke 24:1–53

Main Idea

Knowing the resurrected Jesus encourages us to want to make him known to others.

Question to Explore

How can we more readily experience and share the good news about Jesus?

EASTER LESSON

Knowing the Resurrected Jesus

Study Aim

To identify ways we can experience and share the good news of the resurrected Jesus

Study and Action Emphases

- Affirm the Bible as our authoritative guide for life and ministry
- Share the gospel with all people
- Develop a growing, vibrant faith
- Value all people as created in the image of God
- Equip people for servant leadership

Quick Read

The conviction that Jesus rose from the dead does not arise from listening to others, studying the stories of Jesus' life, or understanding all the mystery involved. Such conviction arises from a personal awareness of Jesus' presence in our lives that brings confident faith.

One of the truly amazing chapters in the history of religion in America is called by historians *the Great Awakening*. This was a time in the middle of the eighteenth century when all around the colonies there was an explosion of great spiritual power. Pulpits were given new life, congregations came back, people's lives were changed, and the topic of spiritual discovery was on the lips of people everywhere.

We have all heard the stories of the religious motives that led many people in the first settlements in the American colonies, but after the initial enthusiasm of settling this nation and the vital religious experiences of those founding days, much of American Christianity had settled into a kind of dull, second-hand experience that was taken seriously by few.

The eighteenth century began in a mood of indifference toward religion by a majority of Americans. All over the colonies the vast majority of people were outside the church. Some felt that we had reached a state in which one did not really need God to get along. The feeling was widespread that if you worked hard enough and applied yourself to wise living, then everything would work out in the end.

This was not a situation of the demise of God's power. It was instead a period of failure of people's spiritual vision. When the first great revivals began to break out in New England, New York, and New Jersey, and later in the South, it was as if people's eyes were opened to the great reality that had been lost from sight for generations. The Great Awakening reached its peak around 1740, as people began to discover God's Spirit working in their lives, their churches, and their communities. Everywhere they turned they met new discoveries of God's grace and power at work.

No wonder it has been called *the Great Awakening*. It was as if people throughout the land had been sleeping through marvelous events and had at last begun to see again eternal truth. Things that should have been evident had been overlooked but were now rediscovered.

Our text for this lesson presents another great awakening, a discovery by two early observers of Jesus that Jesus' power was very much alive and in their midst. Their discovery of the risen Christ has served as a model for many a person's discovery of a personal relationship with the Lord.

Luke 24:13–35

13 Now on that same day two of them were going
to a village called Emmaus, about seven miles from
Jerusalem, 14 and talking with each other about all these
things that had happened. 15 While they were talking
and discussing, Jesus himself came near and went with
them, 16 but their eyes were kept from recognizing him.
17 And he said to them, "What are you discussing with
each other while you walk along?" They stood still, look-
ing sad. 18 Then one of them, whose name was Cleopas,

answered him, "Are you the only stranger in Jerusalem
who does not know the things that have taken place
there in these days?" 19He asked them, "What things?"
They replied, "The things about Jesus of Nazareth, who
was a prophet mighty in deed and word before God
and all the people, 20and how our chief priests and
leaders handed him over to be condemned to death
and crucified him. 21But we had hoped that he was the
one to redeem Israel. Yes, and besides all this, it is now
the third day since these things took place. 22Moreover,
some women of our group astounded us. They were at
the tomb early this morning, 23and when they did not
find his body there, they came back and told us that
they had indeed seen a vision of angels who said that he
was alive. 24Some of those who were with us went to
the tomb and found it just as the women had said; but
they did not see him." 25Then he said to them, "Oh,
how foolish you are, and how slow of heart to believe all
that the prophets have declared! 26Was it not necessary
that the Messiah should suffer these things and then
enter into his glory?" 27Then beginning with Moses and
all the prophets, he interpreted to them the things
about himself in all the scriptures.

28As they came near the village to which they were
going, he walked ahead as if he were going on. 29But
they urged him strongly, saying, "Stay with us, because
it is almost evening and the day is now nearly over." So
he went in to stay with them. 30When he was at the
table with them, he took bread, blessed and broke it,
and gave it to them. 31Then their eyes were opened,

and they recognized him; and he vanished from their
sight. 32 They said to each other, "Were not our hearts
burning within us while he was talking to us on the
road, while he was opening the scriptures to us?"
33 That same hour they got up and returned to
Jerusalem; and they found the eleven and their compan-
ions gathered together. 34 They were saying, "The Lord
has risen indeed, and he has appeared to Simon!"
35 Then they told what had happened on the road, and
how he had been made known to them in the breaking
of the bread.

Two Men and a Journey (24:13–14)

If you could get people in our day talking about the Christian faith, what do you think they would say? Many would profess their appreciation for some of the qualities and sayings of Jesus. They would tell you that they like his words about love and kindness. Some could even stumble through a quote or two of verses like John 3:16. They would be able to tell a few of the stories or parables of Jesus, perhaps the good Samaritan or the prodigal son. They might even be able to quote some or all of the Lord's Prayer.

Most would likely end the conversation, however, with some serious questions. Perhaps they would say, *Why do you Christians make so much of this business of a cross, a tomb, and the resurrection? Those things just don't make sense. If Jesus arose, where is he? Why can't we see more evidence of God's presence in our world? If we could see something we might believe.*

With that kind of questioning mood in the background, we can turn to the story of the two broken disciples who sadly journeyed from Jerusalem to the obscure Judean village of Emmaus. This story, unique to the Gospel of Luke, conveys a powerful truth about vital Christian experience.

The text describes the journey of two pilgrims who, after the resurrection, made their way down the road that ran from Jerusalem to the little town of Emmaus a few miles away. They had been in Jerusalem during the Passover observance. They may have witnessed many of the events of the final week of Jesus in the holy city.

If you could get people in our day talking about the Christian faith, what do you think they would say?

As the two grieving disciples traveled wearily down the dusty road, they were in shock and despair over Jesus' crucifixion. They had not been able to believe the reports of the resurrection. Their minds were consumed with recalling the experiences of the past few days. The week had begun with such promise, only to end in seeming tragedy.

The Gospel of Luke does not tell us in detail what their conversation was. It says only that they were "talking with each other about all these things that had happened" (24:14). Had they seen the triumphal entry? Had they witnessed Jesus teaching and healing in the temple? Had they observed the angry mob who cried for Jesus' crucifixion? Had they seen Jesus trudge out to the hill of Golgotha with his heavy cross? Had they witnessed Jesus' death there? On that very morning before they left for Emmaus, they had heard reports of resurrection. What were they to make of the reports?

We will never know all the answers to these questions, but Luke tells us that they traveled along that road, deep in conversation about all that had happened in that momentous week. We can imagine that there was a mixture of sorrow, fear, disappointment, and even some anger. Such would be consistent with the experience of grief that is common to all of us in the face of some significant loss. Cleopas and his unnamed companion must have grappled to make sense of what they had seen and heard.

They related their own experience, which is the essence of Christian witness.

Jesus Joins the Journey (24:15–27)

Luke tells us that while they walked and discussed the events of the past days, Jesus drew near and walked along with them. For some reason they did not recognize who it was who walked with them. Luke says only that "their eyes were kept from recognizing him" (24:16). Luke apparently intended to convey the fact that their lack of vision was supernatural in origin and not simply that they were preoccupied.

Much to their surprise, their companion inquired of them the subject of their intense conversation. Luke states that upon hearing the question of the Lord, "They stood still, looking sad" (24:17). Perhaps startled that anyone might not know of the events that so consumed them, they stopped in their tracks, trying to take it all in. They could only wonder whether he were the only one in Jerusalem who had not heard the things that had happened.

Puzzled or not, they recalled for him the drama of the Passion Week. They spoke of the resistance of the chief priests and other rulers who had delivered Jesus to be crucified. How they had hoped that Jesus was the Promised One who would lead Israel to restored glory, freed from the domination of the hated Romans. They knew, though, that he had been put to death.

Patiently Jesus opened Scripture and filled it with new meaning as he applied the words of Moses and the prophets to his own life and ministry. Still these travelers did not recognize Jesus as he patiently went through the biblical message related to the coming of the Messiah.

Broken Bread and Open Eyes (24:28–32)

As the two travelers finished their journey at Emmaus, their companion "walked ahead as if he were going on"

(24:28). Is this not always the way of Jesus, the Lord who goes ahead of us in his work among us, waiting to be invited in to our experiences?

The two travelers, however, urged their fellow traveler to stop at their house. The invitation was in the best tradition of Middle Eastern hospitality. Their companion accepted the invitation, and they sat together for a meal.

It is significant that as the Gospel of Luke describes the scene, Jesus "took bread, blessed and broke it, and gave it to them. Then their eyes were opened, and they recognized him" (24:30–31).

How did they come to recognize Jesus? Luke left the mystery of it all for us to ponder. Some have speculated that it was the way Jesus presided over a meal that finally opened their eyes. Others suggest that it was the words Jesus said as he blessed the meal. Still others conjecture that when Jesus put out his hands to break the bread, they saw the nail-scarred hands. Later it would be the sight of the scarred hands that convinced Thomas.

Have you ever stopped to think how important one day can be in human experience?

For Luke it was enough to point out that in the common experience of eating together, particularly in breaking bread, their eyes were opened. They understood who the stranger was. It was as if they relived a meal just nights earlier when, in an upper room, "He took a loaf of bread, and when he had given thanks, he broke it and gave it to them, saying, 'This is my body, which is given for you. Do this in remembrance of me'" (22:19).

No sooner had the blindness fallen from their eyes than Jesus was gone from the travelers' presence. Their hearts were burning with excitement and amazement as they wondered how they had failed to recognize Jesus sooner.

Sharing the Discovery (24:33–35)

Their response was to seek out others who had heard the witness of the resurrection. They made their way back to Jerusalem that very night. As Luke tells us, "Then they told what had happened on the road, and how he had been made known to them in the breaking of the bread" (24:35). They related their own experience, which is the essence of Christian witness.

Every one of our lives has a number of significant days that on reflection show us how a moment in time can shape us forever.

This news was too good to keep. It was the message they had sought but did not know how to understand until Jesus had opened their eyes. The Messiah they had expected from their cultural upbringing was not the Messiah they had discovered. It had become clear to them that Jesus was truly the Christ of God.

Message for Us

For several years our local public radio station has run a little feature that began as a graduate school project and has turned into a widely-distributed feature. It is called *A Moment in Time*. It is put together by Dan Roberts and produced at the University of Richmond. It looks back in our nation's history at some key moments in which decisions were made or events occurred that forever affected our way of life. Some were good and some were questionable, but each has had tremendous impact on us all.

Have you ever stopped to think how important one day can be in human experience? Have there been some pivotal days in your life in which the *before* and *after* were absolutely different? Perhaps it was a graduation day, a wedding day, or a day when your firstborn arrived. Again it might be an employment day, a retirement day, or even an ordinary day with an unexpected visit from someone special. Every one of our lives has a number of significant days that on reflection show us how a moment in time can shape us forever.

The Lord is risen! The Lord is risen indeed!

Of all these special, life-changing days, none can compare to the discovery that Christ has risen, that Christ is alive and in our world, seeking to touch every aspect of our lives. Among the earliest believers, facing hardship and opposition, one thing most sustained them. It was not the teachings of Jesus, or the stories of Jesus' healings or feedings. It was, instead, the unswerving conviction that Jesus was alive and they were not alone. They could do all things and endure unbelievable hardship through Jesus' presence in their lives. They had come to know the resurrected Jesus.

This news was too good to keep.

The Lord is risen! The Lord is risen indeed!

Resurrection

The central affirmation of the Christian gospel is the resurrection. In Jesus' day many died by the cruel means of crucifixion, but we do not know their names today. Without the resurrection, Jesus would likely be forgotten on the rubbish heap of history.

The concept of resurrection is not clearly a part of the Old Testament message. By the time of Jesus, the understanding that all the dead would rise to be judged by the Son of Man was accepted by the Pharisees but not the Sadducees. For Christians, it was the resurrection of Jesus that forever gave insight into the resurrection of believers.

In Paul's discourse in 1 Corinthians 15 about the resurrection, Paul did not speak of the resurrection of the old body. Instead he pointed to a new body, not temporal but eternal (1 Cor. 15:42–47). All of this is tied to the resurrection of Christ, which gives new meaning to both life and death.

Waking Up a Church

Youth complained that church was boring. Young adults sought meaning in other special groups and activities outside the church. Even many of the faithful older members agreed that church had largely become a routine of the same old events and dry, lifeless reports. The arrival of a new pastor led them to appoint a planning group to explore ways of church renewal. Based on your experience, what suggestions would you give this committee and pastor to help bring new life to a sleeping congregation?

Questions

1. What do you feel is the primary meaning or impact of the resurrection of Jesus?

2. What explanation can you offer for the failure of the two travelers to recognize Jesus?

3. Do you think there is a contemporary application of the blindness of these two to the failure of so many in our world who cannot seem to see Jesus as the Christ? Explain your feelings.

4. What do you feel is the most powerful force in helping contemporary skeptics come to see the reality of Jesus as Lord?

5. What are some things that have helped you most to experience the reality of the living Christ?

Our Next New Study

(Available for use beginning June 2004)

Exodus: Freed to Follow God

UNIT ONE: PREPARATION FOR DELIVERANCE

Lesson 1	Just When Things Were Going So . . .	Exodus 1:6–10; 1:22—2:15; 2:23–25
Lesson 2	Excuses, Excuses	Exodus 3:1–14; 4:1–15

UNIT TWO: GOD'S POWER TO DELIVER

Lesson 3	The Futility of Resisting God	Exodus 7:1–6, 14–18; 8:1–3, 16, 20–21; 9:1–4, 8–9, 22–26; 10:3–6, 21–23, 27–29
Lesson 4	A Night Never to Be Forgotten	Exodus 11:1–8; 12:21–32
Lesson 5	Sing to the Lord for Freedom!	Exodus 14:21—15:2, 20–21
Lesson 6	No Longer but Not Yet	Exodus 15:22—16:7; 17:1–7, 11–18

UNIT THREE: GUIDANCE FOR COVENANT LIVING

Lesson 7	Wonderful Offer, Serious Demand	Exodus 19:1–12
Lesson 8	Treat God Like This	Exodus 20:1–11
Lesson 9	Treat People Like This	Exodus 20:12–17
Lesson 10	The Nitty-Gritty of Covenant Living	Exodus 21:12–17, 22–27; 22:21—23:11

UNIT FOUR: CALLED TO WORSHIP ONLY GOD

Lesson 11	A Broken Covenant and a Second Chance	Exodus 32:7–34
Lesson 12	Starting Over	Exodus 34:1–28
Lesson 13	God Dwelling Among Us	Exodus 25:1–8; 29:43–46; 33:7–11, 14–16; 40:16–38

Additional Resources for Studying the Book of Exodus:[1]

Walter Brueggemann. "Exodus." *The New Interpreter's Bible*. Volume 1. Nashville: Abingdon Press, 1994.

John I. Durham. *Exodus*. Word Biblical Commentary. Volume 3. Waco, Texas: Word Books, Publisher, 1987.

Terence Fretheim. *Exodus.* Interpretation: A Bible Commentary for Teaching and Preaching. Louisville, Kentucky: John Knox Press, 1991.

Roy L. Honeycutt, Jr. "Exodus." *The Broadman Bible Commentary*. Volume 1. Nashville, Tennessee: Broadman Press, 1969.

Page H. Kelley. *Exodus: Called for Redemptive Mission*. Nashville, Tennessee: Convention Press, 1977.

Page H. Kelley. *Journey to the Land of Promise: Genesis—Deuteronomy*. Macon, Georgia: Smyth & Helwys Publishing, Inc., 1997.

NOTES

1. Listing a book does not imply full agreement by the writers or BAPTISTWAY PRESS® with all of its comments.

How to Order More Bible Study Materials

It's easy! Just fill in the following information. (Note: when the *Teaching Guide* is priced at $2.45 or $2.95, the *Teaching Guide* includes Bible comments for teachers.)

✦ = Texas specific

Title of item	Price	Quantity	Cost
This Issue:			
Luke: Parables Jesus Told—Study Guide	$2.35		
Luke: Parables Jesus Told—Large Print Study Guide	$2.35		
Luke: Parables Jesus Told—Teaching Guide	$2.95		
Previous Issues Available:			
God's Message in the Old Testament—Study Guide ✦	$1.95		
God's Message in the Old Testament—Teaching Guide ✦	$1.95		
Genesis 12—50: Family Matters—Study Guide	$1.95		
Genesis 12—50: Family Matters—Large Print Study Guide	$1.95		
Genesis 12—50: Family Matters—Teaching Guide	$2.45		
Isaiah and Jeremiah—Study Guide	$1.95		
Isaiah and Jeremiah—Large Print Study Guide	$1.95		
Isaiah and Jeremiah—Teaching Guide	$2.45		
Amos, Hosea, Micah—Study Guide	$1.95		
Amos, Hosea, Micah—Teaching Guide	$2.45		
Good News in the New Testament—Study Guide ✦	$1.95		
Good News in the New Testament—Large Print Study Guide ✦	$1.95		
Good News in the New Testament—Teaching Guide ✦	$2.45		
Matthew: Jesus As the Fulfillment of God's Promises—Study Guide ✦	$1.00		
Matthew: Jesus As the Fulfillment of God's Promises—Large Print Study Guide ✦	$1.00		
Matthew: Jesus As the Fulfillment of God's Promises—Teaching Guide ✦	$2.00		
Jesus in the Gospel of Mark—Study Guide	$1.95		
Jesus in the Gospel of Mark—Large Print Study Guide	$1.95		
Jesus in the Gospel of Mark—Teaching Guide	$2.45		
Gospel of John—Study Guide	$1.95		
Gospel of John—Large Print Study Guide	$1.95		
Gospel of John—Teaching Guide	$2.45		
Acts: Sharing God's Good News with Everyone—Study Guide ✦	$1.95		
Acts: Sharing God's Good News with Everyone—Teaching Guide ✦	$1.95		
Romans: Good News for a Troubled World—Study Guide ✦	$1.95		
Romans: Good News for a Troubled World—Teaching Guide ✦	$1.95		
1 Corinthians—Study Guide	$1.95		
1 Corinthians—Large Print Study Guide	$1.95		
1 Corinthians—Teaching Guide	$2.45		
Galatians and Ephesians—Study Guide ✦	$1.95		
Galatians and Ephesians—Large Print Study Guide ✦	$1.95		
Galatians and Ephesians—Teaching Guide ✦	$2.45		
Philippians, Colossians, Thessalonians—Study Guide	$1.95		
Philippians, Colossians, Thessalonians—Large Print Study Guide	$1.95		
Philippians, Colossians, Thessalonians—Teaching Guide	$2.45		
Hebrews and James—Study Guide	$1.95		
Hebrews and James—Large Print Study Guide	$1.95		
Hebrews and James—Teaching Guide	$2.45		
Letters of John and Peter—Study Guide	$1.95		
Letters of John and Peter—Large Print Study Guide	$1.95		
Letters of John and Peter—Teaching Guide	$2.45		

Coming for use beginning June 2004			
Exodus: Freed to Follow God—Study Guide	$2.35	______	______
Exodus: Freed to Follow God—Large Print Study Guide	$2.35	______	______
Exodus: Freed to Follow God—Teaching Guide	$2.95	______	______
Beliefs Important to Baptists			
Who in the World Are Baptists, Anyway? (one lesson)	$ .45	______	______
Who in the World Are Baptists, Anyway?—Teacher's Edition	$ .55	______	______
Beliefs Important to Baptists: I (four lessons)	$1.35	______	______
Beliefs Important to Baptists: I—Teacher's Edition	$1.75	______	______
Beliefs Important to Baptists: II (four lessons)	$1.35	______	______
Beliefs Important to Baptists: II—Teacher's Edition	$1.75	______	______
Beliefs Important to Baptists: III (four lessons)	$1.35	______	______
Beliefs Important to Baptists: III—Teacher's Edition	$1.75	______	______
Beliefs Important to Baptists—Study Guide (one-volume edition; includes all lessons)	$2.35	______	______
Beliefs Important to Baptists—Teaching Guide (one-volume edition; includes all lessons)	$1.95	______	______

*Charges for standard shipping service:

Subtotal up to $20.00	$3.95
Subtotal $20.01—$50.00	$4.95
Subtotal $50.01—$100.00	10% of subtotal
Subtotal $100.01 and up	8% of subtotal

Please allow three weeks for standard delivery. For express shipping service: Call 1-866-249-1799 for information on additional charges.

Subtotal ______________

Shipping* ______________

TOTAL ______________

____

Your name Phone

____

Your church Date Ordered

____

Mailing address

____

City State Zip code

MAIL this form with your check for the total amount to
BAPTISTWAY PRESS
Baptist General Convention of Texas
333 North Washington
Dallas, TX 75246-1798
(Make checks to "Baptist Executive Board.")

OR, **FAX** your order anytime to: 214-828-5187, and we will bill you.

OR, **CALL** your order toll-free: 1-866-249-1799 (8:30 a.m.-5:00 p.m., M-F), and we will bill you.

OR, **E-MAIL** your order to our internet e-mail address: baptistway@bgct.org, and we will bill you.

We look forward to receiving your order! Thank you!